1750

Anne Robichaud

Aging and Communication

Aging and Communication

Edited by

Herbert J. Oyer, Ph.D.

Professor and Dean
The Graduate School
Michigan State University

and

E. Jane Oyer, Ph.D.

Associate Professor
Department of Family and Child Sciences
Michigan State University

University Park Press
Baltimore · London · Tokyo

UNIVERSITY PARK PRESS
International Publishers in Science and Medicine
Chamber of Commerce Building
Baltimore, Maryland 21202

Copyright © 1976 by University Park Press

Typeset by The Composing Room of Michigan, Inc.

Manufactured in the United States of America by Universal Lithographers,
Inc., and The Maple Press Co.

Library of Congress Cataloging in Publication Data

Main entry under title:

Aging and communication.

  Includes index.
  1. Aged—Addresses, essays, lectures. 2. Interpersonal communication—Addresses, essays, lectures.
I. Oyer, Herbert J. II. Oyer, E. Jane. [DNLM:
1. Communication—In old age. 2. Aging. WT104 A267]
HQ1061.A455   301.43'5   76-14991
ISBN 0-8391-0894-X

Contents

Contributors

Gordon J. Aldridge, Ph.D.
Professor
School of Social Work
212 Baker Hall
Michigan State University
East Lansing, Michigan 48824

Charles K. Atkin, Ph.D.
Associate Professor
Department of Communication
509 S. Kedzie Hall
Michigan State University
East Lansing, Michigan 48824

Daniel S. Beasley, Ph.D.
Associate Professor
Department of Audiology and
  Speech Sciences
207 Audiology and Speech Sciences
  Building
Michigan State University
East Lansing, Michigan 48824

Walter M. Beattie, Jr., M.A.
Director
All-University Gerontology Center
School of Social Work
Syracuse University
Syracuse, New York 13210

Carole O. Bettinghaus, M.A.
Evaluation Integrator
Chronic Disease Module Unit
College of Human Medicine
Suite 40—Nisbet Building
Michigan State University
East Lansing, Michigan 48824

Erwin P. Bettinghaus, Ph.D.
Professor and Chairman
Department of Communication
523 S. Kedzie Hall
Michigan State University
East Lansing, Michigan 48824

James Danowski, Ph.D.
Associate Professor
Annenberg School of Communica-
  tion and Ethel Percy Andrus
  Gerontology Center
University of Southern California
Los Angeles, California 90007

Leo V. Deal, Ph.D.
Chairman
Department of Audiology and
  Speech Sciences
Michigan State University
East Lansing, Michigan 48824

Markham T. Farrell, M.A.
Administrator
Burcham Hills Retirement Center
2700 Burcham Drive
East Lansing, Michigan 48823

Leo A. Haak, Ph.D.
Professor Emeritus and Consultant
Institute for Community
  Development
27 Kellogg Center
Michigan State University
East Lansing, Michigan 48824

John M. Hutchinson, Ph.D.
Assistant Professor
Department of Speech Pathology
  and Audiology
Idaho State University
Pocadello, Idaho 83209

Yash Pal Kapur, M.D.
Professor
Departments of Audiology and
  Speech Sciences and Surgery
111 Giltner Hall
Michigan State University
East Lansing, Michigan 48824

Charles R. Mauldin, Ph.D.
Associate Professor
Department of Advertising
201 Journalism Building
Michigan State University
East Lansing, Michigan 48824

Thomas A. Muth, J.D., Ph.D.
Associate Professor
Department of Telecommunication
320 Union Building
Michigan State University
East Lansing, Michigan 48824

E. Jane Oyer, Ph.D.
Associate Professor
Department of Family and Child
  Sciences
Michigan State University
East Lansing, Michigan 48824

Herbert J. Oyer, Ph.D.
Professor and Dean
The Graduate School
246 John A. Hannah
  Administration Building
Michigan State University
East Lansing, Michigan 48824

Carl Wesley Staser, M.S., M.Div.
Associate Minister
Peoples Church—Interdenomina-
  tional
200 W. Grand River Ave.
East Lansing, Michigan 48823

Helen Taft Staser, B.S.
Director
East Lansing Older Peoples Program
219 Durand St.
East Lansing, Michigan 48823

Natalie P. Trager, Ph.D.
Associate Professor
Department of Psychology,
  Sociology, and Social Work
College of Liberal Arts
Ohio Northern University
Ada, Ohio 45810

Joseph Woelfel, Ph.D.
Associate Professor
Department of Communication
540 S. Kedzie
Michigan State University
East Lansing, Michigan 48824

Preface

One of the most humanizing elements in the adjustment of mankind is the ability to communicate. Communication is important all through life, but it assumes even greater importance as people become more dependent upon others in their later years. Their needs change and their desire to share in communicative exchanges is frequently altered.

Aging and Communication presents a comprehensive set of discussions dealing with the importance of communication with older people. Much of the literature that addresses the many problems associated with aging speaks briefly about the importance of communication between and among older people as individuals, within families, and within community agencies and organizations, but it generally stops short of analyzing the full impact of the need for successful communication.

Communication and gerontology are characterized by multidisciplinary dimensions. For that reason this book has been written by persons representing numerous disciplines and sub-aspects thereof, namely: audiology, education, family science, gerontology, interpersonal communication, law, mass communication, otorhinolaryngology, psychology, sociology, speech pathology, and theology. It continues to be our firm conviction that a comprehensive discussion of aging and communication could only be handled by a team whose backgrounds of education, training, and experience are diverse, and whose interests converge meaningfully at the interface of these two areas. Thus this edited work.

The book is designed primarily for use by upper-level undergraduate, professional, and graduate students who project careers that will deal in some manner with older people. These discussions should also be of interest and benefit to those professionals who in any way work with older people individually or through organizations of one kind or another. This book should also be of genuine interest to the researcher because of the many unanswered questions that are raised throughout. The older segment of the population, as well, should be interested in points of view expressed by the contributing authors.

An attempt has been made to provide internal consistency in the format of the various chapters. Sections devoted to research questions, future trends, and general recommendations are to be found in most chapters. These sections should provide the nucleus for many discussions and for probing the many unanswered questions that abound.

It is our sincere hope that this book will be instrumental in providing the information that leads to greater insights into problems of communication encountered by older people and for stimulating solutions to these problems. We are all deeply indebted to the older people who have contributed substantially to our understanding of this topic.

H. J. O. and E. J. O.

Foreword

The number of people in their later years is increasing faster than any other age group, and this trend is likely to continue in the foreseeable future.

Keeping this group in touch with each other, and with other generations, becomes one of the greatest challenges of our time.

The primary practice of medicine, along with a 20-year chairmanship of the Committee on Aging of the American Medical Association, creates a background for some fairly reliable observations. The primary practice of medicine is made up only in a minor way with pills and potions. It is largely involved with men and women in their relation to nature, to man, and to God. The impact of this environment, and their reaction to it, constitute the warp and woof of everyone's life.

It is awe inspiring and sometimes frightening to realize how important and how dependent people in the later years are on other people. In the later years, there is frequently the problem of lack of communication and understanding between the wife and the recently retired husband; the attempt to take over the woman's work by the retired husband; the relationship with other members of the family both near and remote, who for any number of reasons, would become involved in the life pattern of the oldster; the generation gap; the involvement in community and church activities; the management of estates; the relation of income to needs; the intelligent concern regarding politics and community activity; and, last but not least, the preservation of health by the promotion of good habits, plus physical and mental exercise—prevention of disease by all the means we now have available.

All of these constitute the multiphasic communication challenges in the later years. We in the field often think we are coming on the stage too late, and we are often convinced that the earlier in life good, honest pathways of communication are established, the better will be the results. At the present time, however, the communication in the field of medicine and peoples' life style leaves much to be desired. It would seem that if the Darwinian theory prevailed, the coming generation will be born without ears.

We look forward to the time when the dreams and energies of youth, tempered through communication by the wisdom, judgment, and experience of the oldster, will give us a better foundation for the solutions to our challenging future.

Frederick C. Swartz, M.D.
Chairman,
Committee on Aging of the
American Medical Association

This book is dedicated to the memory of Dr. Leo A. Haak, Professor Emeritus, Michigan State University, who authored Chapter 2. He died while the manuscript was in press.

His creative mind, enthusiasm, and work in the interest of older people serve as an inspiration to those who knew him.

Aging and Communication

chapter 1
Communicating with Older People:
Basic Considerations

Herbert J. Oyer, Ph.D.
E. Jane Oyer, Ph.D.

Communication is an observable characteristic of human beings through-out the entire span of life. As the human being develops, the modes of communicating become more refined. Communicating not only includes the talking and listening that persons do but the reading and writing as well. In addition to these, there is also the tremendous amount of communicating that takes place all through life by way of the nonverbal cues that people pass along to those about them: the raised brow, the sigh, the downturned lips, the smile, the nod, the period of silence following an utterance, etc. It is not an exaggeration to say that as one is involved in the business of living, one is involved in the business of communicating.

Communication in and of itself gives neither assurance of happiness nor enrichment of life. It can, quite to the contrary, contribute to unhappiness and feelings of deterioration of self-worth. Quite obviously the content and the quality of the message make the difference.

As with children, youths, and adults, so it is with the elderly, in that individual differences will determine the frequency with which they wish to and will in fact become engaged in communication situations. Personality characteristics, intelligence, educational and occupational backgrounds are all determinants to some extent of the types of communicative interactions in which the elderly become involved. The point here is that one can expect a great range of communication activities among the elderly, just as one witnesses among those not labeled as elderly.

Communication is central to successful transactions throughout life, and there is no reason to believe that it becomes less important in the later years. Actually, it probably becomes even more important as the elderly enter the ranks of the retired and are, in a sense, set apart from the mainstream of society. Furthermore, there is often a sense of greater dependency on the part of the elderly. Therefore, it is crucial to the integrity of older people that the lines of communication remain open, thus providing for viable exchanges. Unless this occurs, there follows most surely an erosion in feelings of self-worth that dehumanizes the elderly.

Even though there are great individual differences of involvement in communication by the elderly, there are some areas of communication common to all that are vital to their lives.

These areas range from interpersonal communications through small and large groups and on into the mass media. For example, the success of the interpersonal communication that takes place within the family and through age levels, as the elderly interact with children, grandchildren, a young physician, dentist, lawyer, minister, etc., can contribute not only to happiness but also to their actual health.

In order to discuss intelligently the problems of communication as related to the elderly, it is imperative to have working definitions of both terms. These definitions follow in the next section.

DEFINITIONS

What do We Mean by Communication?

As one lives among others, the psychosocial interaction that occurs is based upon communication. It may be intentional or nonintentional. It may be through the medium of verbal messages, written or spoken, or it may be through the multitude of nonverbal cues that one generates as he relates or listens to another's account of an event, walks up to the teller's window at the bank, shows his approval at the concert or football game, etc. Human communication also occurs within one's self. There need be no second or third party involved as one, through the use of language symbols, formulates, evaluates, and reacts to messages that are self generated.

For the purposes of this chapter and those that follow, human communication is defined operationally to include the sending and receiving of messages both verbal and nonverbal within, between, and/or among people. The situations include: 1) an individual communicating with herself/himself or with another person; 2) small group communication among only a few people; 3) large group communication wherein one or several people deliver messages to many people in a face-to-face situation; or 4) mass communication via radio, television, cablevision, newspapers, magazines, books, etc.

What do We Mean by Aging?

Aging might be defined as happiness was in the tune that said it meant different things to different people. Even infants are aging. However, since the adoption of the Social Security Act in 1935, a widely accepted chronological definition is that anyone who has reached the age of 65 automatically attains membership in that sector of the population called "the aging."

Were one to pose the question to medical personnel concerned with older people, the response might be that aging is a slow but continuous process that results in the cessation of growth and in physical decline with a decreased bodily ability to regenerate or renew. Psychologists might respond by saying that their findings suggest aging must be viewed from the assessment of modifications that occur in older persons' sensory processes, perceptions, strategies of adjustment, intelligence, problem-solving and learning abilities, memory, motor skills, emotional states, and related factors. Sociologists are more interested in groups than in individuals per se and in the study of society or social enviroment. Questions the sociologist might pose would be: How do older persons influence the larger society? What groups within society compose older persons' social systems? What are the demographic realities? In other words, what difference does it make to a society such as ours in the United States that over 10 percent of the present population is 65 years of age or older and that theirs is the fastest growing segment of the population? What are the attitudes of other age groups toward the aging, and how do aging persons view themselves?

The social gerontologist is a professional who is concerned with the science of aging in society. Literally, the word gerontology means the logic of aging. Gerontologists are concerned with all aspects of aging in a general way and with the various aspects of older persons' lives as they intersect. In other words, gerontologists are generalists (often with roots in one of the basic disciplines) who are concerned with the way that the various components of older persons' lives intersect or mutually influence each other. For example, the availability of good medical care might mean physically healthier older people who could take part in community life, thereby positively influencing attitudes of younger persons toward them. Or, government policies that provide some forms of financial security might greatly reduce psychological stress, which might, in turn, alleviate biological symptoms (such as hypertension). The gerontologist is concerned in a general way with the sum total of changes that occur in people with the passage of time from birth until death, and especially as they are observed in persons 65 years of age or older.

For the purposes of this book, the segment of the population commonly referred to as "the aging" will be identified chronologically as those persons who have reached 65 or more years of age. The process of aging will be considered to be the slow but continuous changes that occur between birth and death, with special focus upon those who are 65 years of age or older. Where the terms young-old and old-old are used, the age categories assigned to them by Neugarten (1975) will be used. That is, ages 55 to 75 for the former, and 75 plus for the latter.

ATTITUDES TOWARD OLDER PEOPLE

Interest in and concern for older people may be found in historical writings traced down through the years as evidenced in a chapter called "Old Age in Historical Societies" from a recent book, *The Coming of Age,* by Simone de Beauvoir (1972). The interpretation and discussion of opposing points of view bequeathed by Plato and Socrates on the one hand, and by Aristotle on the other, provide some background for the ambivalent attitudes observed in present day developed societies. Plato assumed that the body and soul were not subject to the same forces of decline and that physical aging of the body actually freed the soul for things of the mind (or intelligence). In fact, rulers of city states were not sufficiently mature to deserve their seats until they had lived about 50 years. Socrates was reported to have thought that the young learn by keeping company with their elders. Aristotle, however, entertained very pessimistic notions about older people. Man advances up to the age of 50, and after that time physical decline of the body carries the whole person downhill. Although his descriptions of youth are full of praise and enthusiasm, his descriptions of older people are quite the opposite. Time causes people to accumulate a series of errors that take a cumulative toll eroding self-esteem and courage. The elderly, he thought, live more in the past and possess little hope for the future. This pessimistic view of aging as an accumulation of negative experiences seems to have permeated some present day thinking as well. The old have been undervalued as their capacities to produce have diminished. However, sheer numbers and, hopefully, increased public understanding and enlightenment, may be paving the way toward more positive views of the contributions older persons have made and continue to make.

Only within recent time have interests and concerns for older people become truly national in scope. Population changes are forcing humanitarian and politican alike to take stock. Older people are becoming, in fact have become, a potent political force in this country. About 11 percent of the population is now 65 years of age or older. This proportion has almost tripled since 1900, and some demographers are predicting that it could go as high as 20 percent in the next century (Eisele, 1974). Populations are considered aging when the segment of older persons is increasing at a greater rate than that of younger segments. The United States today, therefore, is indeed becoming a nation of older people.

Lack of unity blunts the power of older people. But even though age may appear to be almost the only common denominator of the heterogeneous group of almost 22 million people 65 and older, there is some evidence that a convergence on some common issues is being effected. The elderly are coalescing into and behind groups that possess high levels of knowledge regarding their needs and political know-how as well. Pratt (1974) mentions some organizations, open to large numbers of people, that are helping to shape and focus the views of the elderly and to exert an influence upon federal policy makers. Included are the American Association of Retired Persons-National Retired Teachers Association (AARP-NRTA), the National Council of Senior Citizens and the National Association of Senior Citizens, and the National Association of Retired Federal Employees.

Contributing to population changes presently being experienced are factors such as: 1) declining birth rates; 2) slowly increasing life expectancy rates; and 3) increasing numbers of people living out their full life spans. Four and even five generation families are not the rare exceptions they once were. But this increase in the number of kin who live to be old does not necessarily mean that aging persons are more apt to find their needs met within the kin network. Power at the polls may mean, however, that older people will have more "say" in ways that their needs are accommodated.

IMPORTANCE OF COMMUNICATION FOR OLDER PEOPLE

Many rewards come to older people. Changing family and work roles bring about the lessening of responsibilities for others, and the luxury of more time and a greater proportion of one's income to devote to self or couple interests. The freedom to control and plan for the use of one's own time is considered by many to be one of the most satisfying aspects of retirement. At long last one can "do one's own thing." Along with this added freedom there are often, however, many problems experienced by older people, many of which are interlinked with communication variables.

Families are frequently confronted with the necessity of making difficult decisions regarding various aspects of the lives of their older members.

The openness or closedness of family communication channels can make a great deal of difference in the emotional costs paid by all concerned. While only about 5 percent of persons 65 or older live in institutions in the United States, many who are living independently are able to do so only because some support services, such as the delivery of meals, make relative independence possible. When independent living is no longer a viable alternative, families must choose from among options about which they may have little accurate information. The communication between generations is a critical factor here. Do adult children "save" mother and/or father the trouble and agony of searching out available community resources, or do they include them in decision-making that may determine how they will live for the remainder of their lives? Communications experts and gerontologists may ask what educational inputs are needed to help people make decisions regarding such crucial aspects of human aging. Spark and Brody (1970) emphasize that the stereotype of families ignoring their aged is a myth insofar as sizable numbers of families are concerned. Although less than 25 percent of older people actually share dwellings with adult children, continuing communication and shared aid are commonly practiced.

The ways that families become informed about and utilize community networks and services, including housing options, are critical questions that will be discussed in the chapters that follow. For example, what are the advantages and disadvantages of each housing option that families need to consider as bases for decision making? Or, how do persons and families learn to use community communication networks? And what kinds of educational offerings would be helpful to people faced with difficult decisions concerning aging?

The way in which the older person is able to deal with benefits available through agencies and bureaus of government is largely a matter of the effectiveness with which these organizations communicate to older people and the ability of the elderly to initiate and respond through networks in the community that are often poorly defined.

Newspapers, radio, and television are tremendously important media that deliver messages to all, including the elderly. Of no small concern are those messages that seek to persuade the listener to purchase commodities of one kind or another. Since the financial resources of the vast majority of the elderly are limited, these attempts at persuasion deserve close scrutiny. Radio and television programming for entertainment and education is important to older people. Likewise, an important area for consideration is the journalistic effort made for older people through the weekly or daily newspaper.

Harris and associates (1975) recently completed an extensive survey on the general topic of the myth and reality of aging in this country. Results revealed that images held by the public of older people tend to be distorted and negative. However, their respondents were not critical, on the whole, of television for the way older people were portrayed. The writers' opinions are that much of the negative image of older people is reinforced by the unkind approach that some buffoons on television will employ merely to elicit a laugh. Three out of four television viewers in the Harris sample agreed that most programs featured young people, but that when older people were featured, they were usually treated with respect and as an important part of the family. However, Arnoff (1974) looked at the television content of dramatic television shows aired at prime time and found that aging was associated with increasing evil, failure, and unhappiness. Older people and their use of and portrayal by the mass media will be more fully discussed in a later chapter.

Atchley (1972) notes that relatively little attention has been paid to older people as consumers, and their impact upon the market has often been overlooked. But sheer numbers and the regularity of their incomes, even when low, give them a special kind of purchasing power or clout. One does not get "laid off" from a pension or Social Security even though they may, singly or combined, keep one below the poverty level.

The public 65 and older has a much lower household income than the younger adult group. Harris (1975) determined that the median income for older people was $4,800, as compared with $12,400 for those 18 to 64 years of age. Large proportions of a small income must be spent for basic survival needs, which means there is little discretionary income for many older people. An extra frill may literally be taking food off the table. Decisions to purchase are of major import. Fraudulent practices, such as the misrepresentation of various health-promoting devices, are cruel indeed. The matter of communicating consumer information to older people is considered in a later chapter.

Although most older Americans are sufficiently healthy to maintain their independent life styles, decrements in health status are distinguishing characteristics between older and younger generations. That this is a youth-oriented culture is communicated frequently in both obvious and subtle ways. Energy level decreases, as do the ability to rebound after stressful experiences, to resist infections, and to return to a state of health following the intrusion of disease. All are related to the aging process. Estes (1969) found, however, that problems associated with the delivery of health care to the population at large have had a more profound effect upon older people than actual illnesses. Major concerns of the Section of

Physical and Mental Health of the White House Conference on Aging (1971) included recommendations for the provision of health education and preventative services as well as diagnostic, treatment, and rehabilitative services for older people. A key problem is *communicating* to older persons the information that health services are available to them, thus motivating them to utilize those services.

A decrease in efficiency of function in the senses often accompanies the aging process. One sense that is highly involved in the human communication process is that of hearing. The deterioration of this input pathway can have far-reaching effects on the extent to which the older person remains in contact with others through interpersonal interactions, organizations, group meetings, and the larger environment through radio and television. It is to these many areas of concern that the remaining chapters of this book are addressed. Eisdorfer (1970) reports that aging persons with impaired audition evidence less mature approaches in dealing with their environment and demonstrate developmentally lower levels of communication. The ability to understand both speech and other environmental sounds may be in question and, hence, the ability to respond appropriately may also be problematic. Hearing loss tends to increase the social isolation of older persons.

The ability to speak may be affected by certain other disorders that often accompany aging. A stroke, for example, may interfere with the language of older persons. The affected person may have difficulty receiving speech as a result of neurological impairment caused by the stroke, he may have difficulty expressing himself through speech, or both problems of communication may manifest themselves. A lessening of the ability to communicate with one's world through the intrusion of sensory impairments has very deep and far-reaching effects upon aging persons and will be discussed more fully in chapters that follow.

Legal rights and responsibilities are concerns that are gaining an increasing amount of public attention as society is becoming more legalistic in terms of its views and dealings with human relationships. Legal services are provided by some senior citizens' voluntary organizations and through local legal aid societies. It is not surprising that many older people are confused by the legal matters with which they are confronted.

Not only do the elderly need assistance with legal matters, but many younger people also share this need. However, as chronological age increases, fears of making errors and feelings of powerlessness frequently increase as well. The inability to hire a private attorney or the pride that prevents one from asking for "free" legal services may be two important barriers with which older people need special assistance. How are the legal rights of older people communicated to them? How do older persons, in turn, communicate, or provide feedback, to express their needs and wishes so that faulty or outmoded laws may be modified? Legal and public policy problems in communicating with the aging are treated later in the text.

Because the aging segment of society is the most heterogeneous one of all segments, persons 65 and older differ considerably in their attitudes toward their participation in religious organizations. Moberg (1972) observed that internalized religious attitudes and feelings increased, but that extra-domicilial religious practices tended to decrease among the aged. Sears (unpublished data, 1975) conducted a study with a sample of low income, urban, black senior citizens and found that 89 percent watched television daily and 87 percent listened daily to the radio. Respondents reported that they were especially interested in programs that focused upon religious topics. Moberg's (1972) analysis suggested that decline in church participation was related to factors such as physical capacities, transportation availability, and economic costs, but that the importance of religion was valued by more adults proportionately in the 65 and older group than in younger groups. Organized religion provided multicommunication channels through the variety of programs it sponsors. These will be amplified in chapters that follow.

Lifelong education (or lifespan education) is a very important concept: an idea whose time has come. At last, it seems, older people are being welcomed back into classrooms in high schools, community colleges, and universities. Data indicate that intelligence does not decline with age (Woodruff and Walsh, 1975), and the ability to learn is not limited to any particular age group. However, older people usually require more time to complete learning tasks and generally do not perform as well as younger people under conditions requiring test completion within preset time periods. New ways need to be found for older people to communicate their information, aptitudes, abilities, and skills.

Ideally, this departure from the stereotype that "you cannot teach older persons anything new" would be the outcome of the accumulation of research evidence to refute the myth. But the rather sudden accelerated interest in providing learning-teaching opportunities for large numbers of older people has not been rooted entirely in either altruism or scientific analysis. The decline in birth rates together with the downturn in the economy has caused educators and governing boards to review optimal uses of their faculties and physical plants. Older people are coming in large numbers to participate in educational enterprises. For example, an aunt of one of the editors is still substitute teaching in an elementary school at the age of 76, and a retired brother is taking real estate classes at a local community college.

Finally, society has come to realize that people from many walks of life have a lifelong need and desire to learn and to teach. New ways to communicate educational information, to provide feedback opportunities, and to stimulate creative thinking must be developed now that the lifelong education movement is underway. Ideas relative to communication and lifelong education for older persons are discussed more fully in a later chapter.

COMMUNICATION AS A PROBLEM AREA FOR STUDY

To study communication as a process demands an interdisciplinary approach, for it is really a study of the variables involved in human interaction. Understanding requires input from psychology, sociology, anthropology, mathematics, linguistics, physics, neurophysiology, and numerous subfields. Through the years, some who have sought to understand the process more completely have constructed models that, in the main, embrace a (1) source, (2) code, (3) transmission medium, and (4) receiver. There is at present a hierarchy of fundamental information relative to communication. But, at best, we have just begun to come to grips with the complexity of the process.

Models portray, in an abstract and general way, that which is common to all communication situations. Therefore, there is no specific model for communication as it occurs with children, with youth, or with the elderly.

BARRIERS TO COMMUNICATION WITH OLDER PEOPLE

Although it is recognized that some of the barriers that make communication with older persons difficult are unique to individual situations, it is also recognized that there are common barriers as well.

Youth-oriented Society

Unlike some other countries of the world, the United States has placed great emphasis upon youth as being synonymous with promise and worth. Retirement in most instances is mandatory upon reaching a particular age. Older persons are perceived as being out of date; thus, how could they possibly make meaningful contributions to society except in rare cases. Therefore, with the orientation upon youth, there is no real need to call upon older people for advice.

Physical Isolation

It is difficult for anyone who is isolated physically from others to engage in much meaningful communication. It is so often the plight of older persons to be set apart from the mainstream of activity and thus to be deprived of the opportunity to communicate. Furthermore, as isolation continues, there is less and less common ground upon which to develop communication when given the opportunity to do so. Therefore, the physical isolation itself and the dehumanizing effects of physical isolation become barriers to communication.

Shifting Societal Values

Most thinking adults would attest to the fact that the values held by society have shifted somewhat in their lifetimes. Some things held as sacred yesterday are not viewed as sacred today. Moral codes upheld by most a decade or two ago are flaunted by many today. High standards set for achievement, which characterized our schools, are in many instances being compromised. Pride in the accomplishment of a piece of work well done is lost as the identity of the workman has been obscured by mass production of commodities. Thus, one who has grown older and maintains the values of yesteryear, may find it difficult to communicate with younger people because of the differences in premises upon which discussions could develop.

Sensory Losses

Although, with advancing age, there is general decrease in acuity and discriminatory function of the senses, perhaps the most devastating to human communication is decrease in auditory function. When this occurs as a sensorineural loss, conversation can become difficult, particularly where there is background noise or the chatter of voices in a group. A later chapter handles this topic in detail, but it is well to note at this point that a hearing loss can loom large as a barrier to communication.

Diminished Power

When older persons are no longer in a position to make those decisions that affect her/him, or that affect the behavior of others, they suffer a loss of power and status and frequently withdraw from situations that normally would have called for communication. When their dollar resources are lessened, they once again suffer from diminished power and are not called upon in the same ways as previously to contribute to society. Once again, this can and often does lead to a reduction in communication opportunities and thus can be viewed as a barrier. Any factor or group of factors that adversely affect the self-concept can have far reaching effects upon communication.

Lack of Transportation

If older persons are not free to move about from one location to another, to church, store, club, visiting relatives and friends, their opportunities for communication are reduced. Thus, the lack of transportation can prove to be a significant barrier to communication.

Retirement

Although retirement does not always serve as a barrier to communication, it can have this effect because the person is removed from the daily contacts and from those persons with whom he has communicated, in many instances, for years. Unless other activities are found to fill the void, retirement can create a substantial hiatus between the retiree and other people, thus reducing the opportunity for communication.

APPROACHES TO THE STUDY OF AGING

The life cycle as it was lived in 1900 has literally been extended with the addition of late middle life and later maturity. Until quite recently, relatively little attention had been paid to education throughout the life cycle. There is concern for making these later years both happy and productive; in other words, adding life to years as well as years to life. Few people have been specially educated to provide leadership and expertise in this area of study.

Social gerontology, the science of aging in society, demands an inter-disciplinary approach. Being an expert in the biological, social-psychological, and physical components of aging while also being able to function at the interfaces of these disciplines would require an almost super human intelligence. Generally, a team approach is employed in the various institutes and centers established to study aging, and team members are experts in rather specific areas while at the same time they are aware of developments in the other dimensions.

Disengagement Theory

Theoretical bases for the study of aging have developed somewhat slowly, but the pace has accelerated as research evidence has accumulated. Cumming and Henry's (1961) work, *Growing Old: The Process of Disengagement,* is the generally accepted source of the first social-psychological theory of aging, i.e., the disengagement theory. The introduction of this theory was an attempt to explain the social withdrawal of many older people. The process of withdrawal was considered to be modal for aging populations, biologically and psychologically inevitable, and a requisite for successful adjustment to aging. Although the contributions of this pioneering work have been many, it became necessary to search for evidence to support a more inclusive theory, one that would account for older persons who do not disengage but have adjusted well to the aging process.

Activity Theory

Busse (1969) and Atchley (1972) provide helpful discussions of a second leading theoretical position referred to as the activity theory. According to the activity theory, the majority of older persons maintain fairly constant amounts of activity or social participation, the amount depending more upon past life style and socioeconomic forces than upon age itself. Maintaining substantial levels of physical, mental, and social activity is considered necessary for successful adjustment to aging. Other theoretical positions are being studied as well, but at this point in time there is no generally accepted theory of aging.

Ecological Systems Approach

The ecological systems approach is being developed at several universities that have organized separate colleges around this theoretical framework (examples are Michigan State University, Cornell University, and Pennsylvania State University). The relationship of man to his near environment is a key notion, and focus is placed upon the interfaces of the social-psychological, physical-technological, and biological support systems as they make an impact upon man. The theory is used as a basis for the analysis of various studies of man that include the study of human aging. One might use it as a basis of analysis, for example, when searching for the answer(s) to a research question, such as: How is the life satisfaction of older people influenced by communication opportunities, communication effectiveness, and other important variables that characterize their environmental subsystems?

RESEARCH QUESTIONS NEEDING ANSWERS

The following chapters will seek to answer many of the questions relative to communication and aging and hopefully will raise many more. It is only through the identification of important questions and systematic efforts made to answer them, that new approaches can be developed that will one day make a difference in the lives of older people whose major problems are linked immutably with communication.

At Michigan State University, a conference was held that had as its principal objective the identification of researchable questions concerning communication and older people. Because of the diversity of interests involved in any consideration of communication and aging, professionals representing many different backgrounds were brought together. The group consisted of older persons and those specifically from the fields of law, medicine, physiology, gerontology, political science, history, education, philosophy, psychology, sociology, religion, nursing, resource development, social work, family science, and specialties in communications to include interpersonal communication, telecommunication, journalism, advertising, and communication disorders. Elected public officials also participated.

Those specific subgroups that discussed the needed areas of research as pertaining to communication and aging focused upon: 1) lifelong education, 2) speech, language, and audition, 3) legal, political, and organizational considerations, 4) health considerations, 5) interpersonal communication, and 6) mass media and aging.

Although at the time of the writing of this chapter the development of the proceedings of that Conference is incomplete, it is of interest to note, as an example, one of the questions arising with reference to health and communication: Where do older persons currently get health information? Who constructs the information? How are they transmitted?

Regarding mass media and aging, a sample of the questions that emerged concerned the effects that news, information, and advertising have on older persons. Does it help them in coping behavior? What effects have the news and informational programs on their political participation?

With reference to the legal, political, and organizational needs and older people, one of the questions that arose dealt with the degree to which one could ensure the necessary support for networks of communication among older persons and between older persons with the larger society. What structures are now existing to facilitate this? What structures should exist?

On the topic of communication disorders, one question dealt with the determination of speech, language, and hearing pathologies most often observed in older people and the effects these have upon communication performance. What is the intelligibility of the speech of older people? How does hearing loss play a role in feelings of security in the communication situation?

The group discussing lifelong education puzzled over, for example, the possible existence of bureacratic regulations that adversely serve the possibilities and needs for lifelong education. Still another question related to the way in which a university could provide for degree and nondegree programs in a way that would be most compatible to needs, aspirations, and energies of older people.

Interpersonal communication and aging as deliberated by the discussion group dealt with, for example, questions concerning the aging from the point of view of their roles and participation in social networks. How much time does the average older person spend in interpersonal communication? How does residential mobility affect the interpersonal network structures? What is the replacement rate in the interpersonal communication network of older persons?

The above examples are but a very few of the myriad research questions that emerged. The hope is that many of the questions will be answered through research efforts.

SUMMARY

Throughout this chapter, the discussion has been focused upon some fundamental considerations that relate to older people and the communication process. The centrality of communication to living is stressed. Individual differences among the older population as regards their abilities and motivations to communicate have been reviewed.

Definitions of both communication and aging have been presented. For practical purposes, the definition of communication includes intrapersonal as well as the traditional categories of interpersonal, small and large groups, and mass media. The label "the aging" encompasses those 65 years of age and older.

A brief resumé is given of attitudes toward older people stemming from the time of the early Greek philosophers. A comparison is drawn between the early philosophic positions and the emergent view in developed societies wherein the older segment of society is gradually being viewed once more as an important resource.

Stress is laid upon the importance of providing for communication opportunities for older people. A brief resumé is provided of the specialized areas that follow in succeeding chapters. Reference is made to research questions that were generated at a multidisciplinary conference dealing with communication and aging.

LITERATURE CITED

Arnoff, C. 1974. Old age in prime time. J. Commun. 24:86–87.

Atchley, R. C. 1972. The Social Forces in Later Life: An Introduction to Social Gerontology. Wadsworth, Belmont, Calif.

Busse, E. W. 1969. Theories of aging. *In* E. W. Busse and E. Pfeiffer (eds.), Behavior and Adaptation in Late Life, pp. 11–32. Little Brown, Boston.

Cumming, E., and W. E. Henry. 1961. Growing Old: The Process of Disengagement. Basic Books, New York.

de Beauvoir, S. 1972. The Coming of Age. Putnam's Sons, New York.

Eisdorfer, C. 1970. Rorschach rigidity and sensory decrement in a senescent population. *In* E. Palmore (ed.), Normal Aging, pp. 232–242. Duke University Press, Durham, N.C.

Eisele, F. R. 1974. Preface. Political consequences of aging. Annal. Amer. Acad. Pol. Soc. Sci. 415:ix.

Estes, E. H. 1969. Health experience in the elderly. *In* E. W. Busse and E. Pfeiffer (eds.), Behavior and Adaptation in Late Life, pp. 115–128. Little Brown, Boston.

Harris, L., and Associates, Inc. 1975. The Myth and Reality of Aging in America. National Council on the Aging.

Moberg, D. O. 1972. Religion and the aging family. Family Coordinator 21:47–60.

Neugarten, B. L. 1975. The future and the young-old. The Gerontologist 15(11): 4–9.

Pratt, H. J. 1974. Old age associations in national politics. Annal. Amer. Acad. Pol. Soc. Sci. 415: 106–119.

Proceedings of the 1971 White House Conference on Aging. 1971. Toward a National Policy on Aging. Section of Physical and Mental Health, pp. 19–28. U.S. Government Printing Office, Washington, D.C.

Sparks, G. M., and Brody, E. A. 1970. The aged are family members. Family Process 9: 195–210.

chapter 2

A Retiree's Perspective on Communication

Leo A. Haak, Ph.D.

This may be an unconventional chapter because it is written by "one of them"—a retiree—who is immediately and vitally concerned with communication in relation to older people.

OVERVIEW

When a retiree learns that a book is being written on *Aging and Communication,* he assumes, at least he hopes, that it will help improve the lot of older people. But he knows that communication is not fixed, that the effects of communication depend on: 1) *who* communicates, 2) *what* is communicated, 3) the *symbols* used, and 4) the *means* of transmitting symbols. Furthermore, these aspects of communication are all deeply embedded in culture, i.e., in customs, behavior, attitudes, social practices and, in some cases, laws. Culture today is the result of development, or change, over many years. Not only has culture changed, it will continue to change. The same could be said about the roles and activities of older people.

Communication—extended and changed as necessary—may be expected to benefit older people. Using the language of the day, it will help *liberate* them. But, speaking more scientifically, the book will help *change* their place in society consistent with generally accepted ideas and goals. This chapter will indicate some of the things necessary to accomplish this end.

Our present culture contains a number of attitudes toward older people including:

1. Prey on them . . .
2. Ignore them . . .
3. Help them (some people favor helping them in ways believed good for them, others favor helping them but only if they "ask," accept "our" way, and are properly "grateful")
4. Accept them as equals, wherever qualified (in a division of labor

17

system); this would include helping in a way desired by older people
insofar as possible

5. Depend on them . . . in their areas of expertise

Naturally, people have these attitudes in various combinations, and some
practice them selectively toward individuals and groups of older people.

Many will reject attitudes 1, 2, and 3 and accept 4 and 5. But to the
extent that this book deals with *how* to communicate with the over 65
population, it could be used by those who would prey on them (1), or to
help them in a way not acceptable to many older people (3). The last two
attitudes toward older people are consistent with the attitude of dealing
with them as people, and not as has-beens. Widespread acceptance of these
attitudes would constitute a change in the position of older people in our
culture today.

When communication is viewed from the standpoint of older people
there are at least eight important areas to be considered. Each is identified
briefly below and will be discussed more fully in the sections following.

1. *Vocabulary* It is important to make vocabulary more accurate, complete, and acceptable. The last involves the reduction of ageism in language.

2. *Lifespan* It is important to recognize the many variations in the period
from age 65 until death . . . within the four systems in which people live:
biological, economic, interpersonal relations, and societal. Biological aging
occurs in only one of them. For instance, some think of the aged only as
the senile, or those in the period of extreme dependency.

3. *Life Styles* Significant variations exist in the life styles among the aging,
and may be accepted and encouraged as being appropriate in this period of
life as well as in earlier periods.

4. *Ethics in Communication* The "right to know" or "truth in communication" is particularly important for older people. To require disclosure of
self-interest by those communicating with older people might be one step.

5. *Completeness of Information* Complete information is needed in order
to make wise decisions. Government may have a responsibility here if this
goal has not been met by other agencies.

6. *Adequacy of the Communications Network* It is well to recognize the
inadequacy of the existing network, in terms of making it possible for
older people to protect themselves, and to work toward an appropriate
extension of the network. A grass roots approach in which older people
provide the volunteer labor and the public pays for the overhead might
serve this purpose.

7. *Equality in Communication* It is important to accept older people as full participants in communication with an equal right to initiate inquiry in any area necessary to their protection, or to the expansion of their useful activities.

8. *Continued Productivity of the Aging* The continued involvement in society by older people should be facilitated and encouraged. This would include individual and social productivity but not necessarily economic productivity.

VOCABULARY

It is fairly easy to talk about aging *and* older people, but it is more difficult to talk about aging *with* older people. So many older people react emotionally to nearly every term used that the discussion often gets bogged down in endless explanations, redefinitions, and word substitutions. Communication is often stopped before it begins. We can speculate as to the reasons.

One possibility is that older people resent growing old, with all the physiological and other changes involved. They just do not want to talk about it and would be more comfortable if others did not either. The denial of age is characteristic of our youth-oriented culture (Percy, 1974) and is manifested in ways such as keeping one's age a secret, using drugs to restore or preserve youthful vigor, coloring hair, and refusing to associate with anyone older than oneself.

A more probable reason is the resentment against the put-down words in our language. This has been identified as ageism (Butler, 1975), and it is similar to racism and sexism. For instance, even the seemingly innocent words "retired" or "retiree" can be derogatory. Most people in our culture think in terms of the dichotomy of work and play. When a person retires he is no longer "productive" and now has endless hours to fill with avocations, limited only by health and wealth. When someone asks, "And what do you do in retirement?" the retiree is well advised to be vague and say something like, "Oh, many things," or "I fish a lot" (which he may not), but not to tell the truth and run the risk of being thought a braggart or a liar. Generally speaking, people are not prepared to accept the possibility that a retiree is a functioning productive person who happens to be no longer "gainfully employed."

When a pre-retiree says to me, "How nice it is of you to do so many things even though you have retired!" I am at a loss as to how to answer. I cannot say, "Did you think I died when I retired?" or, "You are too young to understand." Women's groups have counterattacked their situation with terms such as "male chauvinist pig" and racial groups with the word "bigot," but older people probably feel too insecure to do anything but "take it" and smile. Sadly enough, even older people frequently believe the many stereotypes of aging and spend more and more time doing less and less (Butler, 1975). Perhaps we should become more aggressive and counterattack with "ageist!"—but first we must make the word part of our vocabulary.

The ultimate form of ageism can be observed in many nursing homes when persons are in the stage of extreme dependency and are treated as disoriented children . . . "Their bodily needs are assiduously looked after" . . . but not their minds (Henry, 1963).

A third reason why vocabulary blocks communication is the inaccuracy of the words used to describe reality. For instance, both the words "retirement" and "unproductive" are inexact and may evoke different meanings. It might be more accurate if we always said "occupational retirement" and "economic unproductivity." In fact, after retirement many people are very active; some accentuate other types of activities and some even undertake new types of activities, yet pre-retirees often think of "retirement" as "retirement from life." Furthermore, to specify the kind of productivity leaves open the idea that there may be other types of productivity.

When it comes to words describing "reality," some of them are ludicrous on the surface. In this category are words such as Golden Years, Harvest Years, Senior Citizens, 77 Years Young, Nursing Home, Social Security, Medicaid. Various suggestions have been made to increase the accuracy of descriptions: "the later years" for Golden or Harvest Years; "older people" or "older Americans" for Senior Citizens; "care facility" for Nursing Home. In the interest of accuracy, some think "partial" or "minimum" should be worked in between Social and Security. And despite disclaimers, Medicaid is an acceptable word today for welfare so maybe we should say "Medicaid welfare." Conservatives and some young people like to "bug" social security recipients by calling it welfare . . . which it is, but only partly so. So the war of words continues.

The variation between words and reality in institutions where older people are cared for is interesting. Over time, there have been work houses, poor farms, homes for the aged, convalescent centers, rest homes, retirement homes, nursing homes, and care facilities. The 1975 Lansing, Michigan, telephone book lists five nursing homes, four houses, two residents' homes, two retirement homes, and one each with the following words in their names: home, medical facility, home for elderly people, care center, convalescent center, and storybook acres. This is not to suggest that these facilities are all alike, but the significant differences are probably not indicated in their names. "Home" is used 10 times, "house" is used four times, "center" twice, and "facility" once!

The final concern with vocabulary is the absence of terms or words for concepts, both new and old. Thus, Butler (1975) projects an "Ideal form of care for the old" in his chapter entitled "Houses of Death are a Lively Business," but he does not have a satisfactory name for it; the closest he comes to it is "multipurpose centers or galaxies." Maybe we can call them "Butler's Units" until we have a new name for this new concept! Percy calls his chapter on nursing homes, "Nursing Home or Warehouse?" (Percy, 1974).

This need for words to fit reality (concepts) could be extended greatly. One other example is stages in aging. We all know the final period for some is extreme dependency, but what do we call the earlier periods, closer to 65? Is this "early old age," or "young old age," or "the active years," or what? Words must fit reality!

Regardless of one's age, it is frequently difficult even to think about aging and old people, primarily because of fear and sometimes because of guilt. But to try to think without words for concepts and ideas leaves one literally speechless.

LIFESPAN

By definition, "the aging" are the people over 65. This population can be visualized from the adapted excerpt from the Standard Life Expectancy Table. Starting with 100 people who reach 65, the following can be expected to be alive at each of the specific ages indicated below:

Age	Number of people
65	100
70	78
75	61
80	45
85	33
90	24
95	14
100	4

(Institute of Life Insurance, 1972)

Aging has three different possible meanings. One meaning is in terms of years: each year we become one year older. Another meaning, not necessarily closely related to years lived, is in terms of health or general and specific changes in the body (the biological system). One part of the body can age more rapidly than some other parts; thus, aging in this second sense may be greater in some 65-year-olds than in some 75-year-olds. The third meaning of aging is in terms of the other three nonbiological systems in which we also live: economic, interpersonal relations, and societal. Changes in these systems are not necessarily related to aging in the biological system, or in the time system (chronological age). In fact, chronological age may be an almost meaningless variable, but some group differences should be kept in mind. Life expectancy for those 65 years of age has been calculated to be: male, 13.1 years; female, 16.7 years. Biological aging, however, is a complex variable, or a multitude of variables. Health, or "decline" for those negatively oriented, can be measured on many continua, including sight, hearing, dexterity, mobility, strength, reflexes, mental acuteness, memory, and stamina, to mention only a few.

There is no precise order in which physiological changes take place, no precise time when particular changes start, and no fixed relationship between them (Riley and Foner, 1968; Palmore, 1974). Aging appears to be a highly individualistic happening—at least in the early years after 65. To what extent aging is rooted in genetics, health habits (food and exercise, for instance), disease, and chance is not important in a book on communication. The publications of the Geronotological Society, *Journal of Gerontology* and *The Gerontologist,* deal in depth with all aspects of aging. Not everyone has the same characteristics of physiological aging before death (Manney, 1975), just as not everyone becomes senile, in spite of my young colleague's classification of the subperiods after 65 as soon-to-be-senile, nearly senile, and senile.

Before defining and presenting the case for the other three systems in which we also live, let us note the relationship between biological aging and one non-biological aspect of life, occupation. Do health, strength, reflexes, etc., have any invariable relationship to occupational advancement—except possibly in professional athletics? Health may be a favorable factor, but is probably not a determining factor.

In the preceding paragraph, part of a second system, the economic, was identified. However, there is more to the economic system than occupation, because that is only one way to get income. Income might also come from investments, gifts, or public contributions (welfare). And the other side of the economic exchange system is using income to buy goods and services. Just as the body changes over time, so consumer habits tend to change. For instance, older people usually have the problem of making their money reach, so many use time and energy to buy economically. Furthermore, because money tends to be limited, buying tends to be stable. People buy about the same goods and services month after month. Yet another effect of aging in older people's economic system is the increase in "do-it-yourself" production, which diminishes dependence on the exchange system.

The last two systems, interpersonal relations and society, will be discussed very briefly. It is sufficient to note that we have many types of human relationships and engage in many types of activities. Do these remain constant over time? Are they related in some immutable way to bodily aging, or are there great variations among groups and individuals? In some cases this area of living becomes an extensive and rich experience after retirement.

And, finally, the fourth system in which we all live is society or, more appropriately, culture. For those who are other-oriented, this system provides the opportunity for mutual aid and/or volunteer work, as well as the opportunity to work with others in an effort to change culture in the direction of generally accepted goals.

In these three non-biological areas, change does not necessarily mean decline and deterioration. "Aging" may be appropriate for the biological system, but "change" is more descriptive for the other systems.

The tendency not to consider the whole period of life after 65 is not surprising, for even people over 65 often seem to "make time stand still" and give little thought to the possible, and probable, periods ahead. Furthermore, younger people often think of older people in terms of cases, namely their parents, or grandparents, and tend to generalize from their state of health and activities.

LIFE STYLES

At what age is there the greatest variation among people in their life styles: health, interests, habits, activities? According to Butler (1975), "Physiological indicators show a greater range from the mean in old age than in any other age group, and this is true of personality as well."

He does not give any specific evidence to support his generalizations, but to assume that those differences in life styles that exist at 65 suddenly disappear is illogical. Probably the reason many people generalize about older people and act as if older people were all alike is because they concentrate on the final, rather than the earlier, years in aging. Those who reach a period of extreme dependency—a nursing home phase—are frequently much alike.

This chapter will not consider the factors contributing to divergence in life patterns up to age 65, but no doubt occupation is important. Neither can it fully consider convergence after age 65, but cultural factors are probably important here, especially the stereotype of an older person.

Studies have been made on the types of variation in life styles, including *From Thirty to Seventy* by Maas and Kuypers (1974), and "Disengagement and Patterns of Aging" by Havighurst, Neugarten, and Tobin (1968).

However, two other examples of group differences are easily observable. Some older people segregate themselves into enclaves of the Sun City type. There are, no doubt, significant differences among the various retirement centers, as well as groups, or categories, within these units. But these enclaves constitute one broad life style group.

Another example of people of like interests finding each other is observable in Senior Centers within any neighborhood. Administrators of such centers sometimes wonder why it is difficult to attract more than 5 to 10 percent of the older people in an area to a given center. It could be that the particular life style to which the program is geared may be limited to this number of people. Maybe we need as many programs as there are significant groups in any geographic area.

Still another example of the multiplicty of life styles in a defined group can be illustrated. There are over 500 Michigan State University retirees living in the greater Lansing, Michigan, area. About one half of these retirees are former faculty members. Regardless of widely diversified programs in the eight monthly meetings every year, it is possible to interest less than 20 percent of this group. Maybe if we had 10 to 50 Retiree's Clubs, or that many sections in one club, we could interest all in at least one program.

Probably the lifelong individual and group differences tend to persist well into the later years, even within a home for the aged where many forces tend to reduce or even eliminate differences.

One interesting note with respect to life style variations: Lieberman (1973) found that certain elements in life styles have different consequences, and that those who continue to "fight the system" tend to outlive those who "age gracefully."

Christiansen, in *Dignity in Aging* (1974), makes an ethical case for respecting older people and permitting them to continue decision-making in all areas in which they are competent. He argues: "Families should learn that the decline of their old folks is often gradual. There is no sudden need to take all responsibility from them. At each stage a certain sphere of responsibility remains, and it should be fostered as long as is possible" (p. 8). This section supports the same position: not only *must* we in communication take into account differential life styles in the later years in order to be effective, we *should* do so because variation and choice are basic to human freedom in our type of culture. The section on Lifespan dealt essentially with the quantity of life; this section deals more with quality.

ETHICS IN COMMUNICATION

Older people often feel the increasing strain of living in a world with two types of people at opposite ends of the continuum. At one end are those whose relationships are characterized by love, in which each person tries to do more for others than he receives; this tends to be typical of family and close friendship relationships. At the opposite end of the continuum is the self-interest of the typical business relationships. We can call these two worlds "the friendly world" and "the unfriendly world," even though they overlap.

In the unfriendly world, the ethical issues in communication are more important, and it is in this world that many older people feel increasingly threatened and vulnerable. They know that communication costs money and that those who pay for it expect to get their money back—with a profit. Many older people are painfully aware that their limited resources make it impossible to "buy" the information they need for their own protection.

The unfriendly world can be further divided from a fringe of criminals and near-criminals to the legitimate business interests and the professions. And these elements of the unfriendly world might be arranged in a hierarchy according to the degree they are a felt threat to older people. There are legal safeguards against the worst abuses, and provisions for recourse in the case of deception or certain other practices.

The assumption in our society is that all are equal: buyers and sellers are equal, and so are, or should be, the initiators and receivers of communication. Ideally, anyone on the receiving end of a message can judge whether or not his self-interest is consistent with the self-interest of the initiator. As suggested earlier, however, the relative power to pay for communication can affect this balance. Are we all really equal in communication? At all stages in the life cycle?

There is certainly some evidence of inequality between initiators and receivers of communication, otherwise the existing protective laws make no sense. But short of further and more extensive legal safeguards, one possible response would be to support a program of full disclosure by the initiator of communication. Such a program could be started by individual persons, encouraged through a recommended ethical system, or, in some cases, required by law. Certain disclosures are already required by law in some areas of finance and politics. It has been suggested that age be used in some cases as a basis for requiring the supplying of more information, so that the older person is better able to make an informed judgment between various self-interests.

The particulars of full personal disclosure might include a report of source of income as one verifiable item. If, for example, a doctor recommends a hospital or a nursing home in which he has a financial interest, the prospective patient should probably know about it. And maybe a broker should be required to remind the investor that his income is derived primarily from commissions on the investor's investments.

COMPLETENESS OF INFORMATION

If it is assumed that an objective of communication is to provide all information necessary to make decisions, it must go beyond full disclosure by the supplier of information. All disclosure does is to admit self-interest and indicate that the information provided is limited. The salesman, special pleader, or advocate cannot be expected to present the whole picture.

If full information is important, how does anyone obtain it? In the business world we get part of it from the rival claims of competitors. The government and private organizations provide additional information to supplement or correct, if necessary, this economic information. There are a number of magazines and services covering areas of concern to older people. Some of these national publications are: *Changing Times* (Kiplinger), *Consumer News* (HEW), *Consumers Reports* (Consumers' Union), *Modern Maturity* (AARP), *Money* (Time, Inc.), *Retirement Living* (Whitney Communications), and *United Retirement Newsletter* (United Business Service). If one had enough money to buy these, skill to analyze them, space to file them, and time to look up information in these and related sources, he could protect himself reasonably well. The third source is our own experiences and observations and those of our friends and acquaintances.

We have not systematically evaluated the adequacy and limitations of the above sources, but we believe that older people, for various reasons—

fading hearing, sight, and energy; trustfulness; limitations of friendship circles—need more help than some other age groups, especially if they are also poor and not very well educated.

To illustrate the above generalization, older people often ask, "How much health and hospital insurance do I need to supplement Medicare?" Perhaps every company that sells such insurance can answer this question honestly and fully, and it usually happens that they have just the right policy to supplement Medicare. The older person has the option of buying or not buying the policy, but not the opportunity to make up his mind on the basis of full information. Who is going to help lead the worried older person through the maze of claims and counterclaims and come up with the best policy or combination of policies? This issue cannot be brushed aside by saying that all policies are more or less alike and therefore it does not matter very much which is bought. Even if this were true—which is doubtful—there is still the question of how much protection should be purchased. It is difficult for the layman to understand the exceptions, the exclusions, and what is really covered. For instance, many people think they are buying coverage in a nursing home when they buy hospital insurance. They do not know that custodial care is a noninsurable risk in our society.

Some may have noticed the TV, radio, or other advertisement in which a banker says, "We pay 5.5 percent interest—the highest allowable interest by law." But the "banker" never goes on to say, "According to government reports, inflation is now at a 10 percent rate." People need *both* sets of information to make a wise decision whether or not to put their money in the bank.

One example of more nearly full information is the publication, *Money.* (See articles "A Word to the Wise about Old Age Groups" (March 1975) and "A Concerned Relative's Guide to Old Age Care" (October 1975).) Perhaps our government should be responsible for providing "missing" information. However, it often happens that when a protective law is passed, the enforcement agency is taken over by a segment of the private sector that the agency is set up to regulate. Then, too, it has often been difficult to get the results of research, done at public expense, made available to the general public. For example, information on hearing aids collected by the Veterans' Administration was not willingly released to the taxpayers. Consumers' Union, a private group, took the initiative to make this information part of the public domain.

Sometimes more information is not the only thing needed. In a given item, a list of all the ingredients in technical terms may mean little to the average layman. Information must also be understandable in terms of concepts meaningful to the potential user of the information.

One way the government could serve older people's need for more complete information would be to include in governmental publications the statement, "You will be covered by Medicare after age 65 for approximately 37 percent of your medical bills." (The percentage of coverage is going down each year; therefore, this item would need constant updating.) Older people should also be told that many nursing homes and doctors charge private patients more than those patients paid for by Medicaid. They should be informed that when their resources are exhausted they would get the same care, probably in the same home. This would be more complete, more honest, and might soften the psychological blow an older patient feels if it is necessary to become a "welfare patient."

On this general area of dealing with extreme dependency and medical care, there is an almost total blackout of solid information coupled with a plethora of deceptive words to mask unacceptable meanings. When dealing with older people, advocates of honesty and integrity, including authors Jessica Mitford (1963) and Mary Adelaide Mendelson (1974), all emphasize the need for full and honest information.

ADEQUACY OF COMMUNICATION NETWORK

This is the third section addressed to the problem of defense in a sometimes unfriendly world. The importance of disclosure of the communicator's self-interest has been emphasized mainly on the ethics for implementation. The importance of having all relevant information needed to make decisions has been dealt with, and it has been suggested that the government will take a major responsibility for this as a last resort. This section deals with the need to extend our communications network, and it proposes that older people depend on themselves—a grass roots approach needing financing only to pay the overhead.

This approach has been formulated into a tentative plan which could be called an Information Bank, Information Exchange, or Experience Exchange. There are many retirees now drawing annuities from a common fund who might benefit from participation in such a plan. The communication network already exists.

Retirees need more than money—they need information on hundreds of specific problems they may face as they get older. They cannot secure in advance all the information they need, such as in a pre-retirement program, for they do not know which problems they will have to face and in what order. They can neither purchase the answers in the market place nor work out the problems themselves, for they do not have the money, skills, time, or energy needed. Also, the informal grapevine on which they depended earlier may have shrunk.

If a system can be developed in which the division of labor is practiced and the findings shared, all could benefit. However, there are no answers, even to common problems, that fit all people and all circumstances. People must, after all, make the final choice from the available alternatives. The project would consist of collecting and organizing the known alternatives to various problems to be made available when, and if, needed.

The most logical location for a major "bank" would be in a university community because much knowledge is already stored there (in the library and in the minds of specialists) and is constantly being extended through research. It is also a place where many competent retirees live who might be involved as volunteers.

It is anticipated that knowledge would be secured from examination of the literature, both applied and theoretical (order is intentional), from interviewing appropriate specialists, from communication with appropriate national organizations, and from the older people on the basis of their experience and observations. There would be a volunteer or a minimum-paid coordinator in each of the relevant fields outlined in the four systems. Thus, the money costs should be reasonable.

There could be other primary information banks in university communities that are strong in areas of importance to older people. There could be linked secondary banks in communities of any size, all perhaps connected by a computer. While there would be "deposits" in any bank, it is assumed that there would be more in the university-centered banks. "Withdrawals" could be made from any bank without charge in the usual sense—merely that those who withdraw contribute to building the bank by reporting their experiences and observations or evaluating information in the bank.

Three of the most probable difficulties in implementing this plan are: First, older people may not realize the need for information, because many needs arise as a result of gradual change. Perhaps a series of self-administered inventories could be developed to detect such need. Second, older people often cling tenaciously to the belief that they must help themselves and not even ask others for information. Many accept suffering as inevitable in aging. Finally, many older people may not report their experiences and observations because they believe that everyone is so different that what they have to say could not be of any value to anyone else. Only a trial bank could prove whether or not these obstacles and others can be overcome.

A second suggestion for improving the efficiency of communication has been made in the proposal that a manual on "How to Get the Most Out of the Telephone" be prepared for those over 65. The data would be collected both from the telephone users and from the telephone company. To illustrate, many do not know how to turn up the bell, or that receivers with built-in amplifiers are available, or that especially low rates are available in some areas, allowing limited outgoing calls but unlimited incoming calls. The manual could include suggestions on how to set up a reassurance calls system in a community or how to match homebound people for friendship calls. There are many more. Of course, this proposal would not help the estimated five million older Americans (Butler, 1975) who do not have a telephone.

Such a manual would be printed in large type and the contents would be available orally by telephone during business hours. Various means could be used to inform people of these telephone possibilities for older people.

Somewhat similar proposals have been made in response to an invitation for suggestions about the driving problems of older people from the point of view of an older driver. A manual was also suggested based on the same method of gathering data, i.e., by going to the experts and to the people.

Common driving problems faced by older people could be identified, perhaps on the basis of accident data, with constructive suggestions on how to reduce specific risks. Even the conditions under which a person might consider giving up driving could be indicated. To give up driving is considered by many to be "dying a little," so constructive alternatives are available that are more humane than using the threat approach: "If you have a lot of accidents we will take your license (or your insurance) away." Older people know that; for they live with the fear every day they drive and need not be reminded of possibilities—they need help.

The purpose of trying to improve communication in this area is obviously to make it possible to drive a little longer. An additional service might be to have a sympathetic driver trainer available to monitor driving habits of any who wished this type of assistance. Communication problems may be solved best in reference to specific problems older people face in living.

EQUALITY IN COMMUNICATION

No doubt the balance between talking and listening and listening and talking, which is at the heart of communication, varies considerably during life. Often older people complain, "No one will listen."

The problem here might be clarified by identifying three points of view about younger people's relationship to older people—to those over 65: 1) tell them what (you think) they need to know, 2) tell them, but only if they ask, and 3) tell them, even though they don't ask. The "power versus respect" aspect of a relationship in each of these three cases is perfectly obvious.

Older people frequently need help in asking the right question in terms of their and society's best interest, and younger people (pre-retirees) need reminding that this is a basic right, not an occasion for condescending tolerance. True equality in communication follows only the acceptance of the third position.

If we assume that a person who is aging chronologically has a continuing right to make his own decisions in all areas in which he is competent, then we must grant that he has the right to seek relevant information. He needs to protect himself, as indicated in previous sections, but he also may need to take the initiative as he seeks to develop new roles and activities for himself and for other older people.

As a person gets chronologically older, his biological system may change at a variable rate and in different directions, and his operating in the occupational world may be ended, but his functioning in individual production and making consumer choices may be expanding. Likewise, his relationships with people (and ideas) may be changing, and his participation in social production (mutual aid/volunteer work and decision making) is changing also. In other words, a person may be declining in some parts of life at the same time he is growing in other phases of human activities. In these transitional periods the importance of communication is extremely important.

Another way to depict this relationship between a person and various stages of life is in terms of teaching and learning. The older person may be thought of as a learner: one who takes the initiative in defining objectives, obtaining information, and drawing conclusions. He needs the help of others, not so much as teachers, but as resource people to help him find answers—after clarifying questions.

An attempt has been made to demonstrate this approach in the "Forum for the Over Sixty" in the Evening College at Michigan State University. Participants are assumed to have enrolled because they have specific concerns. They may also have subconscious fears that motivate them. The instructor (for want of a more descriptive term) considers himself a resource person to help them find alternative responses. Those who expect the instructor to present "the questions" older people face and give "the answers" find the Forum of little value.

There is an evident inconsistency between the above brief description of the Forum and the three approaches indicated earlier in this section for this is an example of two! It is believed that the mass media, educational institutions, all who have the necessary expertise (gerontologists), and all who are concerned about old people and life in the later years have the third responsibility: to "tell them even though they do not ask"—at least up to the time they reach extreme dependency, if they ever do.

CONTINUED PRODUCTIVITY BY THE AGING

Life is a continuing series of transitions, of beginnings, continuities, and endings. Some transitions or changes are more dramatic than others, perhaps because of their importance in our value system, or because many areas of life can be affected at once by the same change. Occupational retirement is often a traumatic transition.

Before discussing at any length the continuing productivity of older people, it is necessary to consider the place of older people in our society—not only what that place is, but also what it can be. Only then can the role of communication in this continuing change be profitably examined further.

First, older people are either blamed (scapegoats) for "the mess we are in" or thanked for all things considered desirable in our heritage. Maybe both are logical. Older people are also useful as examples, so middle-aged and younger people can see themselves as they might be when they get older—models to follow, or avoid.

Second, older people are consumers. They tend to stabilize demand in an often erratic economy, because they usually spend all their income for about the same goods and services. Thus, they provide jobs for many people who, directly or indirectly, serve older people.

Third, older people are a source of information, or a window to the past. In a very practical way they are a ready source of information to younger people on countless matters, such as on how to can foods, what are the stages of childhood, and when to plant tulip bulbs. Furthermore, they can often provide historical perspective from memory of changes in society and on their family (become genealogists) to give it roots. Many can go beyond information and offer judgments based on experience. As the wise old man said, "Good judgments are based on the experiences of bad judgments."

Fourth, and finally, they are still producers, and can be even greater producers when this concept goes beyond the limited economic sense.

Although there are many ongoing activities at such a time and many new activities that demand time and energy and are also interesting, the new retiree frequently finds it necessary to place work (economic productivity) in its proper perspective before dealing with new things. Economic productivity is only one type of productivity. There are many things we do for ourselves—tie our shoes, eat, drive our cars, make choices or decisions, and walk—that can be called individual productivity. Even in the most developed economic society there are scores of activities besides the money exchange system. Older people usually increase activities of this sort, especially when reduced income makes it necessary. Another kind of productivity, social productivity, consists of the usual citizenship activities, informal mutual aid, volunteer work, usually through organizations, and helping to make decisions in the public interest.

Economic productivity can go up and up while quality of life declines. War is perhaps the best stimulator of the economy, but there are other, less drastic, behaviors that stimulate economic productivity—new clothing styles and new car styles—none of which guarantee that the quality of life will improve. To turn the argument around for those who think work is the only measure of productivity, that economic productivity is the "most important," where can they buy good government, peace, harmony among groups, love of a child, or protection of the environment with the dollars they earn? There are some things we must do ourselves, often cooperating with others.

Securing these essential intangibles is what most of us do part time while engaged in an occupation, and we can do more after retirement. This writer is less interested in studies of central tendencies than in variations from the average; for it is from identifying what some people *now do* that we can determine what more people *can do*. If what is now minority behavior becomes majority behavior in time, then there is a new norm! Thus, it is in the exceptional that we can look for signs of things that may come in the roles and activities of older people.

Listed below are four specific examples of social productivity that either depend heavily on communication or involve communication. All can be called cultural innovations, involve change in communication, and might increase the well-being of older people. They have several other things in common: 1) they are not designed to produce money income, 2) they are each expected to contribute to increased social status of all older people, as well as to give psychological satisfaction to the individual participant, 3) each is proposed as a demonstration-research project because they require experimentation, change, and adaptation to become a functioning part of our culture.

Re-involvement Day

This proposal was submitted to the Michigan Director of the Bicentennial Commission for the Horizons phase, i.e., a possible contribution to the improvement of American life in the future. The proposal called for the establishment of an annual re-involvement day for older Americans who have retired during the past 12 months from an occupation, (or its equivalent). These people are now free to use their energies for themselves, for others, and/or for society. (Another possible name would be "Increased Involvement Day" on the assumption that most are already doing various things suggested in social productivity.)

If all people in a given community in this stage of life were identified, they could be honored briefly for their past activities and then presented with a report of what other older Americans are now doing in their community.

Each year it would be necessary to: 1) compile the names of people who have retired, and 2) update the record of activities of older people.

Re-involvement Day is a day which, like certain other days in our lives, usually happens only once in a lifetime. Birth, coming of age, graduation from high school and college, marriage, birth of a daughter or son, and retirement are examples of events that can be dated easily. It is true that this day in the year varies for different people, just as do birthdays, but a single day could be arbitrarily selected for every eligible person to move into the next stage. The date selected could become a state holiday, or perhaps even a national holiday.

An added merit of the plan is that the celebration could be shared by the community and as many of the constituent organizations in the community as are interested: churches, service organizations, chambers of commerce, labor unions, and professional organizations. It need not be a threat to existing organizations.

One reason for giving these people-in-transition information on what others are doing in their communities is to present a broader vision of what is possible. Communities would be encouraged to copy or imitate each other, and also to innovate.

Naturally, this proposal assumes that most people who reach this day are reasonably healthy and fairly secure economically. Even when this is not true, there is much anyone can do to help himself and others, as long as the period of extreme dependency is not reached.

Another assumption is that a wide variety of activities would be reported, so that each person could choose those in which he or she is most interested and best qualified to participate. The great variation among people is not only a fact of life but is desirable, for there are many needs in a complex society such as ours.

Banking Maintenance Care Units

This proposal is somewhat similar to the proposal for the Information Bank. Often, older Americans feel trapped after retirement, especially now with rising inflation, for they are probably out of the labor market. An additional fear is that because of the current adverse criticism and pressure from the employed, the existing social security system may be changed. Although they can use political means to try to protect themselves, another alternative might be welcomed.

Such an alternative would be for older Americans to help others and to accumulate credit for doing so. To illustrate: Most older people need transportation, and some can provide transportation. A system could be developed so that a person provides such transportation and thereby builds up or "banks" transportation credits—an example of a maintenance care unit—for the time when he can no longer drive a car. This would not only satisfy an immediate need for people who must get places but cannot drive, it would also take care of a future possible need.

This same principle could be extended to many other areas of every-day-living needs. Much of this helping each other is done informally now by family, neighbors, and friends. But in a society becoming more impersonal and scattered, in which family and friends are far away or perhaps indifferent, there may be a need for a structured system. One step forward might be if the associations now dependent on volunteers would guarantee assistance when and if the volunteers themselves later needed help. Such aid would be an earned right and not merely charity.

Obviously, there are many practical problems, so that further innovations would be required. One problem would be *convertibility*. For instance, someone might help a child learn to read or transport an oldster, but later in life this person might need bedside sitting. Convertibility raises the question of *equivalents,* i.e., how one defines a "maintenance care unit." A third problem would be *portability*. One might make "deposits" in the maintenance care bank in Michigan but wish to live in Florida. This would require a national system, perhaps as an extension of the social security system. Another problem is what would happen if one's credit ran out (as bank accounts and credit in a blood bank run out)? Therefore, the *insurance principle* probably could be added to the banking model on which this is based.

This system is not a panacea for old age, nor is it an alternative to necessary institutionalization or Medicare. It is a proposed innovation in the realm of the things that we normally do for ourselves—at least as long as we can. If this idea were in operation, it might make it possible for some older people to stay in their own homes longer. And it does not require large governmental appropriations, only the cost of the overhead of a records system and a communications system between those who can help others and those who need help.

Communications Facilitator

The root idea for this proposal came from the 1971 White House Conference on Aging. It is proposed that new roles be developed for participating in public meetings, especially those in which the audience has various backgrounds and in which a consensus is desired.

In addition to the chairperson, secretary, and parliamentarian, which are well defined roles now, it is proposed that there be: 1) a semanticist, 2) a resource person, 3) a specialist in group participation, and perhaps 4) a summarizer. Of course, some of these roles might be performed by a single person.

Because of different uses of words by occupations and groups (including minority groups and social class groups) in various sections of the country, a semanticist is needed to translate jargon and special uses of words to facilitate communication. To offset faulty memories or differential knowledge of facts, a resource person at times can be crucial, and perhaps have a calming influence in heated discussions. An expert in group participation can monitor participation and accept some responsibility for full involvement of members of a group. The one responsible for progress summaries and final summaries could be a trained person, and might also double as a traditional secretary.

This proposal is based on the assumption that we desire face-to-face meetings in a democracy. In fact, some are required now by the federal government as a condition for a grant. Many of us have found that successful meetings do not just happen, they are difficult to achieve. Perhaps we do not have enough specialists now to facilitate communication.

Older people could be trained for these roles in communications departments of colleges. An anticipated outcome might be that the people who played these roles of communications facilitators would be recognized as contributors to understanding and order in our society. It would have the added advantage of keeping some older people from talking too much.

Learning Mediator

A little experimental work has been done to see if retired faculty members might usefully attend certain regular university classes for students who are being trained in specialties and obtain information and understanding useful for a non-specialist.

Theoretically, this retiree would be looking for knowledge he could pass on to other older people. He would also get information from other people about their concerns to alert him on what to listen for. One might think of such meetings as piggy-back classes for a different but related purpose.

The logic of such a proposal is that the most up-to-date findings are being reported in training programs. Thus, classes on aging in a medical school were attended Spring term, 1975, to see if something appropriate could be learned to pass on to other older people. The purpose was not to learn to be your own doctor (i.e., to practice medicine), but rather to participate in health education, with emphasis on prevention of health problems. Ideally, it might help the layman to participate with the doctor more intelligently in his own care. The possibilities in this more egalitarian approach are presented in detail in *Beyond the Medical Mystique—How to Choose and Use Your Doctor* by Belsky and Gross (1975).

My proposal is not far enough along to estimate its prospect and limitations. It does emphasize the learner approach and another new non-paid role for older people where they do things for themselves and also share what they learn with others.

In this section, primary attention has been given to innovative roles in social productivity, but more traditional activities should be mentioned, namely, volunteer work and social action through appropriate existing groups. Communication is a key element in both of these. Butler (1975) has a particularly complete treatment of the latter in his section, "An Agenda for Activism."

RESEARCH QUESTIONS NEEDING ANSWERS

Research questions can be general or specific. Obviously, we need both and, as with the recommendations, the following are a mixed bag. Only one basic question is raised in connection with each section.

How varied is the meaning of common words about aging and older people among different social groups in our society? Among different age groups?

What are the correlations between stages in biological aging and stages of change in the other three systems?

To what extent do the variations in life styles after 65 make it necessary to use different techniques in communicating?

To what extent do various categories of older people understand the self-interests of those who communicate with them, whether or not such information is disclosed?

In which areas, and to what extent, do older people lack information essential to sound decisions?

How do various categories of older people secure information in selected essential fields?

To what extent do older people in various categories feel that they are equal, inferior, or superior in obtaining knowledge in selected areas?

In what ways are some older people continuing to be actively involved in life, especially in communication and in social productivity?

FUTURE TRENDS

To attempt to identify trends is always a precarious venture. So many conflicting forces are operating at the same time that changes in our complex world may be speeded up, slowed down, or diverted into different directions. Also, the time element affects reliability. Is a trend predicted in terms of 1 year, 5 years, a generation, or a lifetime? With these cautions the following predictions (trends identified) are made:

People will soon become more aware of ageism in language and realize that the improvement of the lot of older people depends in part on replacing these terms.

It is anticipated that in the long run "age," meaning chronological age, will be replaced by several more meaningful terms indicating the sequences in the various aspects of life.

The concept of full disclosure seems to be spreading in our society, and in a reasonably short time it will become a part of our ethical and legal system.

The state will increasingly monitor knowledge in various areas of importance to older people and accept responsibility for its accuracy and adequacy.

The communication network will continue to be expanded in response to consumer and citizen pressures.

Older people, following the example of the Gray Panthers and certain Nader groups, will take increasing initiative to get information of value and for appropriate social action.

More and more older people will break out of the dependency role assigned to them by tradition after 65 and participate increasingly in society, especially in social production.

RECOMMENDATIONS

Normally, recommendations are made to someone. In this book, then, they are meant for communication specialists and older people. Some of the following recommendations suggest research in a specific area, and some suggest the adoption of a certain course of action. It is recommended:

That an interdisciplinary group be formed to codify the existing vocabulary on aging on two levels, technical and lay, with special emphasis on appropriate words for new concepts. In this way, we no longer will need to "pile up words" to convey new thoughts.

That an effort be made to introduce into our general vocabulary appropriate objective terms to refer to the various life styles, especially in the 5 to 10 or later years after 65.

That we study more exhaustively the stages or sequences of activities in each of the four systems: biological, economic, interpersonal, society.

That a series of conferences on Ethics in Communication be held with experts in ethics, communication, aging, and other fields in order to develop suitable guidelines for communicating with older people.

That full information in all areas necessary to make decisions in everyday problems be accepted as a basic American right (without regard to age, income, or race).

That the grass roots approach of the Information Bank be tried by someone, some place on a demonstration-research basis.

That the right of older people to be heard and to take part in decision-making that affects them be reexamined with attention to phasing out this right only if and when they are no longer competent to exercise it.

That the possibilities of social productivity, with examples and suggestions for those interested, be presented in a book written on a popular level (*A Practical Handbook*).

LITERATURE CITED

Belsky, M. S., and L. Gross. 1975. Beyond the Medical Mystique—How to Choose and Use Your Doctor. Arbor House, New York.

Butler, R. N. 1975. Why Survive? Being Old in America. Harper and Row, New York.
Christiansen, D. 1974. Dignity in aging. *In* The Hastings Center Report. Institute of Society, Ethics, and Life Sciences. 4(1): 6–8.
Donnelly, C. 1975. A concerned relative's guide to old-age care. Money October: 77–86.
Havighurst, R. J., B. L. Neugarten, and S. S. Tobin. 1968. Disengagement and patterns of aging. *In* B. L. Neugarten (ed.), Middle Age and Aging, pp. 161–172. The University of Chicago Press, Chicago.
Henry, J. 1963. Culture Against Man. Vintage Books, Random House, New York.
Ingraham, M. H. 1974. My Purpose Holds: Reactions and Experiences in Retirement of TIAA-CREF Annuitants. Educational Research Division TIAA-CREF, New York.
Institute of Life Insurance. 1972. Life Insurance Fact Book 1972. Institute of Life Insurance, New York.
Lieberman, M. A. 1973. Grouchiness: a survival asset. New insights into crises of aging. Univ. Chicago Mag. July/August: 11–14.
Maas, H., and J. A. Kuypers. 1974. From Thirty to Seventy. Jossey-Bass, San Francisco.
Main, J. 1975. A word to the wise about old age groups. Money, March: 44–48.
Manney, J. D., Jr. 1975. Aging in American Society. The Institute of Gerontology, The University of Michigan–Wayne State University. Ann Arbor.
Mendelson, M. A. 1974. Tender Loving Greed. Alfred A. Knopf, New York.
Mitford, J. 1963. The American Way of Death. Simon and Schuster, New York.
Palmore, E. (ed.). 1974. Normal Aging II: Reports from the Duke Longitudinal Studies, 1970–73. Duke University Press, Durham.
Percy, C. H. 1974. Growing Old in the Country of the Young. McGraw-Hill, New York.
Riley, M. W., and A. Foner. 1968. Aging and Society, Volume One: An Inventory of Research Findings. Russell Sage Foundation, New York.

SUGGESTED READINGS

Butler, R. N. 1975. Why Survive? Being Old in America. Harper and Row, New York.
Manney, J. D., Jr. 1975. Aging in American Society. The Institute of Gerontology, The University of Michigan-Wayne State University, Ann Arbor.
Neugarten, B. L. (ed.). 1968. Middle Age and Aging. The University of Chicago Press, Chicago.

Percy, C. H. 1974. Growing Old in the Country of the Young. McGraw-Hill, New York.
Riley, M. W., and A. Foner. 1968. Aging and Society, Volume One: An Inventory of Research Findings. Russell Sage Foundation, New York.
Journal of Gerontology. Bimonthly journal. Gerontological Society, Washington, D.C.

chapter 3
Exchanging Information within the Older Family

E. Jane Oyer, Ph.D.

The older family has been somewhat neglected by students of family life. However, during the past decade increased interest in older families is reflected by the accumulation of research evidence published in highly regarded professional journals. A noticeable increase is evident in the popular print media as well.

The purpose of this chapter is to look at the role of communication in families of older people. This topic has not heretofore received a great deal of attention. The following questions are explored: With whom do older people live? What factors serve to facilitate or to deter communication within the older family? What kinds of information are communicated between and among family members? Of what value is the kin-family network? Research questions are designed to point up needs for additional information about relationships between various aspects of communication and the family lives of older people. Recommendations are presented, and material covered in the chapter is summarized.

WITH WHOM DO OLDER PEOPLE LIVE?

Families have been partitioned in various ways to provide a common terminology and to permit the systematic accumulation of knowledge about them. Sometimes one finds that the *family of orientation,* the family into which one is born, is used. The second part of this dichotomy of terms is the *family of procreation* or the family one creates by marriage and the parenting of offspring. Another set of terms involves the *residential family,* the family in which one lives, and the *extended family,* the kin-family network based upon blood or marriage ties (Streib, 1972). This extended kin-family network has been described by Shanas (1973) as a social system composed of grandparents, adult children, and grandchildren. Great grandchildren, or a fourth generation, may be present as well, and fifth generation families are becoming increasingly common.

Many older persons live alone or with kin other than spouses, and they too are residential families as well as members of kin-family networks. Others live with unrelated persons and represent yet another family variant. Only about 5 percent of all older persons reside in institutions.

Persons 65 years of age and older form the most heterogeneous segment of the population. Older people have been exposed to and have reacted to a greater number of stimuli than any of their younger cohorts. Thus, it behooves audiences interested in older people, as well as older people themselves, to avoid the pitfall of categorizing older people into a mythical homogeneous group.

Older families show variance in life style as well as in membership. The most common kinds of living arrangements for persons 65 years of age or older fall into five categories (Shanas, 1973; Streib, 1970). About 4 to 8 percent of the older people live alone and have never married. Married couples sharing a home with either married or single children account for 7 to 14 percent. This data confirms an earlier report by Riley and Foner (1968), who stated that only 12 percent of married couples lived with their children. Widowed, divorced, or separated persons comprise a category of 22 to 28 percent. When the group of single persons who have never married is combined with the one that has been widowed, divorced, or separated, a group of from 26 to 36 percent is formed. Thus, about one third of the older people are living alone. The marital pair, however, is still the dominant family form for persons 65 years of age or older. Another interesting point to remember is that most married older people live apart from children or other relatives. Both of these observations from the data stimulate interesting questions relative to communication among both married and single persons about their various kin or primary reference groups.

When one looks at living arrangements for persons 65 years of age and older, however, one finds dramatic differences with respect to sex. Streib (1970) reports 40 percent of the men living with a spouse, but only 15 percent of the women. Life expectancy tables help to explain this phenomeon. Where and with whom one lives certainly influences one's opportunities for interpersonal communication.

WHAT FACTORS SERVE TO FACILITATE OR TO DETER COMMUNICATION WITHIN THE OLDER FAMILY?

Generation Gap

Customs change from one generation to another, and older parents were socialized at quite a different point in social time from that of their children. For example, the acceptability of a wife-mother working outside the home has changed considerably, as has the number of gainfully employed women. This birth cycle differential was spoken of by Davis (1940), who stated that parents would naturally have an historical background different from their children because of the events that occurred during the 20 to 30 years before the children's birth. The reader will recall that persons who are 65 today were born in 1910, and those who are 80 were born in 1895.

The socialization that older parents received as children and young adults continues to serve as a frame of reference for them and contrasts with the later socialization experiences of their now adult children and their grandchildren. The rate of socialization or the rate at which people absorb information from their environment decreases in the older years, so that younger people tend to absorb more from present stimuli than do older ones. By comparison, younger people have more of a tabula rasa, or "blank sheet," that, like a blotter, is ready to absorb the new. But older people possess an experience base that usually permits them to evaluate in a more cautious manner the surrounding events.

The experience base of older people is highly regarded in some cultures, but this cannot be claimed as a general thing for our own. Older ideas are more apt to be considered out-of-date or old fashioned. Mead (1970) noted that certain enclaves of Scandinavian peoples in northern Minnesota still tend to regard grandparents as authorities, but such instances seem to be relatively rare. The generation gap is literally an age-old barrier to communication within the residential as well as the extended kin-family. Older family members are often isolated because of their inability to surmount this social phenomenon.

Changes of Residence

Although evidence is available to attest to the viability of the kin-family network, moving away from kin most certainly affects opportunities for face-to-face communication. The average American has been found to move 14 times in his lifetime, and at least one fifth of all Americans move once or more each year (Packard, 1972). People within the work force move more frequently, and those having the greatest mobility rates are clustered at younger adult ages. Younger people are more apt to move away from older kin, and this may represent a loss to younger generations as well. Mead (1970) suggests that the removal of grandparents physically from the world in which the child is reared shortens the child's experience of his future by a generation and weakens his links to the past. Does this removal from the world of adult children and grandchildren also create a loss for grandparents? Certainly the answer would have to be yes for a majority of older people. Substitutes with whom to communicate may be found, but in most cases this is difficult. Intimacy and long-term commitment are not as apt to be present in relationships with friends. The exchange of services is more difficult to establish as, for example, the exchanging of baby sitting for companionship and the opportunity for face-to-face communication.

Radio, television, or the print media are used by some as substitutes for direct family communication. Grany and Grany (1974) state that "mass media may play a critical role in maintainance of social-psychological well-being among older people when friends and relatives are (often) dead and when churches and favored voluntary organizations are dominated by new and unfamiliar interests" (p. 89). This may hold true for losses created by moving as well. Family members who have moved out of the immediate social orbit of older people usually continue to communicate, exchange aid, and/or gifts, but are not available to satisfy immediate needs for close interpersonal communication. The mass media, for some, is undoubtedly the only available substitute.

In a study that examined relationships between happiness and aging, it was found that the activities highly associated with happiness either involved face-to-face interaction or the potential for it (Grany, 1975). Radio listening was the only mass media activity closely associated with happiness.

A survey conducted by Teachers' Insurance Annuity Association-College Retirement Equity Fund (TIAA-CREF), well known retirement and investment funds, revealed that approximately one third of the retirees changed their places of residence immediately upon retirement (Ingraham, 1974). Loss of family members with whom to communicate in face-to-face situations may have a negative, stultifying effect on many of these older people. If family relationships have been less than satisfactory, however, moving could be a bonus. The reader may recall examples of persons who would fit either case.

Type of Housing

When one is in the process of decision-making with regard to housing for the later years, one may be more likely to think in terms of conveniences the place of residence will afford, its closeness to a shopping center, church, club house, or other services, than to its immediate location within a communications milieu. But most people have experienced loneliness in a crowd as well as in solitude, and moving into a bustling apartment complex guarantees little insofar as neighborliness is concerned, even though it may be located near primary services.

What about the need for privacy, which is experienced to a greater or lesser degree by all of us? Like younger persons, some older people are low communicators. The life styles of older persons who occupy single rooms (SROs) have been studied by social scientists. Men favor this isolated housing arrangement to a far greater extent than women. Stephens (1975) found that the majority of the SRO tennants she studied were life-long social isolates who chose this housing arrangement as an extension of the styles they had established at earlier stages of their lives. It afforded them the extreme amounts of freedom and privacy they desired. Apparently, their low-felt need to communicate was met by this housing option.

Montgomery (1970) found in his studies of housing that "housing patterns are sufficiently relevant to marital interaction to merit increasing concern by professional persons interested in the family. In their work they need to reckon with the significance of housing" (p. 274). Physically, socially, and psychologically, housing often is a major variable in the lives of older people and an important determinant of primary communication partners.

Environments for the elderly have been discussed by DeLong (1974), who concluded that stability was of extreme importance to most older people. He noted that environmental change was stress producing and could affect well-being dramatically.

Certainly, decisions made voluntarily to change houses or environments by older persons hold less potential for the creation of stress than such decisions made by others for them. Lawton and Cohen (1974) interviewed 574 persons at the time they made application to move into senior citizen housing and again after they had spent 1 year in the new environment. Residents experienced a relative decline in functional health, and researchers postulated that this could be the result of the energy expenditures required to adjust to the new situation. Establishing new communication networks is costly of energy as well, and must have been a large part of the adjustment process.

Many older people, however, may improve their environmental conditions by moving. The attitudes of three groups of older people toward their neighbors were determined, and all were found to be negative (Brody, Kleban, Liebowitz, 1975). Two groups moved, and attitudes were sampled again after a 6-month period. The movers' attitudes had improved significantly, but the non-movers remained at the same level of dissatisfaction. All three groups had expressed a desire to move when first interviewed, and this desire was apparently satisfied for those who actually did move. The researchers were not able to pin-point, on the basis of this study, why the non-movers elected to remain in neighborhoods they considered to be unfavorable. However, it is interesting that the *relocation effect,* in which illness and death are manifested, did not occur in the movers. One would suspect that the desire to move, coupled by the viable option to, in fact, move, countered the negative effects that frequently accompany involuntary moves of older people. No doubt the movers were able to substitute new, satisfactory communication links for former unsatisfactory ones.

Attitudes

Resentment at grandmother's continuous presence within the family group, even when an attempt is made to conceal such feelings, is likely to be perceived by both grandmother and other family members. When necessity rather than desire prompts the formation of two or three generation households, negative attitudes are apt to form stumbling blocks to open communication within family groups. Grandmother may exhibit an attitude of tolerance or forebearance toward the ideas and contributions of younger members, implying that they do not measure up to standards from an earlier day. Younger persons may perceive this as a put-down and cease to communicate in her presence. Attitudes may be communicated within the family on many potentially explosive topics such as politics, religion, sex, child-rearing, club memberships, use of alcoholic beverages, dating practices, and uses of leisure time.

When communication takes the form of exchanges of goods and/or services, additional avenues develop for the formation of both positive and negative attitudes. Unequal exchanges may be the breeding ground for dissatisfaction on the part of one or both parties. Older husbands may feel that because they have been faithful breadwinners for many years, they now deserve to be waited upon. Wives may resent this, believing that they have contributed equally to the family through the years. Parents generally do not like to take from children, in that they do not wish to deprive them or their grandchildren. Neither do they like to forfeit any of their freedom and appear to be dependent. When handled sensitively, however, and when accompanied by genuine feelings of affection, one generation may be able to meet the needs of the other in a highly acceptable way through skillful communication.

Role reversal, which frequently occurs between married-child and parent generations, may be another impedance to good communication. How do older parents tell a bossy son or daughter-in-law that they appreciate their concern but are still capable of managing their own affairs?

Attitudes toward retirement are communicated within the family. Retirees mentioned in a recent survey were found to be (Ingraham, 1974) "Neither resentful nor ecstatic, but registered milder degrees of discontent or, much more often, of pleasure with their current lives" (p. 6). Surely those who can look back with more pleasure than pain will communicate much more positive attitudes toward life to those within their family constellations.

Many older homemakers never have worked outside the home, or have not done so for many years. When suddenly the husband who has been absent from the home all day for the past 40 or so years is present all day, she will very likely find she needs to modify her accumstomed routines. Running the vacuum sweeper at 9 every morning may interfere with her husband's reading program or the watching of his favorite television show. The old saw that "I married him for better or for worse, but not for lunch" may appear quite realistic. So the attitude of the wife toward the husband's constant presence, should he elect to remain within the home, is something with which to be reckoned. She may have become accustomed to a dearth of interpersonal communication during the day. Her husband, attempting to readjust his own life, may talk a great deal and demand thoughtful responses from her. Wives' attitudes toward their husbands' retirement are communicated in one way or another and are a very important part of satisfactory family adjustment in the retirement stage.

Douglas, Cleveland, and Maddex (1974) used archival data in an attempt to determine relationships between age and political attitudes at three levels: national, community, and family. They found that age becomes a significant variable only at the most immediate political level, the family. Responses to the more remote issues were not influenced by age, but when issues affected the daily lives of the older people, they displayed significantly stronger attitudes. This might have been a reflection of the centrality of the family for older people. The family might have represented the only level at which true attitudes could be expressed and received in open communication.

Schedule Conflicts

An older couple might find itself running into difficulty because one or the other or both members have become over committed to groups or associations outside the family. Little time or energy may remain for family communication. The couple who can view this situation objectively, diagnose the problem, and act to remedy it may prevent serious family disagreement.

Also children of the grandparent generation might be so committed to jobs and outside activities that they leave no time in their busy schedules for visits with their older parents. If parents do not demonstrate to children (grandchildren) that they value time with their older parents, children are not likely to develop close relationships with their grand-parents. A very informative and interesting source of communication about the past, present, and future may never be opened to them.

Semantic Aspects of Language

Meanings evoked by words in the language develop and expand as vital aspects of the cultural context of the times. Therefore, when grandmother asks Susie when she comes in from an important date, "How did you make out?" she may be rebuffed by a resentful, surprized stare. The term "make out" meant something quite different to each of them based upon their different references in the stream of time.

Or perhaps Susie brings what seems to grandfather a rather unusual young man home to meet him. As soon as he leaves, Susie asks grandfather what he thought about him. Grandfather tries to be somewhat noncom-mital and says, "Well, he seemed a bit queer." Susie thinks grandfather thinks the young man seemed rather like a homosexual, when that particu-lar thought had not occurred to grandfather.

Meanings lie within the minds of communicants and are evoked by language symbols. If generational differences have attributed different meanings to the same words, ideas are not communicated any more than they would be were communicants speaking two foreign languages. Seman-tic obstacles can impede communication between generations, or between social classes or ethnic groups.

Health-related Factors

Communication requires the expenditure of energy (it is sometimes de-fined as a type of energy), and one of the biological correlates of aging is a diminution or lessening of the amount of physical energy available. In rather extreme cases or during periods of fatigue, communicating with a spouse or other family member may be just too demanding. As a result, the older person may appear disinterested, passive, or perhaps even a bit senile when, in fact, he or she may just be very tired.

Speaking with persons who have sustained hearing losses requires an extra expenditure of energy. This author recalls recent experiences inter-viewing women who had sustained losses of hearing. In most cases, after interviews had been completed the author was noticeably fatigued. This fatigue factor may contribute to the isolation of those who are hard of hearing, because it may put considerable stress upon the more normally hearing members of the family. Oyer and Paolucci (1970) found, for example, that the husbands of homemakers with severe hearing losses made higher scores on a test of marital tension.

Mobility problems that often result from arthritis and other diseases of the muscles and joints make physical movement difficult for many older people. If one cannot accompany a physically fit spouse, adult, child, or grandchild on a trip, or even to the grocery store, the family member may seek the companionship of others more able to move about and communicate on the scene.

Zarit and Kahn (1975) found that among a group of persons ranging in age from 38 to 84 who had suffered strokes, that the older persons tended to be more depressed but manifested fewer denial symptoms than the younger ones. Perhaps the seasoning of the old makes them more realistic about a physical impairment and, hence, more depressed about a poor prognosis. The older stroke victim who has a good grasp of the reality of his situation may not be stimulated to communicate with a spouse who is not able to accept the same degree of reality.

Being confined to a bed or perhaps to one room would certainly cut one off from the normal flow of family conversation. Meal times are special times for many families to engage in face-to-face communication. Being denied this opportunity would exclude one from contributing and receiving much information.

Values Conflicts

Kohlberg (1973) noted that one of the most striking things about aging is the way some people grow while others regress. (People never remain the same.) This seems quite logical in view of the fact that older people comprise the most heterogeneous segment of the population. The philosopher of moral values suggests that if some aging persons attain a greater wisdom, then one of the most important jobs of social gerontologists is to clarify and communicate that wisdom to others. What happens in families when one member continues to grow and expand and others do not? How is their family communication affected?

Values have been commonly considered to be ideas or concepts about the desirable things of life. They serve as guideposts for the evaluation of both one's own and others' behaviors. There seems to be some data base for the rather widely held notion that conservatism or traditionalism increases with advancing age. One hundred seventy-eight leaders in cities in developing countries were given a values test, and findings tended to confirm this assumption. Being older generally tended to be strongly related to the holding of more traditional, rather than modern, value orientations (Webber, Coombs, Hollingsworth, 1974). But communicating with those who do hold different viewpoints, be they inside the family or out, is an important and necessary function for both generations.

Within the family as well as other social groups, the tendency toward conservatism may have some very positive, stabilizing effects. Untried, untested ideas may sound excellent in the discussion stages. The conservative opinions or suggestions of experienced older people, however, may save a family from unforeseen pitfalls. They may be able to profit from the experiences of their elders. For example, older people lived through the great depression in the United States and many tend to be conservative with their funds. A younger member's terrific tip on a stock market investment and the impulse of other family members to commit their funds to the scheme may be tempered by the communication of grandfather's more conservative stance.

Undoubtedly, values conflicts stifle family communication, but they can also initiate stimulating exchanges. Additionally, the older communicant then knows through feedback that his ideas have not been ignored. Conflict at least tells the parties involved that their notions have affected others. Conflict also adds to the variety of life: it is preferred to sameness for many people. And an important behavior to be learned that will have wide application in the world outside the family is the ability to handle or deal with conflict. Raush et al. (1974) suggest that "if adults can from their own ongoing experience and action convey to children—as the cycle of development moves to another generation—that communication can maintain individual integrity and mutual regard and even promote growth through the clash of opposition, that is no mean accomplishment. In fact, feeling free to express differing opinions may promote harmony within relationships" (p. 39). Stinnett, Carter, and Montgomery (1972) found in their study of older person's perceptions of their marriages that the most rewarding aspects of present marriage relationships were companionship and freedom to express true feelings to partners.

The reader can think of many topics that have the potential for values conflicts among family members. Perhaps of greater importance than conflicts themselves is the cultivation of an atmosphere within the family wherein members feel free to communicate their opinions and, through family discussion, to develop ways to deal with conflict.

Social Mobility

Oftentimes children move up or down the social ladder and find themselves living on a scale that differs from their parents. Perhaps because of educational opportunities, sometimes provided by parental resources, they are able to obtain jobs that give them incomes higher than their parents. Movement up or down the social scale may also come largely as a result of marriage. A daughter may marry a wealthy man who provides her with a more affluent life style. Or the son of professionals may not wish to pursue a professional career but may prefer to work as a skilled laborer.

Children who find themselves living on a scale different from their parents are cast in the role of the marginal person. That is, they hold membership in two groups with differing values and norms and are expected to perform in conflicting ways. For example, children are usually expected to visit their parents as well as to entertain them in their own homes. However, the couple who was ascended a rung up the social ladder may be too insecure to risk entertaining lower status parents. They may think that mother's dresses are not fashionable or father's speech is too crude and that these somewhat superficial factors would cause people in their new social group to look down upon them. By the same token, parents may be embarrassed because a son or daughter has rejected higher education and instead is working on an assembly line, or has selected a mate who ranks below them on the socioeconomic scale.

Because close communication between parents and children who are cast in marginal positions is frequently fraught with tension, they often cope by using avoidance behavior. Communication may take place, but perhaps in other than face-to-face situations. Gifts or even aid may be exchanged and guilt feelings assauged. But the discomfort felt by communicating directly is avoided.

Some children and parents possess sufficiently strong feelings of social identity, however, to cope with the demands of marginal status, and they actually use their advantages, social and/or economic, to make life more pleasant for older parents or adult children. This comfortable, natural continuation of communication is indeed a very important part of the success or failure of family life for those involved.

Division of Labor

Families adopt different ways of dividing labor within the home. Styles developed relate directly to the opportunities members have to communicate with each other. For example, families that follow the traditional, sex-related division of labor assign tasks on the basis of what they consider to be man's work, woman's work, and child's work. Generally, when this sex-related division of labor is used, tasks are performed singly or by members of only one sex. Presently, the woman's movement, among other factors, has prompted some families to question this previously accepted style. This, too, may be difficult for older parents to understand.

Other families develop an equalitarian division of labor whereby tasks are assumed on the basis of interest and/or expertise. A woman who likes the out-of-doors may elect to assume the responsibility for the yard and garden. A man who likes to cook may choose to prepare the evening meal for the family. Or the couple may decide to do these tasks together. Certainly, the latter alternative increases opportunities to communicate. Children who are included in this pattern of family interaction also have more opportunities to learn to communicate with family members. Hopefully, the establishment of patterns of working and talking together will carry on into later adult life.

The reader can think of other areas of family life and ways in which they facilitate or deter communication. Classes or groups may wish to examine them in greater detail. Any one of the factors could be greatly expanded. For example, "type of housing" is a topic with a tremendous number of facets. In a chapter devoted to the topic of family communication it is not possible to exhaust any one of them.

WHAT KINDS OF INFORMATION ARE COMMUNICATED WITHIN THE FAMILY?

Families talk about all sorts of things, and older families are no exception. Couples who have grown old together have shared many experiences that they use to interpret or to compare with events in the present. Couples who have married late in life and who have come from different walks of life have separate frames of reference about which to communicate. These observations hold true for single adults and their primary communication partners as well.

When researchers look at the content of communication, that is, what information is exchanged, they have to formulate categories to cover the broad range of topics discussed by families or groups. Hare (1966) used two broad categories. The first he labeled *task behavior,* and this included communication directed toward the completion of various tasks or jobs. The second broad category Hare called *social emotional,* and this included communication directed toward relationships between group members. An example of this type of communication might be asking one's housemate how he/she were feeling today, or some other friendly greeting that conveyed a note of concern for the other person as well as for his relationship to or effect upon the group.

Bales (1966) used four main categories to study what people said and/or did. These he called: 1) positive reactions, 2) problem-solving attempts, 3) questions, and 4) negative reactions. His research dealt largely with small, unrelated groups. On the other hand, Raush et al. (1974) developed a six-category coding scheme for interpersonal conflict within marriage. These he labeled: 1) cognitive, 2) resolving, 3) reconciling, 4) appealing, 5) rejecting, and 6) coercive. Data thus categorized revealed, for example, the percentage of husbands' and wives' communicative acts that were conciliatory in nature.

Studying the content of communication within the family is a very difficult and complex task. Sometimes the way something is said negates the meaning of the words. Someone who shouts goodbye and slams the door on a guest's coattails is not a friendly host even though he has extended the proper fare-well greating. Communication may be contra-dictory and it may not fit easily into predetermined categories. Within the family a full range of communication content is likely to take place. Wahlroos (1974) recently authored a book, *Family Communication: A Guide to Emotional Health*. He attempted to show how communication influenced marriage, child rearing, and personality formation.

Space permits a few general kinds of information communicated within the older family to be discussed here. The reader may elect to expand the list.

Food, Clothing, and Shelter

Meeting physical needs is a concern that, of necessity, extends throughout the life cycle. When the world of older people shrinks, as it does for many, undue emphasis is often placed upon them. For example, a preoccupation with the relationship between food and health may occur. A great deal of discussion between older family members as to the importance of eating or not eating certain foods is not unusual. Such topics are not necessarily of much interest to younger family members, however, and may stifle or *turn off* communication among them.

Clothing needs generally decline with age in that fewer are needed when work outside the home is less common. Perhaps an interest shift also partially explains a common tendency to *make do* with the old things. Personal clothing may seem less important than alternatives such as a contribution to a worthy charity. Adult children often have to convince parents that they should spend some of their savings on themselves and that they need to replace worn items of clothing. Attempts at persuasive communication are not uncommon features of intergenerational dialogue.

The home in which older people live becomes increasingly important to them. Housing also represents a major expenditure with its rising maintainance and utility costs. As new housing options present themselves, discussion of this vital environmental aspect often occupies considerable attention.

Attitudes and Morale

Older people are sometimes preoccupied with self-interests and well-being. The ability and opportunity to discuss these with family members is very helpful. Morale, or life satisfaction, in the older years is likely to be a reflection of that developed at earlier stages. Communication skills that assist older persons to discuss attitudes and morale are extremely important in terms of mental hygiene.

Uses of Leisure Time

As hobby clubs, recreational centers, and adult education courses have proliferated, the able older person has been presented with an array of options for the use of time and talent. Work and/or community service opportunities are often available for the taking. What to do, when, and with whom are topics that occupy the communication of many older persons.

Health

Economic pressures may promote a strong desire on the part of many to maintain the highest degree of health possible. Some literally cannot afford to become ill. Health is known to rank high on the list of concerns of older people and is reflected in communication about medicines, diet, sleep patterns, exercise routines, and the like.

OF WHAT VALUE IS THE KIN-FAMILY NETWORK?

The kin-family network (extended family) is essentially a series of communication links through which family members exchange information. Although to outsiders exchanges often appear unequal or assymetrical, family members do not necessarily regard them in that way. For example, an older parent who sacrifices to give an adult child a costly gift may feel well repaid by the child's expressions of appreciation and affection. The parent is saying I still care about you, and the child is returning this demonstration of affection in kind.

Services as well as material goods are exchanged. Time is a resource that older persons sometimes choose to exchange for companionship, perhaps by baby sitting or performing household tasks. But behind exchanges of material goods and services there is generally a social-psychological motive as well. Affection and attention are accompaniments of most positive exchanges. Patterns established during earlier stages of family life usually hold for the retirement stage as well. If affectionate relationships were established and maintained, they will likely be continued, and it follows that unfriendly relationships will likely be perpetuated if they have been the family's mode. Unpleasant relationships often provide the basis for the discontinuance or lessening of extended family communication, however, the friendship groups may replace them. Hill (1968) noted that in times of crisis such as disaster, illness, or accident, family members communicate first with those in their kin network as they search for help.

RESEARCH QUESTIONS NEEDING ANSWERS

What are outstanding characteristics or correlates of families who have established satisfactory communication links across generations?

How can the generation gap be bridged to restore a greater appreciation on the part of younger family members for the contributions older people have made and are making to family life?

Does dependence upon mass media increase for older people with changes in places of residence? Does media use increase for older people as a result of residential moves of close extended family members?

Would tests designed to measure needs for face-to-face communication be useful in predicting adjustment of older people to various types of housing situations?

How can younger family members promote the development of interpersonal communication skills that will serve them well throughout the life span?

Would pre-retirement cablevision courses designed to assist homemakers adjust to husbands' retirement contribute to over-all family adjustment?

Would family life education materials or courses designed to point up relationships between the division of labor within the home and the development of family communication skills be helpful to young families? Over time, would young families who had had such exposure communicate with greater skill in the later stages?

Are there relationships between the *kinds* of information exchanged within the older family and over-all marital adjustment?

What is the content of the communication of older persons who express a high degree of satisfaction (morale) with their family lives? Of those who express dissatisfaction?

What communications substitutes are used by families who make little or no use of the kin-family network?

SUMMARY

The study of the older family has not claimed the attention of many scholars up until the past decade; however, the role communication plays in the later stages of family life still has not received very much attention by scholars in either field.

An overview of the persons with whom older people live reveals that about one third of persons 65 years of age and older live alone. The marital pair is the dominant family form. Close family members, other housemates, or the absence of a housemate influence opportunities older people have for interpersonal communication.

Certain factors related to the lives of older family members facilitate or deter their communication within the family. Factors discussed include the generation gap, changes of residence, types of housing, attitudes, schedule conflicts, health, values conflicts, social mobility, and the division of labor within the home.

The content of the communication of older people is discussed, that is, what information is exchanged by family members. Selected topics of general concern to older people, such as food, clothing, and shelter, attitudes and morale, and health, serve as examples of important concerns of older people that are reflected in their communications exchanges.

The kin-family network functions as a series of communication links between and among extended family members. The uses of the network for exchanges of material goods, services, and social-psychological satisfactions are noted.

Research questions are designed here to point up needs for additional knowledge about the relationships between various aspects of communication and the family lives of older people.

Recommendations include the suggestion that younger people listen to older people, value, and appreciate their contributions to family life. Another recommendation points up the need for longitudinal research that would discover relationships between the development of communications skills in the early stages of marriage and their carry-over into the later years.

RECOMMENDATIONS

This author recommends the following general proposals:

Longitudinal research should be initiated to point up relationships between the development of communications skills in the early stages of marriage and their carry-over into the later stages.

Younger family members should be taught by example to listen to, value, and appreciate the past, present, and future contributions older members make to family life.

Communication needs of older people should be considered when advising them about housing in the later years. Social isolates may prefer to be single room occupants (SROs), but many other older people need the reassurance of daily face-to-face communication.

Consideration should be given to the greater use of cablevision as a teaching tool for the development of positive attitudes toward retirement; for example, wives' attitudes have an important bearing upon husbands' adjustment to retirement.

LITERATURE CITED

Bales, R. F. 1966. How people interact in conferences. *In* A. G.. Smith (ed.), Communication and Culture. Holt, Rinehart, and Winston, New York.

Brody, E. M., M. H. Kelban, and B. Liebowitz. 1975. Intermediate housing for the elderly: Satisfaction of those who moved in and those who did not. The Gerontologist 15: 350–356.

Bultema, G. L., and V. Wood. 1969. Normative attitudes toward the aged role among migrant and nonmigrant retirees. The Geronotologist 9: 204–208.

Davis, K. 1940. The sociology of parent-youth conflict. Amer. Soc. Rev. 5: 523–535.

DeLong, A. J. 1974. Environments for the elderly. J. Commun. 24: 101–112.

Douglas, E. B., W. P. Cleveland, and G. L. Maddex. 1974. Political attitudes, age, and aging: A cohort analysis of archival data. The Gerontologist 29: 666–675.

Duvall, E. M. 1971. Family Development. 4th Ed. J. B. Lippincott, Philadelphia.

Graney, M. J. 1975. Happiness and social participation in aging. J. Gerontol. 30: 701–706.

Graney, M. J., and E. E. Graney. 1974. Communications activity substitutions in aging. J. Commun. 24: 88–96.

Hare, A. P. 1966. The dimensions of social interaction. *In* A. G. Smith (ed.), Communication and Culture. Holt, Rinehart, and Winston, New York.

Hill, R. 1968. Social stresses on the family. *In* M. B. Sussman (ed.), Sourcebook in Marriage and the Family. Houghton Mifflin, Boston.

Ingraham, M. H. 1974. My purpose holds: Reactions and experiences in retirement of TIAA-CREF annuitants. Teachers Insurance and Annuity Assoc. and College Retirement Equities Fund, New York.

Kohlberg, L. 1973. Stages and aging in moral development: Some speculations. The Gerontologist 13: 497–502.

Lawton, M. P., and J. Cohen. 1974. The generality of housing impact on the well-being of older people. J. Gerontol. 29: 194–204.

Mead, M. 1970. Culture and Commitment. Doubleday, Garden City, N.J.

Montgomery, J. E. 1970. Impact of housing patterns on marital interaction. Family Coordin. 19: 267–274.

Neugarten, B. L. 1975. The future and the young-old. The Gerontologist 15 (Part II): 4–9.

Oyer, E. J., and B. Paolucci. 1970. Homemakers' hearing losses and family integration. J. Home Econ. 62: 257–262.

Packard, V. 1972. A Nation of Strangers. David McKay, New York.

Palmore, E. 1975. The status and integration of the aged in Japanese society. J. Gerontol. 30: 199–208.

Raush, H. L., W. A. Barry, R. K. Hertel, and M. A. Swain. 1974. Communication Conflict and Marriage. Jossey-Bass, San Francisco.

Riley, M. W., and A. Foner. 1968. Aging and Society. Vol. I. An Inventory of Research Findings. Russell Sage, New York.

Shanas, E. 1973. Family-kin networks and aging in cross-cultural perspective. J. Marriage and the Family 35: 505–511.

Shanas, E., P. Townsend, D. Wedderburn, H. Fris, P. Milhoj, and J. Stehauwer. 1968. Old People in Three Industrial Societies. Atherton Press, New York.

Stephens, J. 1975. Society of the alone: Freedom, privacy, and utilitarianism as dominant norms in the SRO. J. Gerontol. 30: 230–235.

Stinnett, N., L. M. Carter, and J. E. Montgomery. 1972. Older persons' perceptions of their marriages. J. Marriage and the Family 34: 665–670.

Streib, G. F. 1970. Old age and the family. Amer. Behav. Sci. 14: 25–39.

Streib, G. F. 1972. Older families and their troubles: Familial and social responses. Family Coordin. 21: 5–19.

Wahloos, S. 1974. Family Communication: A Guide to Emotional Health. Macmillan, New York.

Webber, I. L., D. W. Coombs, and J. S. Hollingsworth. 1974. Variations in values orientations by age in a developing society. J. Gerontol. 29: 676–683.

Zarit, S. H., and A. L. Kahn. 1975. Aging and adaptation to illness. J. Gerontol. 30: 67–72.

SUGGESTED READINGS

Atchley, R. C. 1972. The Social Forces in Later Life: An Introduction to Social Gerontology. Wadsworth, Belmont, Calif.

Blake, R. H., and E. O. Haroldsen. 1975. A Taxonomy of Concepts in Communication. Hastings House, New York.

Field, M. 1972. The Aged, the Family, and the Community. Columbia University Press, New York.

Institute for Interdisciplinary Studies. 1972. Indicators of the Status of the Elderly in the United States. Institute for Interdisciplinary Studies, Minneapolis.

Kantor, D., and W. Lehr. 1975. Inside the Family. Jossey-Bass, San Francisco.

Klemer, R. H., and R. M. Smith. 1975. Teaching about Family Relationships. Burgess, Minneapolis.

chapter 4

Communication across Age Levels

Joseph Woelfel, Ph.D.

This chapter examines communication among people of different ages. It asks three important questions: 1) How often do people of different ages, such as children and adults, or adults and the aging, talk to each other? 2) What are the *consequences* of such communication, or lack of communication, for both of the persons involved and for the whole society? 3) What can be done about it? As will be shown, these turn out to be very simple questions to ask—and, for that matter, very easy to answer, given the effort and resources—but they may well be much more important questions than most would realize. To understand why these questions are so important, a very simple model of what a society is like is presented, and the role of communication in that model is illustrated.

SOCIETY AND ITS MEMBERS

When a person is born, it is obvious but important to realize that he or she is born into a society that already exists and that has a history. Over a long period of time the society has learned to survive in its environment. It grows, manufactures, and distributes food, clothing, shelter, and other goods and services to its members and in general has discovered or invented ways of doing things that allow it to survive as long as it has. Over the lifespan of the society—which is, of course, much longer than the lifespan of any member of the society—it will have learned to do an extremely long list of things. These may be everyday things that are taken for granted, such as cooking food (or, for that matter, even knowing what things may be eaten and what things may not, which is very valuable knowledge indeed), or very special things, such as complex surgical procedures, or scientific and technical things, such as how to produce electricity. Some of the knowledge a society has built up is very general, and everyone must learn it, such as the language of the society, or the pattern of nonverbal gestures used to show feelings and which controls communications with others. Some of the society's knowledge is very specific and known only to a few, such as bricklaying or lens grinding. This body of information, accumulated throughout the history of the society, is the *culture* of the society. This culture makes the society what it is: its ways of doing things, of thinking, and of behaving.

The Locus of Culture

Where is this knowledge? Some of it is contained in written records (at least in literate cultures), such as constitutions, laws, deeds, titles, books, and other symbolic recordings; some of it is recorded in the things people have built, such as architectural styles, manufactured goods, etc. But mostly the culture of a society is knowledge in the minds of its members. To be sure, each person holds only the smallest fraction of the total pattern of social knowledge but, taken together, culture is mainly ideas in the minds of people. This fact takes on a fresh importance when it is realized that societies usually outlive their members many times over. In a very short time in the lifespan of a major society like the United States— say every 100 years—*every member of the society is replaced.* A major problem for every society, therefore, is to maintain the system of knowledge and beliefs called its culture as members of the society grow older and are replaced by new members. This process, in which new members of the society learn the basic beliefs, values, and ways of doing things that the society has developed over its lifespan, is called *socialization.* It should be easy to see that socialization is a *communication process* in which adult members of a society communicate the culture of the society to younger, newer members. Any society, then, is held together by communication; communication is the "social glue" that binds people together, that coordinates their activities, and makes organized social life possible. If anything goes wrong with the basic communication systems by which people are socialized into the society and their roles in society, the survival of that society is in jeopardy. If we are concerned with our survival as a society, we must pay close attention to the system of communication—and changes in the system of communication—by which the culture of our society is communicated across generations (Durkheim, 1947).

A Model of Cultural Communication

As mentioned earlier, there are two kinds of information a society has in its culture: 1) general ideas, language, beliefs, values, and so forth, that need to be communicated to every member of society regardless of position or "status" in the society, and 2) specific ideas, beliefs, practices, and skills—such as carpentry or brain surgery—that need to be communicated to some persons—such as carpenters and doctors—but not to everyone. By and large, these kinds of information are communicated by different communication systems. In this chapter, information that is distributed to every member of the society and that controls general activities like talking, dealing with others, etc., is called *primary,* or *core information.* The communication channels that carry such information are called *primary communication systems.* On the other hand, specialized information, such as the knowledge needed for specific occupations or people, is called *secondary information,* and the communication systems that carry this sort of information are called *secondary communication systems.*

Not long ago, many, perhaps most, sociologists in the United States believed that these two kinds of communication systems automatically grew and adjusted to the society's needs, but this view (called "functionalism") is now losing ground. Recent events here and abroad have made scholars once again realize that things do go wrong with societies, and sometimes things go wrong so seriously that the society, or major parts of it, fail to survive. The rest of this chapter deals with how these two communication systems, the primary and secondary communication networks, have been affected by changes in our society, and makes some guesses about what might happen in the future if these trends continue.

MOBILITY AND SOCIAL CHANGE

The distinction between primary and secondary information—and with it primary and secondary communication networks—was not always as sharp and distinct as it is today. Before the industrial and scientific revolution, societies were not divided into as many specialized statuses and roles (jobs) as they are today. Members of society were more similar to each other in what they did and what they believed in than they are now. Division of labor was small, and the major divisions occurred by age (the very young and the very old could not hunt, for example). Most members of the society performed the same basic tasks as every other member. Accordingly, secondary communication systems were less well developed, and most communication within the society was primary and not specialized. To be sure, highly specific information about special hunting or agricultural techniques might be passed on selectively to only a few specialists, but by and large there were few special secondary communication systems.

Within these societies, communication was, overwhelmingly, face-to-face and verbal. This is important because primary face-to-face communication systems have a very valuable property: they allow for high rates of error-reducing feedback. *Feedback* is the process whereby the receiver of a message repeats, or "feeds back," his or her understanding of the message to the sender so that the sender can know how accurately the listener has understood the message. Moreover, because these societies were generally small and immobile (i.e., the members did not move frequently except as a group), rates of communication were probably high, and turnover in conversation partners was probably small. It is easy to see that, after years of high rates of low-error, face-to-face communication with a small set of the same people about a wide range of topics, members of these societies would be come very similar. The communication of cultural beliefs and ideas across generations would be quite secure and involve little "error" or change. Such societies should be expected to be, and generally are, very stable. Some societies like these, in fact, when local environmental conditions are stable and contact with other societies is small, have survived essentially unchanged for hundreds of years.

This, of course, is not the way American society looks today. Over the past few centuries (which is really only a few moments in human history), all that has been changed fundamentally and radically. While the number of changes in society over this stretch of time is very large, we are interested mainly in two changes. First, our society has grown vastly larger, from about 3,000,000 at the time of our founding as a nation to 215,000,000 now, a 7,000 percent increase. Second, the degree of specialization of work, the number of different jobs and roles people fill, has multiplied even more dramatically. These trends are not only continuing, but appear to be speeding up. Since 1940, for example, over 30,000,000 people left farms to take up other occupations.

We know these changes have been rapid and we are even accustomed to calling them a "revolution," but it is difficult to conceive even now of just how rapidly they have taken place. If we were to view the growth and spread of people and the roles of people as a movie, say, 1 hour long, with the movie beginning with the building of the pyramids and ending today, the entire industrial revolution would take place in only two minutes, and the population of the United States would have increased by 70,000,000 in the last 15 seconds of the movie.

These figures are perhaps of some help in understanding how rapidly the communication networks, both primary and secondary, have had to grow and develop to distribute primary and secondary cultural information among a population that has grown so dramatically in both numbers and specialization. In fact, as we shall see, even though many people have marveled at the rate of development of new mass media like radio, television, newspapers, books, etc., over the recent past, we may still wonder in the face of this gigantic increase in population and division of labor whether our communication resources have been able to keep pace. We would be unwise to expect a smooth and orderly development of such new communication systems, and there is evidence that the rapid development of such systems of communication has left some people out. Among these people are certainly the aging. The consequences of leaving this very special and growing group of people out of the major communication systems may well have profound if unforeseen consequences both for the aging and for the society as a whole. It is well worth understanding how this has happened.

CHANGE AND STABILITY IN COMMUNICATION PATTERNS

As suggested earlier, divisions between primary and secondary communication patterns on the scale they are now known are very recent. Only moments ago in human history, almost all communication took place on a face-to-face basis in a small geographic area among a few people who knew each other well. Almost all socialization took place within a context of extended family and near neighbors. The rapid division of labor made this pattern of socialization impossible for several reasons. First, the increase in number of different kinds of jobs has meant a great increase in the amount of information in the culture that needs to be provided to different workers. This new, formal, and technical information required different communication systems, which are provided in part by schools and more specialized media. This results in children being withdrawn from the family and neighborhood for education—a fact that itself results in a substantial drop in face-to-face communication among children, parents, grandparents, and across ages in general.

This specialization of jobs has had another important effect—it has dramatically increased the frequency with which people move. Instead of spending a lifetime in one spot among a few people they know well, people must now relocate quite frequently. Children must change schools several times, and many attend colleges in cities different from their own; in the job market, relocations are frequent: last year 40,000,000 Americans moved. What is more, these movements are not the nomadic wanderings of a whole group, but moves of individual persons and small families. More than any other factor, the mobility of Americans has so modified the extended family that children may seldom see grandparents or other extended relatives, and frequently children do not live in the same city as any of their relatives other than their parents. These factors further reduce the amount of cross-age communication. The result of all this is that, in the contemporary United States, *the vast majority of all communication occurs among people of the same or very close age.*

In fact, research has shown that almost half the people high school students consult about their future educational and occupational careers are other children of their own age. Of the remainder, about 30 percent are either parents or people whose job it is to interact with children, like teachers and guidance counselors. This leaves only about 20 percent of all sources of information to children who are *older* than the child (Woelfel, 1972). As the age discrepancies increase, communication between young and old are nearly eliminated. These patterns appear to be common, since the rapidly developing secondary communication systems (e.g., schools) group children together in age cohorts. High mobility patterns break up extended family systems and act strongly against developing extensive interpersonal roots. These results all tend to cluster people of similar ages together and to prevent communication among those of different ages. By and large, what cross-age communication does exist is largely on-the-job communication. In the case of those who are not formally employed (e.g.. housewives, retired persons), even these few cross-age contacts are missing.

What kinds of effects does this insulation between old and young have? Two important effects can be seen: on the society as a whole and on the aging as individual persons.

SOCIAL CONSEQUENCES

It has been said here that the culture of a society is mainly ideas in the minds of people, and that it must be communicated from one generation to the next. But the events just described show communication between generations to be diminishing, perhaps seriously. How is the culture maintained in the absence of communication across generations?

The answer to this important question is not completely known. To a very great extent, secondary communication systems have grown up as communication networks within formal organizations (where people work), but these communication systems are usually very specialized in the kinds of topics they carry, and in any event certainly do not perform the basic socialization into primary values, beliefs, and ideas of the society. Schools, particularly, are able to present at least a formalized approach to primary socialization, but the extent to which schools contribute to the process is not known. What has played a role in this primary socialization, many researchers believe, is the mass media, particularly television. Television presents people each day with dramatized examples of primary values and ideas. In fact, because it is a mass medium, it cannot portray secondary information: information specific to certain people and not to others. Certainly the amount of time people of all ages spend viewing television is very substantial, and unquestionably much of that time was time formerly devoted to interpersonal communication.

If schools and mass media provide the largest part of primary socialization, at least two interesting effects might be expected. First, because both schools and the media are basically mass communication systems—that is, they are centralized sources that distribute common information to many persons at once—they should be expected to minimize systematic subcultural differences. Mass media have to present standardized information, and they are not well suited to tailoring special messages for individual persons. At the same time, though, to some extent schools and to a much greater extent the media are low feedback communication systems. Low feedback systems usually have a high rate of misunderstanding or "error," however. What is more, these errors are not systematic, like the differences between special groups in a society, but are more or less random. This kind of error can lead to unpredictable changes in culture over time, if they are substantial enough. In a sense, large amounts of random error in communicating cultural information across generations is much like suffering a partial loss of "social memory" in the society. Unfortunately, not enough is known about either of these effects to judge how serious they may be. It is true, however, that most observers agree that internal social conflict in the United States has been increasing very seriously, and such effects could be attributed to the kinds of communication systems that have been discussed here.

PERSONAL CONSEQUENCES FOR THE AGING

However little may be known about the consequences of society at large of isolating the aging from the younger society, the effects of this isolation in the aging themselves is quite clear (Mettlin and Woelfel, 1974). The loss of communication is not merely a loss of entertainment or interest. Communication may be seen as a kind of energy, because all human activity is a response to information received. It is not the *having* of information that is important, but the *receiving* of information. Almost all daily activity is a direct result of information received during or immediately before the activity. A status, like a job, is a place in the communication system through which a variable stream of information passes and that directs the person who holds the status to perform activities organized into a role. The organization of activities follows the organization of the information that flows through the status.

As long as a person remains in a status in the communication system, she or he is exposed to the information flow that calls out activities from the person. Removal from the information stream, which happens more and more with the aging population, stops this flow, and the person is *cut off from the source of activity*. When out of the system, the person does not perform role behaviors that are a part of the social pattern in the culture. Removal from the system results in increasing inactivity. What this means in practice is that whether or not a person is active and productive when removed from a position in the communication system, that person is likely to *become* inactive as a result of being taken out of the communication stream. There is an important body of medical opinion that holds that simple inactivity worsens general health, and may even speed the aging process. If this is true, then removal from the information stream may well lead to important declines in the health of the aging population and perhaps shorten lifespans to an unknown extent.

RESEARCH QUESTIONS NEEDING ANSWERS

The most important question of all is: What is happening to our social communication system? Unfortunately, this question has no single answer, just as there is no single answer to a question like, "What is happening to our economy?" Yet, while thousands of economists concern themselves with the economy, and tens of thousands of sociologists and psychologists study culture and personality, human communication scientists number only in the hundreds. Those who concern themselves day to day with the scientific study of the large-scale social consequences of communication patterns number perhaps only a few dozen.

The first important research question, therefore, is: Where will the communication scientists needed to answer the rest of the questions be found? Certainly, at the minimum a relatively large cadre of Ph.D.-level communication scientists will be needed who have at their command the most powerful of quantitative mathematical research techniques.

Second, society will need to address itself to the mapping of its changing communication systems over time. How does information about basic values, beliefs, and other cultural components travel through society now? What major groups and constituencies (like the aging) are left out of the current communication patterns? What are the effects of communication isolation on those forgotten groups? How does the flow of information affect the individual human life cycle? What are the consequences for the old of being isolated from the young? What are the consequences for the young of being isolated from the old? What factors affect the shape and functioning of the social communication system? To what extent can new technologies of communication reduce the need for travel?

These are not tightly focused research questions, but it is unrealistic to expect more precision given the tiny amount of hard knowledge now available. They are answerable questions, though, and it is certainly time to begin asking them.

FUTURE TRENDS

Predicting the future is always hazardous, and the absence of careful large-scale measurements of past trends of the kind discussed here make such guesses doubly tentative. Nevertheless, some educated guesses are needed, if not fully justified. First of all, it seems likely that specialization, division of labor, formal education, and training outside the home are likely to continue, although current knowledge is too hazy to predict whether the trends will accelerate or slow down. The important question is whether these trends will result in still further geographic mobility of the population. If mobility does increase, trends toward the isolation of the aging population will continue. While the best guess is that mobility will continue to increase at least over the short-range future, developments in communication technology could conceivably reduce and even reverse these trends.

As sketched in this chapter, virtually the *only* reason for increased mobility within the society has been the need to obtain specialized information needed for increasingly specialized roles and jobs. This means traveling away from home to go to schools, jobs, etc. Furthermore, much of the geographic mobility connected with changing jobs results from the need to get people with specialized knowledge or training to the places where this knowledge is needed. The development of new individualized communication systems with greater information-carrying capacities could reduce or even eliminate the need to *travel* to the place where specialized knowledge can be found. Mass media, by their mass nature, cannot efficiently carry specialized or secondary information, because they are best suited to sending the same information to many people at once. But with the development of specialized information systems, such as telephones that permit *pairs* or *groups* of people to communicate with each other *cheaply,* specialized information and training could be given or received without the need to travel. Hardware for such systems now exists, at least in early stages. Cable television has the capability for such uses if the cable is connected to central switchboards like telephones, and has the capacity to carry far more information than telephones. Hard-copy capability from the cable (i.e., the ability to transmit printed matter instantly across the cable) also exists. The only drawback to these systems now is their initial cost, which is very high. Perhaps in the light of increasing costs of transportation and decreasing costs of sophisticated electronic equipment, cost/benefit ratios for these kinds of systems will soon be very favorable.

SUMMARY

The communication system of a society is its core. It determines its shape, its beliefs, its collective character, and the individual thoughts, beliefs, and actions of its citizens. Rapid changes in the structure of the society have dramatically changed that communication system in our lifetime. Some of these changes, by all appearances, have been very undesirable, and key among these has been an apparently serious reduction in the extent to which people of different age levels communicate with each other. This effect is most pronounced among the aging, who, as a group, have become highly isolated from the rest of the society. The probable consequences of this isolation seem serious both for the society and for the aging. Our general knowledge and understanding of these matters are very low indeed, perhaps less is known about these important problems than is known about any of the other major social problems. Our greatest need in this area is for basic, quantitative knowledge about social communication processes.

RECOMMENDATIONS

The problems discussed in this chapter are not isolated events, but long-term social trends affecting the entire structure of the society. On the surface, some of these trends clearly seem to be undesirable to the aging population in particular and to society in general. Nevertheless, very little that is precise and quantitative is known about these events. Even if we were sure of what should be changed, we know very little about how to redirect social forces of such magnitude. These recommendations, therefore, do not call for specific actions as much as for devoting resources to answer important questions and to determine certain facts.

LITERATURE CITED

Durkheim, E. 1938. The Rules of Sociological Method. University of Chicago Press, Chicago.

Durkheim, E. 1947. Division of Labor in Society. The Free Press, Glencoe, Ill.

Mettlin, E., and J. Woelfel. 1974. Interpersonal influence and symptoms of stress. J. Health Soc. Behav. 15: 311–319.

Woelfel, J. 1972. Significant others and their role relationships to students in a high school population. Rural Soc. 37: 86–97.

SUGGESTED READINGS

Bruner, J. S. 1958. Social psychology and perception. *In* E. Maccoby, T. M. Newcomb, and E. L. Hartley (eds.), Readings in Social Psychology. 3rd. Ed. Holt, Rinehart, and Winston, New York.

DeTocqueville, A. 1961. Democracy in America. Vol. II. Schocken Books, New York.

Morris, C. W. (ed.). 1934. Mind, Self, and Society. University of Chicago Press, Chicago.

Parsons, T., E. Shills, K. D. Naegele, and J. R. Pitts. Theories of Society. The Free Press, Glencoe, Ill.

Woelfel, J., and A. O. Haller, 1971. Significant others, the self-reflexive act and the attitude formation process. Amer. Soc. Rev. 36: 74–87.

chapter 5
Available Communication Networks for the Aged in the Community

Natalie P. Trager, Ph.D.

> Data make it clear that effective provision of service must be based on effective communication to the people to be served. . . . There is also evidence that once all people know of services and programs, those who need them will in fact tend to take advantage of them (Administration on Aging).

The United States has the most sophisticated and far-reaching communication networks available anywhere on this earth. Technology has advanced to the point that closed-circuit lectures on medical research can be beamed, via satellites, to foreign countries and, via telephone lines, to all parts of the United States (Cass, 1975; Hechinger, 1975). Why then, do workers in the field of aging often find that their clients are unaware of what is going on in their immediate neighborhood, or their county, region, or state? Is it because aging people lack newspapers, telephones, radios, TV sets? Or, if the tools are present, is it because aging cohorts are not interested in the outside world?

Before discussing these matters, it might be wise to consider some of the constraints endemic in services to the aging, constraints that often frustrate both workers and clients in their efforts to communicate.

Most programs designed to serve the aged 1) lean heavily on volunteer labor, 2) require local match funding, 3) are time-limited, and 4) require pre-performance evaluation criteria built into all proposals. These mechanisms are defended as producing maximal effectiveness with minimal expenditure of public resources. The burden of contacting and interesting aging residents rests squarely on local initiative. To assist such efforts, this chapter lists and describes the existing sources of information and expertise already available. A large community may have all of these; the smallest town has some of them.

75

SOURCES: FORMAL ORGANIZATIONS

Economic Organizations

Many workers in the field of aging overlook their most obvious resources: economic organizations. Large corporations, particularly those with retirees living in the community, maintain benefit departments as well as public relations departments. Members of these departments should be recruited to serve on advisory councils and executive boards. "Enlightened self-interest" is at work. Corporation in-house journals, mailed out to stockholders, often print items of interest to retirees.

Most cities and towns have a Chamber of Commerce, a loosely organized group, with varying degrees of "clout," depending on the locality. They usually print brochures listing local business outlets in the area. If persuaded that such a service is a reasonable extension of their role, most directors of these Chambers will include a special section listing organized groups of senior citizens, such as local chapter address and telephone numbers of the American Association of Retired Persons, the local chapter of the National Council of Senior Citizens, the Retired Telephone Workers, and others. Copies of these yearly listings by Chambers of Commerce are available in libraries or directly from the Chamber offices.

Vocational groups (nurses, dieticians, prosthesis suppliers, etc.) exist in metropolitan area; and in less densely populated areas, they sometimes organize regionally. These groups often need a "project" to develop esprit de corps, as well as to interest new clients. What should appeal more to such groups than aged citizens who have an increasing need for their services? Discount arrangements for group service delivery have sometimes resulted from opening communications with such organizations.

Unions are particularly interested in doing well by their retirees, and in many cities, notably Detroit, the dominant union opens its doors to retirees in general, not just to their own members. Union members are traditionally knowledgeable in developing communication networks; retired members should be recruited by members in the field of aging to serve as advisers and troubleshooters.

No community is too small to be without at least one retail merchant, the "crossroad" store, perhaps, that sells gasoline, groceries, hardware, or whatever else is in demand in the locality. Such stores often serve as neighborhood centers, featuring notice boards for local events, one of the surest "traffic attractors" known. Such entrepreneurs are usually delighted to serve as message centers, and they gladly tack up posters and brochures. Larger retailers, including some of the chain grocery stores, also donate large notice boards, and they even set up racks of free brochures donated by public and private agencies.

The Farmers Cooperatives are another often unexplored resource that regularly send out sales information and reports to their members. Notices of the activities of the rural aging can be included. Even if the retired farmer may not see the bulletin, his son or daughter may and can pass along the information.

One of the most honored economic organizations, the banking indus-try, is now cooperating in making information available to seniors. How much this trend is the result of Maggie Kuhn's *Gray Panthers* pioneering pressure, or how much is the result of the banking community adding up total purchasing capacity of the aging population is a moot question. Regardless of why, bankers are now making their services and facilities more available to seniors and are advertising their efforts on TV and in other media. One of the most effective methods to identify unserved but eligible Supplementary Security Income (SSI) persons was discovered by setting up SSI Information tables in a metropolitan bank that serves a low income minority area in Detroit. The table was manned by volunteers (naturally!), but the lobby space and amenities were donated by the bank. A new and effective method of communication about special services to the aged cohort was thus established.

Finally, under this category of economic organizations must be men-tioned the powerful professional organizations. The American Medical Association, the American Bar Association, and others exist primarily to serve the professional interests of their members; but more and more are contributing sincere and highly skilled attention to the special problems of the elderly. Most have subcommittees devoted to exploring the obligations of their particular society to the current needs of aging citizens; most have produced research papers of depth and probity; most are willing to share their findings with bona fide workers in the field of aging. Their special publications can be secured in large university libraries or by writing directly to headquarters (see Appendix).

Government Organizations

The federal bureaucracy charged with the administration of Congressional appropriations for special services to the aged is the Administration of Aging (AOA). It is housed in the Department of Health, Education, and Welfare (HEW). Following the proconsul approach of recent administra-tions, further administrative duties are assigned to 10 regional HEW offices. These offices, in turn, delegate and oversee administrative control to offices on Aging in each of the 50 states; the Virgin Islands, Puerto Rico, Guam, Samoa, and the Trust Territories are absorbed into either Region 1 (East) or Region 9 (West). Administrative authority is then further subdivided by requiring each state to "regionalize." Some states (e.g., Michigan) are fully regionalized, with each of its 83 counties assigned to an "Area Agency on Aging." At this penultimate level of the hierarchy, local programs enter the system, and proposals are submitted for funding (with required local matching funds), competing for approval with those submitted from other local programs.

It is not the purpose of this chapter to scrutinize the advantages or disadvantages of this method of distributing the very minimal funds allocated to the AOA for distribution to states on a demographically defined formula. However, it is the purpose of this chapter to improve communication between thse bureaucracies and the local aging citizen. Contact addresses of the federal and regional bureaucracies are in the Appendix. In most cases, letters to them will be answered, telephone calls will be accepted, and available brochures and other government sponsored research papers will be mailed out.

The best publicized and monolithic federal agency, the Social Security Administration (SSA), advertizes its services widely and effectively. It administers the Trust Funds accumulated from the paychecks of all American workers. The funds are distributed according to carefully de-signed actuarial tables, which, of late, have shown some instability because of double-digit inflation. The SSA also administers the Supplemental Security Income Program, which was designed to homogenize the minimal income throughout the United States to be made available to the elderly, the blind, and the permanently disabled. Communication with SSA in large metropolitan areas is difficult; their telephone lines and waiting rooms are clogged with traffic. Presently (October, 1975), also, some of the computer problems have not been entirely resolved. In smaller com-munities, the SSA functions more efficiently than other federal bureaucra-cies, and the individual aging citizen should have no trouble getting service. The services of many other federal agencies, including the Office of Equal Economic Opportunity, the General Services Administration, the Bureau of the Census, and the Department of Labor, are occasionally involved in programs that benefit aging citizens, but the bulk of their efforts goes to other age cohorts.

There are certain federal resources available that most workers for the aging overlook. Surplus army equipment can be secured by negotiation with local army installations, either active or reserve units. The National Guard is often able to furnish not only supplies but manpower for qualified senior projects. Army Reserve Hospital units can sometimes, by special arrangement with their commanders, supply expert medical and dental service to fill community needs, including those of the aged. Setting up the necessary lines of communication is time-consuming and arduous, but rewards for such effort can be significant.

At the state level, communication between the individual aging citizen and the administrative bureaucracies is most effectively established through personal letters to elected representatives and senators. These letters are then sent on to the staff of the state agency responsible for particular services. Services such as vocational rehabilitation, however, where federal matching funds are tied to employability, are unlikely sources of services. Even services to the blind may suffer certain constraints. For example, one Midwestern state, with an estimated 8,000 elderly blind citizens, served only 35 persons aged 45 and older during fiscal year 1974 to 1975 (to the great distress of the Director of these services, who must abide by "regulations" or risk cut off of federal funds). Most elderly clients of the gigantic Social Services state systems are acquainted only with their local caseworker, who may or may not be able to fill needs, since "minimums" are a matter of state option. Again, personal letters to elected officials are a time-proven method of establishing some sort of dialogue, often resulting in benefit to the individual aged person.

Some programs (e.g., Project Find, subcontracted to the Red Cross) uncovered many cases of elderly couples or singles who had no idea that they were eligible for food stamps, SS1, or Medicaid. In one county in Michigan, 70 percent of the elderly called on by a Red Cross worker had gross unmet needs at the survival level. Such programs were designed as joint federal/state/county/local mobilization to identify needs. The very fact that such a massive effort was needed is clear evidence that many old people do not communicate their needs to those who are in a position to fill them.

Of all county departments the ones most traditionally ready to respond to the needs of older citizens are the county departments of Public Health and the county Extension Services. Again, a personal letter to an elected official is the most effective method of opening a channel of communication, but smaller or rural county officials respond to personal or referred telephone calls.

Most local tax-funded programs for aged citizens are run by the Parks and Recreation departments. Because they have been serving the aged in their own fashion for many years, it is sometimes difficult to change or refocus their present emphasis on bingo, checkers, and other leisure-time activities. However, some of the departments involved now run year-round programs, and/or combine with federal Title VII (congregate meals) to offer more varied activities. A telephone call to city hall should bring in the mail (in metropolitan areas) a brochure listing all local tax-funded activities; in rural areas, the individual senior citizen usually can talk personally with the director of all such programs for the aged.

Education Organizations

The effect of many congruent events (e.g., inflated gasoline and fuel prices, the drop in young cohort enrollments anticipated within 15 years as a reflection of today's zero birth rate, new research on the continuing mental capacity of older people) has shown most clearly in the changing stance of educational institutions toward older students. Community colleges have suddenly discovered that their obligation to be a "community resource" extends to senior citizens. Regulations limiting free public transportation to and from community colleges to young students are quietly being breached. Community college offerings to older citizens range from cake decorating to Transcendental Meditation. Some community colleges are open from early morning to late evening, accommodating their schedules to suit the preferences of both young and old students. Most community colleges advertize in newspapers, on radio, and even on TV.

The way is open; older citizens, however, are not flooding in—in time, perhaps, when the present aging cohort is succeeded by better educated seniors. What is lacking, so far, is any nation-wide commitment to offer the basic three "Rs" to the many illiterate, low income aged. Professor Emeritus Howard McClusky of the University of Michigan, School of Education, is a pioneer in such work. He is convinced that ways must be found to bring basic reading and writing skills to aged citizens (McClusky, 1971). Here is a real communication gap; what is needed is not offered, and neither side appears to be much aware of the hiatus. Basic English *can* be taught on TV; in certain metropolitan areas Spanish-speaking instructors will be necessary. Community colleges can develop teaching cassettes to show at senior centers or public libraries. They can develop home-study kits. None of these methods is new; they have been used successfully in several European countries and in a few pilot programs in this country.

The universities, on the other hand, are not as welcoming to older students as the community colleges. With the exception of Berkeley's Extension department under the dynamic leadership of Milton Sterne, and New York's financially sinking City College's policy of open admission, few universities have joined in a dialogue with older students. What they have done, and with mounting enthusiasm, is to develop programs devoted to biological, sociological, and psychological research into all aging processes. Universities also have contributed much research into such age related topics as alternative income maintenance methods, alternative health insurance schemes, and nursing home or mental hospital quality of care. By all this, the aged may be properly awed, but there is no real contact or communication between them and the large university. Their greatest point of congruence is when large or small groups of aged citizens serve as "sample groups" in the proliferating doctoral studies on various facets of aging. This is not the place to debate the proper role of the modern university. Citizens over 65, however, should not expect much two-way communication from this particular setting.

Adult education groups are traditional in certain parts of the United States, particularly in middle class communities. However, there are many "adult education groups" that depart from this "genteel" tradition. Many start out because of some special interest, or are sparked by some charismatic local personality. Storefront city locations are favored; participant age range is wide. They might be described as temporary/permanent communes with vague educational goals. Rent is usually donated, and all "teachers" are volunteers. Within the limits of geographical and class distribution, adult education groups are available to those elderly citizens who seek them out.

Many communities offer opportunities for older citizens to serve in organizations devoted to better public schools. Such service requires strong nerves and an abiding sense of humor because the schooling of the young has never been as controversial as now. Even parent-teacher groups have opened their membership to grandparents; a reflection, no doubt, of the growing number of broken families in which a grandparent is assuming the parental role. Even great-grandparents are sometimes acting as surrogate parents, particularly in minority subgroups.

Religious Organizations

Church groups are the most "open" to participation by older men and women. All faiths know that their congregations are, in most cases, serving more of the elderly than the young. When crises arise, priests, ministers, and rabbis are among the first sources of help sought out by older people. Genuine faith and belief in the mercy of God are typical of the older generation, particularly among black and other minority parishioners. The church auxiliaries carry on the tradition of neighborly helpfulness and cooperative fund raising (the ladies bake cakes and the men buy them!). Even the ecumenical associations, fostered by clergyman associations, boast a majority of older members.

Bible study groups are less common than in earlier times except in black communities, and they are patronized mostly by women. Groups such as the Jesus freaks and underground Catholic gatherings, while not hostile to the older generation, are almost exclusively patronized by young men and women.

Various churches, however, sponsor certain secular activities (summer camp, athletic teams, etc.), and older men and women are invited to participate, usually as spectators. In Utah, however, the Mormon sect has developed regular summer camps for the elderly, and has expanded the originally church-funded program by supplementary federal grants.

Cultural, Fraternal, and Recreational Organizations

Any attempt to describe the multiplicity and variety of these types of organizations is futile. This section will be sketched out; the individual reader must apply shadings and background. There are forum or current events clubs to which the elderly are welcome. The elderly are particularly welcome in library groups and, because services are usually entirely free, many older persons participate. The whole world of creative activities (art, music, drama) has traditionally drawn no age-correlated entrance requirements. Local amateur and community organizations recruit retired carpenters and painters with guile and persistence. In the area of the arts anyone is welcome, and almost every skill is eventually usable. Summer theatres, summer art shows, summer pottery and plant shops—the elderly are more than welcome because their "out-moded" hand skills have come back into fashion.

The fraternal associations (Elks, Police Benefit Leagues, Grange Societies, etc.) have no "retired"; a member remains in good standing as long as he pays his dues. All offer opportunities for fellowship and community service. Many "take care of their own" as well, having formed their own benefit systems, including private "memorial societies" that cover total or partial burial expenses. However, these organizations are not for "Johnny-come-latelys"; full membership is based on present or previous occupational requirements. For those aged persons who continue these previous associations, social benefits accrued are highly dependable.

There is also no age limitation on hobby clubs, weight watcher groups, or minority service clubs, though full membership is not for the older person with a limited income. Some senior citizen clubs, however, manage to sponsor hobby groups at minimal cost to the participants, but these are age-correlated activities and may not fill individual needs.

For vigorous and healthy oldsters, particularly those residents of warm climate senior retirement towns, all sorts of athletic activities, competitive or non-competitive, are available. Jogging, calisthenics, and folk dancing are popular, as well as more expensive exercises such as golf or tennis. In colder climates, curling, bowling, Bocce, indoor swimming, and the traditional hunting and fishing expeditions are popular. The greatest obstacle to expansion of these activities appears to be that many older people do not realize that age per se is no barrier to athletic or sporting participation; only medical limitations apply. Even some permanent residents of nursing homes have been introduced to gentle calisthenics, with considerable benefit to their morale and muscle tone.

Civic Organizations

For the older man or woman who rejects purely recreational activity or still feels the need to be more seriously involved in solving social ills, there are innumerable opportunities to serve his fellow man. Good government leagues, regional planning groups, taxpayers organizations, watchdog committees, neighborhood planning groups, nature and/or conservation versus pollution groups—all are eager to recruit conscientious members. Age is no barrier.

All political campaigns require cadres of volunteers to do the often dull work of canvassing, signature gathering, envelope stuffing, typing, etc. An older man or woman can be competent at these chores and may find great pleasure in working alongside persons of varying ages and life styles. A telephone call to the local political headquarters of choice should bring an assignment, perhaps not the most interesting job available, but one that must be accomplished.

For retired men and women whose interests remain fixed in the occupational field in which they spent their working lives, there are many local, regional, and national organizations happy to recruit new/old members. Some examples are real estate associations and housing associations. Retired persons have the time to perform the all-essential tasks of research into precedent-setting legal decisions that often have great impact on neighborhood zoning and limited-use developments.

For older men and women who are particularly interested in serving as advocates for their own age group, membership in the local councils on aging is highly satisfactory. These groups not only provide a free intensive course in grass roots politics but also can keep members busy seven days a

week. Conducting local surveys of needs, identifying local available resources, coordinating with other local agencies, and, above all, being *vocal,*
using all popular media, are long-drawn-out and essential parts of the job.
No one who serves on a local council on aging can ever again complain that
he is "not needed," or that life is dull and lacking in challenge.

Health and Welfare Organizations

These groups are part of the health service delivery network. Many older
men and women find them hard to deal with, particularly as clients. The
multiplicity and complexity of their systems defy the best efforts of
administrators to avoid "overkill" or "underkill" in delivery of services. A
maze of conflicting eligibility and accountability requirements confront
both clients and service deliverers. Nevertheless, older citizens are subject
to a high percentage of medical needs and should receive treatment.

The privately funded groups are usually freer to respond to expressed
needs. Groups such as the Salvation Army, the Red Cross, the Black
Panthers and the special disease organizations (cancer, arthritis, etc.) are
more responsive to crisis situations.

The Community Mental Health movement, which recently admitted
that, nation-wide, less than 1 percent of their total cases deal with clients
aged 45 or older, is obviously not much interested in treating older clients.
In its defense, however, it should be noted that its case load is heavy and,
given a choice of clients, tends to choose younger cohorts with the hope of
feeding them back into the working population. Some pilot programs in
metropolitan areas are now testing the feasibility of drop-in crisis centers
for elderly poor clients.

State-funded agencies such as safety councils and consumer protection
departments do not deny services to older people, but they have a long
way to go before they tailor their programs to include the special problems
of seniors. Most such agencies are in the process of absorbing the plethora
of research on special handicaps accruing to the elderly because of sensory
deterioration, low educational levels, and technological ignorance. (It is
not always that the elderly driver does not see the new sign forbidding a
left turn; it sometimes may be that the unfamiliar logo means nothing at
all.) However, both of these types of state agencies have field representatives who will come to senior and/or neighborhood centers to describe and
lecture on new developments. Letters to the state directors are not
ignored; teaching is available.

Legal aid societies in metropolitan areas are swamped with cases, many
involving young children. In most cases, an older man or woman needing

legal assistance finds himself on a "waiting list." Some pilot projects, federally funded, are experimenting with providing free legal assistance to the aged by use of (what else?) volunteer law students and volunteer layman coordinators. Once the initial screening and "crank" aspects are cleared away, the case is then "recommended" to the lawyer staff of the society. The Public Defender system limits itself to serving indigent clients accused of a misdemeanor or a felony. Few older clients fit this category. The whole matter of legal guardianship, surrogate property managers, etc., for aged mentally incompetent persons is haphazardly handled, often to the permanent pauperization and institutionalization of the client. Here is a field where communication between the aged and the legal establishment is in great need of expansion.

The powerful health associations (nursing home association, pharmaceutical associations, optometric and hearing aid associations, among others) are most involved in lobbying to protect their greatest source of income, i.e., private and public monies spent on health care of the aged. Nevertheless, local or state chapters of these groups, even if motivated only by a desire to improve their public image, can be approached by representatives of the local aging population. Letters to elected officials also can help.

There are two associations that appear to deliver services to the aged while also responding to the heavy demands of younger clients. They are the Visiting Nurses Association and hospital social service workers. Because no one ever became rich in these professions and because the great majority of their members are female, it may be fair to assume that a spirit of nurturance still prevails, in spite of bureaucratic regulations and low status on the professional totem pole. The aged are better served by these workers than by most other members of the medical profession. They respond to telephone calls; they respond to crisis situations; they are indispensable.

Community Service and Planning Organizations

There are a number of public and private agencies that, at least in the public mind, appear to both plan and serve, though their laws and charters try to differentiate between the two functions. Community planning agencies, regional planning bodies, and area agencies on aging are primarily expected to develop centralized, coordinated plans for a community or a specifically designated area. On the other hand, United Funds and/or Community Chests, community action agencies, club federations (such as the League of Women Voters, the Association of Business and Professional

Women, the Federation of Women's Clubs, and others) expect to provide service (or the funds to subcontract for service) to specifically designated areas.

Most responsive to the specialized needs of the aged, at least in recent years, have been the private service clubs, the Kiwanis, Rotary, Exchange, Quota, Altrusa, etc. Because membership in these organizations is for life (provided dues are paid) and because many long-term and highly respected members of these clubs are now in the over 65 age bracket, continuing support can be anticipated. The National Exchange Club has been particularly active in promoting free optometric screening for seniors; Kiwanis International has just completed a year in which the "Most Emphasized Service Goal" was special services to the aged. These nation-wide service clubs have tremendous resources of manpower and political influence; it is a very good omen for the future that they devote time, effort, and money to serve the aged citizens of their communities. Communication with these clubs is gratifyingly easy; usually all that is required is a telephone call to the reigning president, who refers the matter to the proper subcommittee chairman, who then proceeds to respond to requests for help.

Advocacy, Lobbying, and Research Organizations

The largest advocacy and lobbying organization for the aged is the American Association of Retired Persons-National Retired Teachers Association (AARP-NRTA). An auxiliary group to AARP is Action for Independent Maturity (AIM), directed toward persons approaching retirement, age 45 to 65. Present total membership, including AIM, is over eight million. Chapters of AARP-NRTA are in every state of the union. An international alliance with retired groups in other countries is still in the formative stages, but it is advancing rapidly. The established goal is to improve every aspect of living for older people. AARP-NRTA-AIM has minimal yearly dues ($2.00 per year per single or couple) but has tremendous financial resources from Colonial Penn Life Insurance, which sells specially designed insurance programs for pre- and post-retirees. Also available is a nation-wide pharmacy service for both prescription and brand name drugs. Special touring group rates to all parts of the world are available to members. AARP-NRTA publishes *Modern Maturity* and the *NRTA Journal.* AIM has its own magazine, *Dynamic Maturity*. AARP-NRTA's members are almost 90 percent white and middle class, but legislative efforts, backed by an able research staff, are directed toward fostering changes in congressional attitudes that will be beneficial to all aged persons.

The black aged have formed their own association. While still an infant compared to AARP-NRTA, the association's input to Congress carries considerable weight because they are officially bringing the views of their black constituents to the attention of influential members of the House and Senate.

The second largest advocacy and lobbying organization for the aged is the National Council of Senior Citizens, which is a loosely connected group of over 3,000 senior citizen clubs, associations, and councils. Combined membership is over three million. The NCSC encourages the aged to participate in social and political action activities; this characteristic may be attributed to its early beginnings when it was totally financed by a powerful labor union (the UAW) and threw all of its considerable muscle into the campaign to pass the Medicare legislation. Since 1969, however, it has become a dues-paying group, is self-supporting, and offers drug service and other benefits at reduced cost to members. Basically, its major goal is the same as that of AARP-NRTA: to improve every aspect of living for older people. However, methods employed (mass rallies, working in behalf of selected political issues, etc.) do suggest the "honorable adversary" tradition of labor unions.

The National Council on the Aging was organized in 1950 to provide leadership services for organizations concerned with the aged. It has no individual memberships. It sponsors the National Institute of Senior Centers and the National Institute on Industrial Gerontology. The latter group publishes the journal *Industrial Gerontologist,* which is by far the best publication available in its particular field. The Council is funded by grants (public and private), dues, and the sale of its many excellent research publications.

These four organizations are the most influential of all the advocacy and lobbying groups, but there are some newcomers, one publicly funded, one privately funded. The Federal Council for the Aged, Chaired by Bertha S. Atkins, was created by Congress under the 1973 amendments to the Older Americans Act. Its function is to advise the president, the secretary of HEW, the Commission on Aging (present incumbent Dr. Arthur S. Flemming) and Congress on all matters relating to the special needs of older Americans. It is also required to review and evaluate the impact of federal policies on all federally funded aging programs. It is to serve as advocate for the aging and as an information clearinghouse. Finally, it must provide public forums for discussing and publicizing the problems and needs of the aging.

The National Organization for Women (NOW) has recently created a Special Task Force to lobby for the rights of older women. The national coordinator, Tish Sommers, works out of the Oakland, California NOW headquarters. Each regional, state, and local chapter of NOW is in the process of developing such subcommittees. It will be interesting to monitor this offshoot of the women's liberation movement, and to observe what response will come from the great mass of American older women.

The leading research organization on aging is the Gerontological Society. It is a professionally oriented group that promotes the scientific study of the aging process. The Society publishes the *Journal of Gerontology* and *The Gerontologist.* It sponsors an annual conference for all professional gerontologists and professional field practitioners. The Gerontological Society works closely with the International Center for Social Gerontology, headed by Dr. Wilma Donahue, Professor Emeritus from the University of Michigan, who is devoting her remarkable and brilliant talents to the development of international coordination and cooperation among gerontology specialists.

This list of organizations working to improve the quality of life for the aged would not be complete without mentioning the many state and regional societies that advocate, lobby, and do research in behalf of their aged constituents.

SOURCES: INFORMAL ORGANIZATIONS

With so many "official" spokesmen and resources for the aging, why, then, do workers in the field often find that their clients are untouched by these official efforts? What is lacking in the communication network?

In practice, many workers have come to rely on informal sources, gossip, and tips from concerned average citizens. This is the communications network that is most unstructured, most flexible, yet most attuned to the older life style in which today's aged citizens were raised. A young man worried about his marital situation may look in the Yellow Pages for a "Marriage Counselor." An old man worried about his wife's unusual behavior will either brood in silence or, as a last resort, talk to his minister, priest, or rabbi. When older people have problems to be solved they do not turn easily to quasi public or public agencies. The aged were socialized into a scheme that stressed self-reliance, reticence, and pride. The Great Depression irretrievably marked many of today's aged; anything smelling of "charity" is automatically rejected. Therefore, when many of the aged apply for social benefits, whether it be Supplemental Security Income, food stamps, or for participation in a Title VII meals program, they are shamed by all the "personal questions" they must answer. Workers in the field are sympathetic, but "accountability" is required, "eligibility" must be established, and "management by objectives" approaches must be maintained. (Or so read the rules; in fact, many programs for the aged maintain only a slight resemblance to the proposals under which they were funded. Most old people have independent spirits; it is not easy to cudgel them into governmentally defined and restrictive cubbyholes.)

How do workers in the field get most of their leads on old people in trouble? In metropolitan areas the police are usually the referring agency, particularly for mentally confused "wanderers." The aged involved in serious crime are a very small percentage; most arrests are for moving traffic violations, particularly driving under the influence. Many states still require their police force to arrest the aged "wino," but others now have substituted "delivery to one's home or to a treatment clinic." Sometimes these ragtag old persons are then referred by the police to some form of custodial or semicustodial home care arrangement. Large cities specialize in converting dilapidated old hotels into "rooms for singles," mostly aged men and women. The police also refer and transport aged persons to social service departments, mental hospitals, hospitals, and nursing homes. When all else fails, the policeman is the "friend in need" for many aged citizens.

This sort of "last ditch" intervention is averted, however, by referrals from all sorts of concerned laymen. Postmen usually know the aged people on their route, and they report to the authorities if they suspect trouble. If a utility service man, delivering oil or checking meters, is unable to rouse an aged resident, he often takes steps on his own to check on the person's health. There are innumerable cases of aged people, helpless after a serious fall, being saved a lingering, lonely death because their regular delivery man was worried and did something about it.

Some referrals to field workers come from door-to-door canvassers, from Boy and Girl Scout fund raising supervisors; public housing complex managers report on special trouble; hotel managers call the social service workers or the police. Pharmacists, lawyers, landlords, bartenders—all have been known to take the trouble to call help for an aged man or woman who in their opinion "just ain't makin' it so good." The number of aged poor who collapse because of acute malnutrition is documented in the records of hospital emergency wards of every large city. The great bulk of the referrals come from the informal sources mentioned above.

There is another level of the communications network that is in between the formal and informal systems described. It has elements of each, but its major strength is the dedicated work of volunteers. (Surprised?) These networks are the Friendly Visitor and Telephone Reassurance programs. Volunteers make regular visits to old people confined to home, nursing home residents, long-term patients in terminal hospital wards or mental hospitals. Volunteers also make regular telephone calls, at pre-arranged hours, to an assigned list of home-bound aged persons; if the phone is not answered within a reasonable time, a personal visit is made to the home to check up on what, if anything, is wrong.

How do the Friendly Visitor and Telephone Reassurance volunteers learn who needs their services? In most cases, what is dubbed the "gossip network" is operating, particularly outside of metropolitan areas. In cities where there are local chapters, Maggie Kuhn's Gray Panther youth auxiliary does a lot of snooping about in their determination to uncover the aged isolate who falls between the cracks of formal outreach systems. In many cases, a "nosy neighbor" is the best safeguard an aged person can have, because signs of trouble (broken locks or windows, no shades raised, no smoke from a chimney) rarely escape the eyes of such a neighbor.

All informal systems have a lingering aura of neighborliness, of the helping hand stretched out in human sympathy. It is sad that all the formal systems do not absorb some semblance of that same sympathy; aged persons, particularly the poor and poor minority members of our society, have great needs. The two-way communication system, so necessary for fulfilling those needs, is not in the best working order.

COMPILING AND PROCESSING
INFORMATION: COST AND EFFECTIVENESS

Workers in the field of aging are attempting to design communication systems so that needs of individual clients can be identified and these clients can be referred to available service agencies. This activity, everywhere referred to as "I and R" (Information and Referral) is the heart of all social work agencies. Either the worker responds directly or finds somebody else who can. Ideally, the worker "follows up" to make sure that the referred client actually received service to fit his need.

At present, depending on the funding source and the dedication of overseeing personnel, accountability (or responsiveness) is crucial. It is mandated in tax-paid programs; it is stressed in all privately funded agencies. Management personnel have learned that a systems analysis approach to I and R not only provides accountability data, but also a built-in method of evaluation technology, measuring performance and efficiency of both the program and staff members.

In the field of aging, workers have run head on into the undeniable fact that programs designed specifically for the aging cannot afford computer technology; they must "hitchhike" on existing technologies used by the Social Security Administration, the various state employment commissions, the state departments of social service and, in some metropolitan areas, transportation authorities. Leaving aside the theoretical argument that such systems simply do not fit the special needs of the elderly (based as they are on assumptions of widespread literacy, familiarity with technical language, general ability to fill out forms, and other common skills of citizens educated to handle such things) the systems are available to the elderly as much as to any other citizen in need. I and R is supplied without charge at any Social Security office. Mechanization of the system is evolving. To judge by the 5-year experience of the United States Employment Service, mechanization requires many years to pass the "learning stage." The best, or at least the kindest, way to describe national I and R systems for the aged is that they are still in their expensive infancy and that compatible systems between agencies are the exception rather than the rule.

While 800 "hot line" setups (leased, subsidized with public funds) are available, few states have installed them. The technology is available; services are not. These systems are too expensive unless genuine referrals result.

State subsystems are being developed, but they are still wrestling with the "privacy issue." While both national and state systems have immense numbers of data banks, there is continued pressure to hold down costs, and often non-use of available information is justified because privacy may be breached. Even the use of passwords, locked doors, scrambling devices, and 24-hour guards has been unable to assure compliance with federal requirements of confidentiality.

Regional systems are even further removed from the magic blend of computerization/confidentiality and service delivery. Some area agencies on aging have invested in elaborate card index and needle-pick systems, spending precious hours debugging the systems themselves and then training special staff to keep records current and useable. These efforts are admirable, but more and more are exercises in futility because actual services to the aged do not appear just because an agency has devised a semi-mechanized listing of those persons who have requested them. Area agencies keep fine lists of those who telephone them for help in solving problems; such agencies, however, are restricted by federal regulations from actually providing service unless no other agency in the area is capable (Federal Register, 1973). In rural areas where there are no other agencies to refer to, area agencies could give services, but their meager funding makes it impossible.

Local councils on aging, with their extensive familiarity with a very small section of a state have the best record of actually meeting needs with appropriate services. Someone knows someone who knows someone else, and the old fashioned neighbor/gossip network is still effective.

RESEARCH QUESTIONS NEEDING ANSWERS

Since I and R systems have one thing in common, i.e., that telephone service is taken for granted, it appears that the first and most essential task for workers in the field of aging is to verify how many aged persons in their individual area of responsibility are without phones. Once this basic data is gathered, how can we provide phones? What funding can be garnered, public or private, donated or client part-pay?

Which of the many already identified factors (ignorance, fear, indifference, feeling of shame) that constrain the elderly in their use of public agencies is most easily broken down? What mechanisms are most effective in such an attack?

What effect has general inflation had on the readiness of the elderly to approach public agencies for assistance? Which agencies have had the greatest increase in requests from the elderly?

How many illiterate or non-English speaking aged persons live in each aging area agency's jurisdiction? Are educational institutions and state departments of education prepared to offer suitable remedial programs and bi-lingual teachers?

What progress has been made on making existing data bank systems compatible? How much cooperative service is available on an inter-agency basis?

FUTURE TRENDS

Workers in the field of aging have been much heartened by the fact that more and more states are using homestead tax cuts and other fiscal devices to allow older people to keep their homes. This, of course, transfers the burden to the working people, because tax revenues must come from somewhere. Relieving grandpa of taxes lays a heavier tax bill on son and grandson.

Nevertheless, it appears that no other mechanism is easily available. The same device may be extended. For instance: special discount postal rates. Items to be mailed would be brought to the post office and mailed over the counter; this would minimize the possibility of fraud and/or collusion. Mailing of Christmas cards and birthday greetings to absent family members, gifts to grandchildren, etc., are a source of pleasure and involvement for aged family members; some sort of "senior discount" should be worked out.

Along with special discount postal rates, special phone rates should be made available to the aged poor, particularly for home-bound elderly. This subsidy would be reimbursed to the telephone companies out of general federal tax revenues.

More and more the young-old will be recruited to work as volunteers for the old-old, particularly in health care settings. They will be asked to serve as adjunct aides (unpaid), as adjunct social workers and data gatherers, and as monitors or watchdogs to report negligent practice. The young-old have a vested interest in improving the lot of the old-old who are institutionalized. Unless our systems are improved it will soon be their turn to exist under inhumane and dehumanizing conditions. Young-old volunteers will be a tremendous force in upgrading the quality of life for the old-old bedridden aged. Physical therapy and rehabilitative calisthenics will become the rule, rather than the exception. Overuse of tranquilizers will be cut. The young-old are far better educated than the old-old; they will communicate reports of ongoing abuses to the regulating authorities and to elected representatives.

Communications systems in general are inevitably becoming more and more complex. Workers with the aging will be forced to use considerable ingenuity to translate complex systems into the old fashioned and time-honored methods still favored by the older generation. The mass media should be the teaching instrument of choice. Older citizens watch TV, can learn from it, and would have no fear of appearing publicly "stupid." Many state departments of social service advertize their wares on TV and do an effective job. Extended use of this media is certain, and area agencies will follow the trend. Public service announcements, community calendar programs, etc., will proliferate. Much more use of the "neighborly approach" can be made with local elderly taking the spotlight as announcers of local services. Some rural-based stations are already using this technique very effectively.

SUMMARY

There are a multitude of formal and informal organizations that, according to their stated goals, are available to serve the aged. That so few of the real needs of the elderly are met by these organizations is a source of continuing frustration for both practitioners in the field and their aged clients. Expansion of two-way communication appears to be a necessary solution.

Mechanized systems, while diffuse, are not well adapted to serve the elderly because they depend upon technologies that are unfamiliar to aged clients. Their tendency to regiment and dehumanize service is their most obvious defect.

Special efforts should be made to make the aged aware of what services are available, using television and radio as teaching devices. Other communications media, particularly the postal system and the telephone, should develop subsidized services for the aged, particularly those who are poor and/or house-bound.

RECOMMENDATIONS

Methods selected by area agencies to offer I and R services to their area clients should be those best suited to the needs and mores of the particular area. In areas of minority concentration, the particular mores of the group must be respected. For example: Bible study groups are an excellent contact point for members in the city of Detroit. In other sections of Michigan, no minority population 60 years of age and older is large enough to warrant funding of special programs. The few 60 and older minority citizens are widely scattered through the area and are integrated with existing programs.

The least rigid method of I and R service should be the method of choice. No more than any other group, the elderly do not enjoy being treated as statistical items. The human touch is essential.

As soon as possible, divorce I and R service from dependence on federal funding. Continued cuts in budgets are promised, and expectations of improvement appear unrealistic.

All area agencies should expand their media presentations. If budget cuts interfere with this suggestion, the agencies should develop more use of the excellent publications available at moderate cost (*Aging,* AARP-NRTA Newsletter, etc.).

LITERATURE CITED

Administration on Aging. Knowledge and Use of Social Clubs for the Aging. Department of Health, Education and Welfare. Publication #7, p. 14. Washington, D.C.

Cass, J. 1975. Lifelong learning: The back-to-school boom. Saturday Rev. 9(20): 14.

Federal Register. 1973. Title 45. 903.67(a). 10:11:1973. V. 38, No. 196.

Hechinger, F. M. 1975. Education's "new majority". Saturday Rev. 9(20): 14–16, 18.

Kelley, V., and H. Weston. 1975. Computers, costs and civil liberties. Social Work 20: 15–19.

McClusky, H. Y. 1971. Education. Background Paper for 1971 White House Conference on Aging. Washington, D.C.

SUGGESTED READINGS

Adult Services of Alleghany County. The Friendly Visitor, 429 Forbes Avenue, Room 406, Pittsburg, Pa. (free).

Butler, R. N., and M. I. Lewis. 1973. Aging and Mental Health. C. V. Mosby, St. Louis.

Carp, F. M. 1966. A Future for the Aged. Rustin and London: University of Texas Press, Austin.

Lindsay, I. B. 1971. The Multiple Hazards of Age and Race: The Situation of Aged Blacks in the United States. Study for the U.S. Senate Special Committee on Aging, U.S. Government Printing Office, Washington, D.C.

Manney, J. D., Jr. 1975. Aging in American Society. The Institute of Gerontology, The University of Michigan-Wayne State University, Ann Arbor.

Maxwell, J. M. 1962. Centers for Older People: Guide for Programs and Facilities. National Council on the Aging, Washington, D.C.

Office of Economic Opportunity. Establishing Telephone Reassurance Services. National Countil on Aging, Washington, D.C. (free).

Rosow, I. 1967. Social Integration of the Aged. Free Press, New York.

U.S. Senate Special Committee on Aging. 1975. Developments in Aging: 1973 and January—March 1974. U.S. Government Printing Office, Washington, D.C.

APPENDIX

Useful Addresses

Action, 806 Connecticut Ave., N.W., Washington, D.C. 20525. (202)655-4000.

Administration on Aging, Department of Health, Education, and Welfare, Office of Human Development, Washington, D.C. 20201. (202) 245-0724.

AARP-NRTA (American Association of Retired Persons-National Retired Teachers Association), 1909 K Street, N.W., Washington, D.C. 20006. (202) 872-4700.

American Bar Association, 1155 East 60th Street, Chicago, Illinois 60637.

American Medical Association, 535 North Dearborn Street, Chicago, Illinois 60610. Liason: Herman W. Gruber, Secretary, Subcommittee on Aging.

Bureau of the Census, Suitland, Maryland 20233. (202) 655-4000.

Bureau of Labor Statistics, 441 G Street N.W., Washington, D.C. 20212. (202) 961-2221.

Federal Council on the Aging, 400 6th Street, N.W., Room 4022, Donohoe Building, Washington, D.C. 20201.

Federal Regional Offices

Region 1: (Connecticut, Maine, Massachusetts, New Hampshire, Rhode

Island, Vermont). J. F. Kennedy Building, Government Center, Boston, Mass. 02203.

Region 2: (New Jersey, New York, Puerto Rico, Virgin Islands), 26 Federal Plaza, New York, N.Y. 10007.

Region 3: (Delaware, District of Columbia, Maryland, Pennsylvania, Virginia, West Virginia). P.O. Box 12900, Philadelphia, Pa. 12900.

Region 4: (Alabama, Florida, Georgia, Kentucky, Mississippi, North Carolina, South Carolina, Tennessee). 50 Seventh Street, N.E., Atlanta, Ga. 30323.

Region 5: (Illinois, Indiana, Michigan, Minnesota, Ohio, Wisconsin). 300 South Wacker Street, 29th Floor, Chicago, Ill. 60606.

Region 6: (Arkansas, Louisiana, New Mexico, Oklahoma, Texas). 1114 Commerce Street, Dallas, Texas 75202.

Region 7: (Iowa, Kansas, Missouri, Nebraska). 601 East 12th Street, Kansas City, Mo. 64106.

Region 8: (Colorado, Montana, North Dakota, South Dakota, Utah, Wyoming). 1 Grand Stout Street, Federal Office Building, Denver, Colo. 80101.

Region 9: (Arizona, California, Guam, Hawaii, Nevada, Samoa, Trust Territories). Federal Office Building, 50 Fulton Street, San Francisco, Calif. 94102.

Region 10: (Alaska, Idaho, Oregon, Washington). Arcade Building, 1319 2nd Avenue, Seattle, Wash. 98101.

Gerontological Society, One Dupont Circle N.W., Washington, D.C. 20036. (202) 659–4698.

International Center for Social Gerontology, Inc., Suite 350, 425 13th Street, N.W., Washington, D.C. 20004. (202) 393–0347 Telex 89–2407.

National Council of Senior Citizens, 1511 K Street, N.W., Washington, D.C. 20005. (202) 783–6850.

The Senate Special Committee on Aging, G-225 Senate Office Building, Washington, D.C. 20510. (202) 225–5364.

Social Security Administration, 6401 Security Blvd., Baltimore, Md. 21235.

Subcommittees with Legislative Authority over Older Americans Programs

U.S. House of Representatives (Select Subcommittee on Education of The Education and Labor Committee) Chairman: John Brademas (Ind.), Lloyd Meeds (Wash.), Shirley Chisholm (N.Y.), William Lehman (Fla.), Robert Cornell (Wisc.), Edward Beard (R.I.), Leo Zeferetti (N.Y.), George Miller (Calif.), Tim Hall (Ill.), Alphonzo Bell (Calif.), Peter A. Peyser (N.Y.), James Jeffords (Vt.), Larry Pressler (S. Dak.).

United States Senate (Subcommittee on Aging of the Labor and Public Welfare Committee). Chairman: Thomas Eagleton (Mo.), Alan Cranston (Calif.), Edward M. Kennedy (Mass.), Jennings Randolph (W. Va.), Harrison A. Williams, Jr. (N.J.), Claiborne Pell (R.I.), Gaylord Nelson (Wisc.), J. Glenn Beall, Jr. (Md.), Richard S. Schweiker (Pa.), Robert Taft, Jr. (Ohio), Robert T. Stafford (Vt.).

The following committees do not have legislative authority, but are empowered to study and analyze problems of the elderly and make recommendations to their respective Houses:

U.S. House of Representatives (Select Committee on Aging) Chairman: William J. Randall (Mo.), Claude Pepper (Fla.), Spark M. Matsunaga (Hawaii), Edward R. Roybal (Calif.), Fred B. Rooney (Pa.), Mario Biaggi (N.Y.), Walter Flowers (Ala.), Ike F. Andrews (N.C.), John Burton (Calif.), Edward Beard (R.I.), Michael Blouin (Iowa), Thomas Downey (N.Y.), James Florio (N.J.), Harold Ford (Tenn.), William Hughes (N.J.), Marily Lloyd (Tenn.), Jim Santani (Nev.), Don Bonker (Wash.), Bob Wilson (Calif.), William C. Wampler (Va.), John Hammerschmidt (Ark.), H. John Heinz III (Pa.), William Cohen (Maine), Ronald Sarasin (Conn.), William Walsh (N.Y.), Charles Grassley (Iowa).

United States Senate (Special Committee on Aging). Chairman: Frank Church (Idaho), Harrison A. Williams, Jr. (N.J.), Jennings Randolph (W. Va.), Edmund S. Muskie (Maine), Frank E. Moss (Utah), Edward M. Kennedy (Mass.), Walter F. Mondale (Minn.), Vance Hartke (Ind.), Claiborne Pell (R.I.), Thomas F. Eagleton (Mo.), John V. Tunney (Calif.), Lawton Chiles (Fla.), Dick Clark (Iowa), Hiram L. Fong (Hawaii), Clifford P. Hansen (Wyo.), Edward W. Brooke (Mass.), Charles H. Percy (Ill.), Robert T. Stafford (Vt.), J. Glenn Beall, Jr. (Md.), Pete V. Domenici (N. Mex.), Bill Brock (Tenn.), Dewey Bartlett (Okla.).

chapter 6

Mass Media and the Aging

Charles K. Atkin, Ph.D.

What roles do the mass media play in the life of the older person in our society? How can channels of mass communication provide improved services for the elderly audience member? In the past few years, researchers have accelerated their pace of investigation into some of the basic questions involving the mass media and the aging. This chapter presents a thorough review of the research evidence that has been accumulated about older people's exposure and responses to mass communication messages, followed by a listing of important research problems requiring theoretical and applied research. The chapter is designed to provide the reader with an overview of the current state of knowledge about media and aging and an agenda of questions that remain to be answered.

REVIEW OF RESEARCH EVIDENCE ON MASS MEDIA AND AGING

There are an increasing number of empirical research studies dealing with topics involving mass communication and the elderly. Unfortunately, most have dealt only with patterns of exposure to the major mass media, although some researchers have also attempted to explain the functions of this consumption. Almost no research describes the effects of the media on elderly audiences, nor the impact of portrayals of the aging upon the remainder of the population. The research evidence will be presented in four basic categories: 1) content analysis of the way older people are portrayed in media messages, 2) exposure patterns of older segments of the audience, 3) older people's evaluation of mass media offerings, and 4) functions and gratifications of mass media exposure for the aged.

Content Analysis of Aged Characters in the Media

Although there have been numerous content analyses of mass media messages, only a handful of studies have described findings in terms of the age of characters. Because television is the most important medium, the results of several TV studies are briefly examined. Three studies dealt with entertainment programming and commercial messages.

Aronoff (1974) reviewed archival video tape evidence from three sample weeks in 1969, 1970, and 1971, focusing on network television drama. Of 2,741 characters, 5 percent were judged to be "elderly" with equal proportions for each sex. Compared to younger age groups, elderly men were more likely to be "bad guys" and less likely to be "good guys." Elderly females were more frequently failures than successes, while other age groups tended to be predominantly successful.

Petersen (1973) assessed older people's visibility and directionality of image in a sample of 30 half hour time slots in the 1971–1972 television season. Persons over age 65 constituted 13 percent of all television characters, slightly higher than the real-life amount of 10 percent. Unlike the actual sex ratio, only one of every 10 older characters was female. These findings were essentially replicated when total program time rather than frequency of appearance was analyzed. The expectation of an unfavorable image was not supported, as measured on 21 evaluative bi-polar attributes. Overall, 18 percent of the attribute ratings were negative, 23 percent were neutral, and 59 percent were positive along a seven-step scale. The most favorable ratings occurred for "active/passive," "good health/bad health," "independent/dependent," "competent/imcompetent," and "strong/ weak," with more than 75 percent of the ratings on the positive side of the scale. Old characters received the lowest ratings on "socially accepted/ socially rejected" and "friendly/unfriendly," with slightly more than one third of the scores on the unfavorable side of the continuum.

Francher (1973) randomly sampled 100 television commercials and assessed the aging message presented in those ads. He found that 43 percent featured characters who were both young and attractive. Only two commercials portrayed older characters, and in both cases and ads showed a number of people in montage fashion. Among the promises implied in the monitored commercials, 57 percent pledged youth, youthful appearance, or the energy to act youthful.

Mass Media Exposure Patterns of the Aged

Since the 1940s, audience researchers have measured the amount of exposure and the content preferences of older citizens. Some of these studies have examined the general population and provided breakdowns by age, while other investigations have focused on varying types of elderly audiences. In this section, a large set of evidence is summarized from a wide variety of samples; the more comprehensive multi-media studies are presented first.

Chaffee and Wilson (1975) surveyed a representative sample of 544 adults in Wisconsin, including about 100 respondents 65 or older. They found that television viewing time increased consistently from age 40 until the 80s, with people over age 60 scoring above all other age groups. Although attention to news programming was well above average in the over 65 age segment, there was a slight decline from the late 60s to the oldest respondents. Among the elderly, news exposure was relatively greater than general TV exposure, compared to younger age groups.

According to the Wisconsin data, newspaper reading time began to increase above the overall adult average in the mid-50s, reached a peak at age 65 that held until the early 70s, after which a precipitous drop occurred in very old age. Attention to political and public affairs news in the newspaper followed a similar age pattern, although attention was relatively lower than overall exposure time. Magazine reading reached its highest level during the 60s, but dropped very sharply after age 70. Radio listening began to decline after age 60, and steadily decreased through old age.

A state-wide survey of 3,000 noninstitutionalized persons aged 60 and over was conducted in Michigan by Market Opinion Research (1975). One question asked how the respondent spent leisure time. Thirty-five percent named 'television as the predominant activity, with no other behavior scoring above 12 percent. Combining first, second, and third choices, the mass media achieved a central role. Sixty-seven percent named watching television, 45 percent said visiting with others, 39 percent indicated reading, 25 percent chose hobbies, 24 percent selected travel, and 17 percent picked church activities. Only 4 percent reported that movies were an important leisure pastime. Seventy-five percent claimed that they read a newspaper on all 7 days before the interview. Television viewing averaged slightly more than 2 hours per day.

Danowski (1975) conducted interviews with 162 residents of a Michigan retirement community averaging 72 years of age. Most were working class and lower middle class, and four fifths were female. Mean television viewing time was 6 hours per day; radio listening accounted for slightly more than 2 hours. Three fourths of an hour was devoted to newspaper reading and a half hour to magazine exposure, along with several minutes of book use. The most frequently viewed content on television was news, followed by game shows, sports, situation comedies, crime shows, movies, and soap operas.

Beyer and Woods (1963) interviewed more than 5,000 social security beneficiaries in four areas of the United States, asking how the person had spent time the previous day. Among those over 65, 70 percent watched television with viewers spending a median 3 hours with TV. Reading was reported by 61 percent, totaling 1 hour. Only 17 percent listened to radio or records, but the exposed persons apportioned 1.5 hours to this activity. These media exposure behaviors constituted 45 percent of all available leisure hours. The proportion viewing the previous day did not differ between those in their 60s, 70s, or 80s. On the other hand, they found a slight upturn in reading time in the 70s and 80s.

Cowgill and Baulch (1962) surveyed 224 persons 60 years old and over in a midwestern city several years after television was introduced. When asked to describe their leisure time activities on the previous weekday, 52 percent said they have viewed television. This was by far the most frequent leisure pursuit. Reading was the second most popular activity for women and third most often cited by men. On weekends, television was superceded by visiting and entertaining, thus falling to second most favorite activity.

Bower (1973) reported on interviews conducted with a national sample of 1,900 adults to provide authoritative data on television viewing. The 1970 survey found that weekly television viewing time on evening and weekends totaled more than 28 hours for those aged 60 and older. This was slightly lower than the 29 hours for respondents in their 50s, but was similar to the sample-wide average. A comparable baseline survey in 1960 found that the 60 and older age group viewed 25 hours per week, well above the overall average. A cohort analysis of the segment aging from their 50s to 60s between 1960 and 1970 indicated that this age group increased their viewing by 3 hours.

In terms of content exposure patterns, the Bower study discovered that 34 percent of the 60 and older age group watched public television at least once a week; this was somewhat below the overall level of 40 percent. In addition, another 29 percent viewed public TV at least once. Television diet was also gauged in a supplementary "diary" survey of 344 persons, including 82 who were 55 years or older. In terms of percentage of total viewing time, the older subgroup saw 27 percent comedy-variety, 19 percent news, 16 percent action, 13 percent movies, 12 percent light music, and 8 percent sports. They were above average on news and light music, but below the norm on movies.

Steiner (1963) reported on media exposure diaries of 237 New York City residents, showing that the proportion of television viewing of informational versus entertainment content rose steadily throughout the life cycle; while less than one third of the program exposure of those under 55 was informational, this type of content exposure was 44 percent for the 55 to 64 age group, and 48 percent for those 65 and older.

Schalinske (1968) received questionnaires from 85 residents of a retirement community, with an average age of 80. They watched over 3.5 hours of television daily. He reported that these very old persons were not attracted to documentaries, panel discussions, or other serious public affairs content, although they relied on TV for news.

Davis (1971) distributed questionnaires to Southern California members of the American Association of Retired Persons, highly educated persons ranging in age from 55 to 80. Three fourths of the 166 respondents were female, and all lived in private housing. Respondents indicated that news and public affairs programs were the preferred type of television content, followed by music, drama, educational, and travelogue programs. Only four of the top 15 programs most popular with the general public were listed as favorites by the elderly. Surprisingly, 75 percent of the viewers indicated that they watched only 5 hours or less per week.

A national survey of newspaper readership was conducted by the American Newspaper Publishers Association (ANPA, 1973), with interviews of more than 1,700 randomly selected adults across the United States. The proportion of the public who had read a newspaper the day before increased with age, from 67 percent among those 18 to 34, to 83 percent in the 35 to 64 group, to 84 percent for elderly respondents. The most and least widely read topics were broken down for readers aged 50 and older. This analysis showed that the average item dealing with accidents, disasters, and natural phenomena was read by 43 percent of these older respondents, followed by letters to the editor (42 percent), obituaries (41 percent), crime stories (36 percent), and articles concerning public health and welfare (35 percent). In each of these cases, older respondents scored somewhat higher than the overall sample. On the other hand, only 12 percent of the older readers consumed sports stories, and just 21 percent read comics, relatively less than the remainder of the sample.

Schramm and White (1949) examined newspaper reading of 750 adults in Illinois. They found that 19 percent of the news content in the daily paper was read by respondents aged 60 years and older; this was slightly less than in middle age groups but higher than the youngest segments of the sample. There was a positive relationship between age and the proportion reading public affairs news content.

Parker and Paisley (1966), in a survey of 574 California adults, found that 18 percent of the 60 and older age group listened to the radio for one or more hours daily. This was compared to 32 percent of younger and middle aged groups. In an expanded sample of almost 1,900 Californians, Parker and Paisley discovered that half of the older age segment selected information on the radio, in contrast to the one third rate in the rest of the sample.

Two earlier studies of radio listening preferences showed strong inverse relationships between age and liking for popular music. Lazarsfeld and Kendall (1948) found that less than one third of those 50 and older regarded currently popular music as a favorite form of programming; the rate of preference was twice as high among younger segments of the sample. A decade later, Whan (1957) discovered the same trend; preference for popular music declined from 68 percent in the 19 to 30 age group to 26 percent in the over 60 age group.

Some aging evidence on motion picture attendance by the elderly was presented in a report by Meyersohn (1961). Examining sample surveys from 1945, 1947, and 1957, he demonstrated that movie viewing decreased dramatically as people grew older; just 15 percent of the 50 and older subgroup had gone to the theater at least once a week.

Handel (1950) studied the tastes in motion picture stories among 2,000 persons, with the oldest age category including those more than 45 years of age. Compared to younger age segments, the older respondents were more likely to prefer serious drama and history-biography themes, and less likely to express liking for mystery-horror and slapstick types of movies.

Evaluations of the Mass Media by the Aged

While the previous set of findings clearly shows that older people spend a considerable amount of time with the mass media, this does not provide direct evidence of their opinions and level of satisfaction with the media. In the last decade, researchers have begun to measure evaluative responses of the elderly toward the dominant medium of television. There are also some limited results comparing television with other mass media. The data base for several of the following studies has been described in the previous section.

The Bower (1973) national survey provides a variety of evidence about older persons' opinions toward television. Respondents were asked which of five things they were most satisfied with (fashions for women, automobiles, television programs, movies, and popular music). In 1960, 43 percent of those aged 60 and older chose television programs, but the 1970 total dropped to 27 percent. This difference may have been partly the result of a cohort effect, because only 30 percent of the 50 to 59 age segment selected TV programs 10 years earlier. In both years, the older age group was far above the other age levels in satisfaction with television. Another question asked which things they could least do without for several months. Among the older subgroup, 21 percent in 1970 and 25 percent in 1960 gave television first or second choice; again, these ratings were somewhat higher than for the younger respondents. General attitude toward television was also highest in the older age group in both years, although a moderate decline occurred over time that could not be accounted for by cohort differences.

Other Bower questions dealt specifically with news programming. When asked to identify which medium provides the fairest, most unbiased news, 34 percent of the older age group chose television, and 25 percent picked newspapers. The television figure was similar to the overall average, but the newspaper percentage was slightly higher than the norm. Another question dealt with the extent to which respondents felt there was too much news coverage of United States social problems, such as racial conflict and student unrest. There was a strong tendency for older persons to object to this type of content: 45 percent said there was too much coverage, and only 32 percent of the overall sample felt this way.

In his survey, Danowski (1975) asked elderly respondents several questions about changes they would like to see in television programming. When asked whether there should be more senior citizens as regular TV performers 66 percent agreed and 17 percent disagreed, with the remainder uncertain. In addition, 43 percent agreed that there should be a soap opera specially designed for the older audience, while 43 percent disagreed. In response to a question about preferred program types, 38 percent wanted more musical shows, 20 percent sought more travelogues, 14 percent desired additional news and public affairs programming, and 13 percent preferred more comedies. Other categories were mentioned by less than one tenth of the sample.

The Schalinske (1968) study of very old residents of a senior citizens community reported that the elderly expressed both appreciation for television and devotion to this medium. According to the findings, old persons were far more likely to name favorite programs than to identify disliked programs; action-adventure shows were the target for most criticism.

In his study of higher status retired persons, Davis (1971) described the level of satisfaction with television programming. Almost two thirds said that television was "satisfactory" to them. The majority recognized that television provided a companionship service to a moderate or strong degree. Almost one half felt that television presented a factual and honest image of older persons, although many negative responses were expressed to commercial representations of the elderly. Among the various types of program content, the most frequent objections involved violence, sex, commercials, and over-exposure of minorities.

Steiner (1963) asked a representative national sample of 2,500 adults which of the mass media was "most important" to them. Older respondents tended to cite newspapers, while younger respondents chose television. In the 65 to 69 age group, 45 percent selected newspapers, 38 percent picked television, and 11 percent chose radio; among those 70 or older, the distribution was 44 percent for newspapers, 33 percent for TV, and 15 percent for radio. These findings were almost identical in the 45 to 64 age group, while the relative position of television and radio was reversed for those in their 20s and 30s. Older people were also more likely than younger age groups to rate newspapers as the "most entertaining" medium, but television was still most enjoyed by a three-to-one margin over newspapers.

Functions and Motivations for Mass Media Usage by the Aged

Many researchers have tried to explain the reasons *why* the elderly are so dependent on the mass media for entertainment and information. They have identified many factors that seem to motivate people to expose themselves to several hours of mass media content each day. They have relied on the functional approach to understanding mass media usage patterns, exploring the uses and gratifications that are sought and obtained by this segment of the audience. Much of the theory has dealt with the elderly person's need for para-social interaction through mass media as a substitute for declines in direct interpersonal communication. In this section, some of the discussions of motives and functions are briefly described and then the recent body of research findings is reviewed.

Schramm (1968) proposed that much media exposure is undertaken to combat loneliness and alienation characteristic of old age. In particular, the loss of access to channels of local news dissemination on the streets or at work may be compensated by attention to news content in the media.

Graney and Graney (1974) suggest that the mass media may serve a critical role in maintaing social-psychological satisfaction when older people lose contact with friends and relatives and when churches and voluntary organizations become dominated by new and unfamiliar interests.

Petersen (1973) proposes that TV personalities, particularly soap opera characters, can compensate for lost personal relationships because television allows the older person to reduce isolation and to feel a part of a populated world.

Danowski (1975) argues that the primary relationship between mass media use and interpersonal communication is substitutive; mediated and personal communication are inversely related over the life-span, with greater use of the media at the young and old extremes.

Somewhat in contrast, Meyersohn (1961) forwards the notion that a crucial function of television is to provide universal conversation pieces. Exposure to TV content gives people of different generations a common basis for social interaction when few other shared experiences may exist.

Another idea proposed by Danowski is that older persons' seeking of news and reality content can be traced to the high degree of stability, predictability, and homegeneity in their personal environments. There is a lack of stimulation to maintain adaptive functioning, particularly with regard to engagement with the immediate time and space context.

Chaffee and Wilson (1975) argue that television becomes the dominant preference among the mass media as the elderly become very old, because it is a two-sense medium that can be understood by those having trouble hearing and seeing.

In the study by Danowski (1975), respondents were given a list of eight functions of television and asked to respond on seven-point Likert scales. Three items scored at or above the midpoint on the scale: watching for excitement, to avoid thinking too much, and because of boredom. In order, the remaining functions were to calm nerves, to take the mind off things, to gain knowledge, to relax, and to see new things.

Graney (1974) sought to test the hypothesis that mass media exposure serves as a substitute for participatory activities in his small sample of female public housing residents. Because the data showed small positive correlations between visiting friends outside the neighborhood and amount of exposure to television, radio, and reading, he concluded that the compensitory explanation was not tenable.

Graney and Graney (1974) conducted a follow up survey 4 years later with 46 of the original sample of 60 described above. In general, changes in viewing, listening, and reading were positively related to changes in attendance at meetings and telephone use; changes in organizational membership, church attendance, and social visits were not strongly or consistently related to media changes. Inverse relationships were not obtained, with the exception of mild negative correlations between radio listening changes and alterations in church attendance and visiting friends. Thus, the substitution of media behavior for more active forms of participation was not widespread in the sample studied.

In a later conceptualization, Graney (1975) proposed that there are three types of behavior exchange: complementary, supplementary, and substitution. He reported that losses in reading were replaced by the complement of television viewing, and that decreases in attendance at religous services and voluntary association meetings led to substitution of television and reading, respectively. Surprisingly, increased religious attendance substituted for declines in reading time. He argues that these types of findings support the activity exchange theory (because different behaviors replaced each other) and the disengagement theory (because each exchange was less effective in meeting the lost activity). In his view, television viewing is a "substitute of last resort" at the end of the chain for the elderly as they disengage from active life.

Danowski (1975) discovered that intra-community conversations were positively related to newspaper use, but that no other media use variables were substantially associated with interpersonal communication. He concluded that there is little evidence to support the proposition that mediated communications substitutes for interpersonal, and he observes that there is limited evidence showing that newspaper use facilitates interpersonal communication. This is consistent with the hypothesis of Atkin (1972) that people seek out mass media informational content for the purpose of subsequently discussing it with others.

Cassata (1967) studied 177 older people in New England to examine the interrelationship of interpersonal and mediated communication. The research showed that as degree of retirement and leisure time increased, respondents were more likely to use the mass media. Self-perceived decreases in interpersonal conversations and writing letters were related to increase in media usage.

Gregg (1971) sought to determine if television served as a para-social substitute for face-to-face interaction unavailable to older people. In a random sample of 277 persons aged 60 and older, he found that the degree of social isolation was related to preference for TV content classified as having attributes that would encourage para-social interaction with the medium.

RESEARCH QUESTIONS NEEDING ANSWERS

The literature review yields a narrow range of largely superficial research evidence on issues of mass media and aging, indicating that extensive work must be undertaken before scientists and practitioners adequately understand these problems. In this section, some of the most significant future research priorities are presented and explained. Each is stated in a question form, accompanied by a brief rationale describing the need to study the problem. The research questions are divided into theoretical and applied categories. Many of these questions were formulated in a 1975 workshop on mass media and aging sponsored by the College of Communication Arts at Michigan State University. Among the academic participants were Bradley Greenberg of Michigan State and James Danowski of the University of Southern California; professional members included Leonard Biegel of the National Council on Aging, Penny Sahara of the University of Michigan, and Elmer White of the Michigan Press Association.

Social Science Research Questions

Do Television Entertainment Programs Present Stereotyped Images and Role Portrayals of the Aged? Careful content analyses must be undertaken to accurately describe the quality and quantity of portrayals of older persons on television entertainment programs. Because of the wide viewership and potential impact of television programming, this form of mass media content is most important to study. Television advertising is another worthy subject of study, along with children's readers. Dimensions of analysis might include: absolute incidence of older characters, diversity of characters in terms of sex, occupational category, social status and economic productivity, competitiveness between older and younger characters, and the favorableness of the depictions.

How Are Older People Depicted in the News, and What is the Nature of News Coverage of Problems Among the Aged? Because aging people are frequently the subject of feature stories in the news media and the political and social issues of aging are increasingly significant news stories, systematic analysis of the news content of the mass media would be useful. This might examine how often older people are presented on television radio newscasts and in newspaper and magazine articles, and give qualitative dimensions of these presentations. The relative ranking of issues and problems of the aged among other news developments would provide evidence of the priority of this topic area on the news agenda; comparisons across time would be particularly valuable.

What Are the Basic Mass Media Usage Patterns of Older Audiences in the United States? Empirical information is needed to document the amount of exposure to television, radio, newspapers, and magazines among the aged under the changing conditions of the mid-1970s. Standard media rating services seldom provide detailed reports on this subgroup of the population, and a general survey with a representative sample is needed to provide benchmark data on their consumption patterns. This should be obtained within the context of a total leisure time allocation analysis, describing day-long behaviors involving the mass media and other activities. Analysis of content preferences among various types of mass media presentations would allow more insightful conclusions about media usage.

What Is the Social Context of Mass Media Consumption Among the Aged? Little is known about the interpersonal context of aged receivers of mass media messages, although some have suggested that much institutional television viewing occurs in groups and that much print media use involves sharing of newspapers and magazines. Patterns of sharing may facilitate greater access to the mass media, which is currently inhibited by economic factors. Furthermore, the social context of media use may significantly affect enjoyment, comprehension, and learning of the content presented.

What Is the Impact of Stereotyped Entertainment Content on Aged Audiences? When older audience members see stereotyped presentations of the aged in dramas or situation comedies, this might have implications for their changing self-image, their norms for appropriate social behavior, and their perceptions of reality. Social effects research is necessary to assess whether exposure to entertainment serves more than a transitory enjoyment function and actually influences cognitions, attitudes and behaviors. Furthermore, lack of media portrayal of the aged in entertainment programs (i.e., game shows, variety shows) may also have indirect effects on the thinking of older audiences. These effects should be considered relative to the contributions of other institutions.

How Do News, Information, and Advertising Content Affect Aged Audiences? Although much research has examined the effects of the mass media on social, political, and economic orientations, few studies have specifically tested the impact on older people. Researchers must learn more about the impact of news content on political participation, social consciousness, awareness of current developments, and interpersonal conversations. The impact of information campaigns on knowledge and coping behaviors and the effects of advertising on product consumption would also provide valuable data for understanding the implications of mass media messages for the aged.

How Do Mass Media Depictions of the Aged Influence the Perceptions, Attitudes, and Behaviors of Younger Audience Members? Portrayals of older people in the mass media may be an important input for many younger members of society in forming their orientations toward the aged.

The impact may be particularly great in cases in which younger people have little interpersonal contact with older people. The stereotypes in entertainment messages may shape perceptions of how older people think, feel, and behave, and may influence the development and change of attitudes toward the aged. The types of older people presented in commercials may also exert a significant influence. This information and affective learning may have implications for the way younger people act toward older people. Thus, the role of the mass media must be considered broadly to encompass the effects on younger audience members.

What Are the Implications for Mass Media Coverage Issues on Aging as News? As the problems of the aged attain more frequent treatment in the news media, social science researchers can examine the impact of these messages on both old and young audience members. For instance, the portrayal of the aged as beset with overwhelming problems might lead to sympathy, increase support for reforms, or reinforce stereotypes about the helplessness of older persons. Mere coverage of aged political leaders might serve to confer status and legitimization of these actors and their demands. Research is needed to discover what kinds of impact (or lack of impact) occur as the result of news treatment of topics such as nursing home crises, social security bankruptcy, or Grey Panther activities.

Applied Research Questions

What Are the Needs of the Aged for News, Information, and Advertising Messages? Before media practitioners can design messages appropriate for older audiences, the needs of this subgroup should be thoroughly probed to determine what kind of informational material is most relevant. In particular, they must identify which problems require guidance information (i.e., retirement, housing, health, crime), which consumer decisions require advertising inputs, and which forms of public affairs participation require news orientation (especially for local events and issues). Research must identify the needs, determine the extent to which they are satisfied, and suggest how the gap can be bridged.

What Are the Tastes of the Aged for Entertainment Content? More effective entertainment messages can be designed for older persons when creators and producers have a more precise knowledge of their interests and tastes. Research should explore the extent to which the aged desire escapist and enlightening materials for enjoyment, filling time, avoiding loneliness, stimulating their imaginations, and providing relaxation. Because of the large age gap between aged message receivers and younger message senders, systematic research data is most useful in supplying media personnel with an understanding of this distant subgroup of the audience.

How Do Older Audiences Evaluate Current Media Offerings? As a concrete step in examining how the mass media can satisfy the needs and tastes of the older age categories of society, reactions to current media content can be measured. While this approach is limited to the range of offerings currently available rather than to the potential scope of innovative media presentations, the research will indicate the extent of satisfaction at this point in mass media development. Evidence of dissatisfaction that is uncovered should provide insight into those areas in which the mass media must strengthen their services to the aged.

What Roles Should the National versus Local Mass Media Play in Delivering Information to the Aged? The relative merits of nationally and locally originated mass media information programs should be assessed by researchers to determine which functions each can serve most efficiently. Studies can indicate how the aged use current (and potential) information presented in generalized form by highly capable national columnists, producers, and writers, and how they make use of more localized sources that try to relate the material to the specific situations in various towns or states. In particular, the utility of a weekly newspaper column by the state aging agency should be explored.

What Are the Capabilitities of Print versus Broadcast Media in Reaching the Aged with Information? Research can demonstrate the optimum combination of the two basic types of mediated communication in informing older persons. Studies might examine whether substantive information can be transferred via television and radio, or whether the capabilities of these media are limited to making people aware of opportunities and more detailed information sources by presenting short public service messages. The scope and depth of material that can be disseminated via newspapers and magazines can be assessed, along with the role of these media in stimulating awareness and interest.

How Can Mass Media and Interpersonal Institutions be Combined to Facilitate Delivery of Information and Services? Rather than considering the mass media capabilities in isolation, the linkage between the impersonal media messages and interactive personal sources should be studied to evaluate the optimum overall system for informing and helping older persons. First, researchers should test the best procedures for follow-through by institutions after the media create awareness and interest, to determine how they can estimate the amount of response and serve the needs that have been activated. Second, the role of the media as a "referral service" to various agencies might be explored to determine how much the media should present and how much the agencies or consultants should provide.

What Are the Most Effective Substantive Information Campaign Strategies with Aged Audiences? Although there is considerable research indicating that entertaining and relevant informational presentations are most successful with children and typical adult audiences, there is little evidence concerning the basic strategies that might be appropriate for the aged. Specifically, data can show which forms of entertainment attract attention to informational messages, and which linkages to the aged receivers' needs allow for the greatest learning. Such research can indicate whether a "Sesame Street" approach would be more or less effective than a more sedate and serious format for presenting information to this subgroup of the population. New formats, such as live on-the-air telephone call-ins or town meetings in the studio, can be evaluated.

What Are the Technical Adjustments in Broadcast Media Presentations that Can Facilitate Impact on Aged Audiences? Experimental research can provide data on the changes in program pacing, sound levels, repetition, and redundancy that contribute to greater learning of the content by older people. Because of their more limited capacities for information processing, a variety of technical alterations in presentational style and format may be necessary to communicate effectively with the aged via the media. In particular, the optimum amount of time that a name, address, or telephone number is shown on the screen can be used in simple experiments. Scheduling of messages on radio and television might be adjusted to maximize reach, based on techniques of measuring audience flow patterns. Finally, research can be useful in determining how to facilitate older persons' tuning of UHF channels with special instructions, because they under-use these channels at present.

Which Print Media Techniques of Message Presentation Can Best Serve the Reading Needs of the Aged? The reading capabilities of the aged can be studied to assess how newspapers and magazines might make technical adjustments to increase exposure to and understanding of messages. Experiments could vary type size, layout, use of photos, and standardized location within an issue in an attempt to define the best techniques to meet the special needs of the aged.

What Are the Needs of Mass Media Professionals for Research Information about Characteristics of the Aged and Strategies for Communicating with the Aged? Exploratory research would be useful to determine the precise role that social scientists can play as resource persons for those working in the mass media who are producing messages about the aged or for aged audiences. In particular, procedures for reaching technical personnel such as engineers must be delineated if improvements are to be implemented. Studies of the behavior of media personnel can determine the decision points where research information is most useful, and the most intelligible formats for presenting research information so that they can readily use the knowledge gained by social researchers.

What Are the Optimum Methods of Involving Older People in Planning and Evaluating Mass Media Presentations? Pilot studies by researchers can provide evidence regarding the best procedures for using aged persons as advisory board members or part-time consultants to mass media institutions. Research can suggest methods for overcoming the coorientational problems arising in communication between the older advisor and the younger decision makers with dissimilar backgrounds, interests, attitudes, and knowledge. Techniques for setting up panels of older people might be explored, such as liaisons with retirement organizations. The utility of "brainstorming" conferences can also be assessed. Methods that organizations involved in aging issues can use to get publicity in the media can be tested and taught to these groups. Other researchers might determine the feasibility of measuring the preferences of the aged with special audience surveys or breakdowns of data about aged subgroups from conventional broadcast rating reports or newspaper readership surveys.

Which Measurement Procedures Are Most Useful for Gauging the Effectiveness of New Techniques for Communicating with the Aged via the Mass Media? Methodological studies can assess the success of various procedures for pretesting specific information campaigns, broadcast programs, or print media features before they are disseminated to wider audiences of older persons. Measures can be developed to post-test the actual impact of media presentations in relation to the goals of the writers or producers.

FUTURE TRENDS

During the next few decades, predictable changes in the nature of the mass communication system and of the elderly component of the population will have profound implications for issues relating to media and aging. In the United States, there will be a larger number of older people with higher levels of education and leisure time. Mediated communication will continue evolving beyond the mass audience popular stage of development into a more specialized phase where mini-media beam specific messages to small and homogeneous segments of the public, using modern technological hardware such as cable, cassette recorders, and home information terminals.

Havighurst (1975) predicts that there will be more leisure time for everybody in the next 25 years, including the elderly. He expects that increasing numbers will take "early retirement" at age 55, and those working beyond that age will reduce time on the job. The typical 65-year-old in the year 2000 will have 30 hours of free time each week. The elderly of the future will diversify their activities because the mean level of education will be greater with each new cohort. Because Havighurst predicts that there will be increase in voluntary service, working around the home, traveling, patronizing of the arts, and educational enrichment, the time devoted to the mass media might not be expanded.

Schramm (1968) feels that adequate service to older people is unlikely in the youth-oriented "mass" media dependent on advertising dollars targeted to the under 50 market; specialized media such as public television, neighborhood newspapers, and special-interest magazines may play a more important role in the future. Hess (1974) also argues that media oriented to mass advertisers will not program for and about the elderly. Her analysis indicates that old people are not attractive as consumers because of low income, uncertain futures, and unwillingness to invest in long-term products that might not be fully enjoyed. In addition, the elderly do not provide good material for news, entertainment, or persuasion, because they tend to remind the rest of the population of role loss and deprivation. Nevertheless, Schamm (1968) suggests that a major challenge to the news media in the near future is reporting the emergence of an elderly segment of the population that is non-working, non-wealthy, non-contributing, and socially disengaged.

Marshall and Wallerstein (1973) are not optimistic about the role of conventional television in serving the health needs of the elderly. They claim that programming devoted to older people focuses on senile, incapacitated nursing home residents and ignores the vast majority of the elderly who do not fit the stereotype of the incompetent, pathetic, and debilitated older person. Furthermore, they observed that only 7 percent of commercial television time is devoted to health-related matters, and that three fourths of this information is misleading or inaccurate. They suggest that cable television is the most advantageous medium for delivering a specific message for the small specific audience of elderly that has the greatest health needs. They specify three dimensions of these health needs: clinical services, information and education, and ego support. Cable TV can provide for many aspects of these needs, especially when two-way interactive cable becomes more widely available. However, they are cautious about the cost-effectiveness problem in dealing with the elderly through this medium.

Schramm (1968) observes that an important priority is for the media to determine how their services can be physically adjusted to facilitate use by the aging audience. Among the suggestions are print media editions in large type for those with failing eyesight, headphones for electronic media to compensate for deafness, and talking books for the aged who have difficulty reading.

SUMMARY

Elderly people in our society spend from 3 to 6 hours daily with the media of mass communication, allocating more time to this activity than anything except sleep. The aged are very dependent on television for entertainment, and they are particularly devoted to news and information content in several media; generally, they approve of the offerings that are consumed. Mass media exposure serves a variety of important functions for older persons, providing a needed link to the outside world and occasionally substituting for direct experiences and social interaction.

Little is known about the effects of the mass media on the aged, nor is there sufficient evidence concerning the impact of portrayals of elderly characters on the rest of the population. Social scientists must investigate the various effects of the media on the attitudes and behaviors of the audience. Applied researchers should endeavor to increase available knowledge about the techniques for delivering information to the aged through optimum combinations and communication channels. Future technological developments such as interactive cable show promise for more effective service to the increasing number of elderly persons in the United States.

RECOMMENDATIONS

The available research evidence provides satisfactory answers to few of these research questions raised in the preceding section. In general, fairly adequate information exists regarding issues such as the images of the aged in entertainment content, the media usage patterns of older people, and the reasons why the elderly use the entertainment media. Other areas are barren of directly relevant research, although general mass communication theory can be useful in answering many questions.

Recommendations for subsequent social science research efforts focus on generating knowledge about two important problems that are not well understood by scholars: the effects of stereotyped entertainment content, particularly television programming, on both the elderly audience and the younger segments of the audience, and the impact of news coverage of aging issues on the knowledge, attitudes, and behaviors of young and old alike.

Older people may be particularly susceptible to mass media influence, because they have less extensive social communication. According to Hess (1974), elderly audience members have fewer opportunities to test the validity of media messages in informal conversation. Very little effects research has been conducted, however. For instance, in the Bower (1973) national survey, people were asked to introspectively report on the importance of television's role in helping them decide who they wanted to win the election. Among those aged 50 and older, 10 percent said TV played a very important part in their decision, 24 percent said it played a fairly important part, and the remainder said it played no part at all. Correlational studies would be particularly valuable in assessing this type of mass media effect.

In the realm of applied research, researchers should emphasize the development of multi-channel strategies for delivering information and services to the aged by combining national and local, print and broadcast, and mediated and personal forms of communication. A secondary effort might be initiated to explore technical methods of improving message transmission to the aged, especially those with restricted decoding capabilities.

Certainly many other topics deserve close examination by theoretical and applied researchers, but these appear to be of greatest priority at present. Future technologies that become practical in the next few years will also require research investigation to determine the means of facilitating acceptance, the ways that they are used by the elderly, and the consequences of exposure to their knowledge, attitudes, and behavior.

LITERATURE CITED

ANPA News Research Bulletin. 1973. News and Editorial Content and Readership of the Daily Newspaper. April 26. American Newspaper Publishers Association, Washington, D.C.

Aronoff, C. 1974. Old age in prime time. J. Commun. 24: 86–87.

Atkin, C. 1972. Anticipated communication and mass media information-seeking. Public Opin. Quart. 36: 188–199.

Beyer, G., and M. Woods. 1963. Living and activity patterns of the aged. Research Report No. 6. Center for Housing and Environmental Studies, Cornell University, Ithaca, N.Y.

Bower, R. 1973. Television and the Public. Holt, Rinehart, and Winston, New York.

Cassata, M. 1967. A study of the mass communications behavior and the social disengagement behavior of 177 members of the Age Center of New England. Unpublished doctoral dissertation, Indiana University.

Chaffee, S., and D. Wilson. 1975. Adult life cycle changes in mass media use. Presented at Association for Education in Journalism convention, Ottawa, Canada.

Cowgill, D., and N. Baulch. 1962. The use of leisure time by older people. The Gerontologist 2: 47–50.

Danowski, J. 1975. Informational aging: Interpersonal and mass communication patterns in a retirement community. Presented at Gerontological Society convention, Louisville, Kentucky.

Davis, R. 1971. Television and the older adult. J. Broadcasting 15: 153–159.

Francher, J. 1973. It's the Pepsi generation . . . : Accelerated aging and the television commercial. Intern. J. Aging Human Devel. 4: 245–255.

Graney, M. 1974. Media use as a substitute activity in old age. J. Gerontol. 29: 322–324.

Graney, M. 1975. Communication uses and the social activity constant. Commun. Res. 2: 347–366.

Graney, M., and E. Graney. 1974. Communications activity substitutions in aging. J. Commun. 24: 88–96.

Gregg, P. 1971. Television viewing as parasocial interaction for persons aged 60 years or older. Masters thesis, University of Oregon.

Handel, L. 1950. Hollywood Looks at Its Audience. University of Illinois Press, Urbana, Ill.

Havighurst, R. 1975. The future aged: The use of time and money. The Gerontologist 15: 10–15.

Hess, B. 1974. Stereotypes of the aged. J. Commun. 24: 76–85.

Lazarsfeld, P., and P. Kendall. 1948. Radio Listening in America: The People Look at Radio Again. Prentice-Hall, Englewood Cliffs, N.J.

Market Opinion Research. 1975. Survey of the aging in Michigan. Report No. 4812. Market Opinion Research Corporation, Detroit.

Marshall, C., and E. Wallerstein. 1973. Beyond Marcus Welby: Cable TV for the health of the elderly. Geriatrics 28: 82–86.

Meyersohn, R. 1961. A critical examination of commerical entertainment. *In* R. W. Kleemeier (ed.), Aging and Leisure. Oxford University Press, New York.

Parker, E. B., and W. G. Paisley. 1966. Patterns of adult information seeking. Institute for Communications Research, Stanford University, Stanford, Calif.

Petersen, M. 1973. The visibility and image of old people on television. Journalism Quart. 50: 569–573.

Schalinske, T. 1968. The role of television in the life of the aged person. Unpublished doctoral dissertation, Ohio State University.

Schramm, W. 1968. Aging and mass communication. *In* M. Riley, J. Riley, and M. Johnson (eds.), Aging and Society. Vol. 2: Aging and the Professions. Russel Sage Foundation, New York.

Schramm, W., and D. White. 1949. Age, education, and economic status: Factors in newspaper reading. Journalism Quart. 26: 150–158.

Steiner, G. 1963. The People Look at Television. Alfred A. Knopf, New York.

Whan, F. 1957. The 1957 Iowa Radio-Television Audience Survey. Central Broadcasting Company, Des Moines.

chapter 7
Communication and the Aging Consumer

Charles R. Mauldin, Ph.D.

The impact of increasing knowledge and developing technology appears to result consistently in social and economic conditions that have special implications for the aged. The state takes increasingly direct responsibility for the economic security of the dependent aged; the family takes increasingly less direct responsibility. Growing numbers and population proportions of the aged and increased mobility of residence have been linked to lower and more ambiguous status for the aged. Characteristics of modernization have been shown to vary with the aging phenomenon described as "disengagement" or "withdrawal," a phenomenon not characteristic of agrarian or primitive societies (Cowgill and Holmes, 1972).

The complex economic and administrative structures of modern societies mean that responding to the needs of the aging will be complex, involving the necessity for monitoring needs at aggregate and individual levels and the operation of complex systems to respond to those needs. The complexity of such response systems places an important burden on the effectiveness of communication within systems in meeting consuming and health needs of the aging.

Much effort has been invested in determining basic consuming needs of the aging population. The crucial influences of income and health and transportation have been recognized and translated into massive efforts to provide income and services to the aging population, particularly as basic needs of food, health, and housing are concerned.

Collateral research efforts have been mounted to measure the success of and constraints on the success of governmental efforts, dealing, for example, with some of the constraints that the complex response system itself places on the achievement of its objectives (Administration on Aging Fact Sheet, 1974).

Such research must determine how persons are to communicate their needs to appropriate system inputs. Crucial variables include the person's ability to recognize need symptoms and to translate them into behaviors that access the system: knowledge of "appropriate" channels, constraints on accessing channels, compatibility of individual and system language, and criteria for describing and dealing with needs.

Such research must deal with how the response system is effectively and efficiently to decide what response mixes—money, products, services, counsel, information—are appropriate to what needs or need-mixes.

Such research must deal with the conditions under which the needs of persons can be accurately and efficiently transmitted through the response system and translated into appropriate responses.

Because in operation, complex response systems are expected to respond to individual needs, it is important to have an adequate understanding of the impact of aging effects on individual consuming processes. Data based on such understanding, aggregated, would also provide important parameters for allocating resources and measuring system effectiveness. Ultimately, the effectiveness of response systems may be constrained by the understanding of the impact of specific consequences of aging, in interaction, on consuming needs, consuming resources, and consuming processes. This chapter examines research related to this problem, and particularly to the communication aspects of the problem.

RESEARCH QUESTIONS NEEDING ANSWERS

There appears much of importance yet to be learned about the interaction of aging and consuming. The consequences of aging are numerous and interactive in their influence on consuming, a condition that could be expected to hinder development of a concrete understanding of these influences. Many studies, which have used age to operationalize aging, add little to understanding because the effects of aging vary greatly across individual persons, and consuming needs have not been linked to specific aging effects.

The influences of aging on consuming can be observed on three levels: in the impact on consuming needs for products and services; on consuming resources, such as income and consuming skills, and on the process of consuming itself. A single consequence of aging, such as loss of physical capacity, may have an impact at each level, for example on need for a changed diet, on the ability to earn financial resources, and on the effort required to solve consuming needs. Neither the literature on aging nor the consuming behavior literature reveals direct evidence of the interactive effects of the consequences of aging on consuming. But each reveals variables of apparent importance in research to establish such relationships.

Aging is defined as a slow and continuous process that results in the cessation of growth and in physical decline, with a decreasing bodily ability to regenerate and renew. The aging process is accompanied by modification in sensory processes, strategies of adjustment, problem-solving capacities, perceptions, emotional states, and memory. There is no consensus of agreement on these effects. Kriauciunas (1968), for example, found no age differences for memory span, learning and memory, memory storage, or trace decay. He found that memory shows decline with age only for subject matter presented with competing stimuli, which he held might appropriately be attributed to diminished motivation, speed of performance, and energy.

Physical aging is accompanied by less energy in reserve, slower recovery of energy, and medical histories showing declines in physical functions (Schramm, 1969). Aging is associated with changes in life circumstances: a long period in which a couple lives alone after the last child is married and a long period after one partner dies in which the surviving partner lives alone or with grown children or in an institution (Wolfbein, 1963). The latter circumstances are more often the result of disability than of death of a spouse or retirement, and many of those changing living arrangements report at least one major associated problem, most commonly problems of caring for the disabled person (Newman, 1975).

Many of the problems of aging are economic. Kutner (1956) documented increasing fear of financial problems as retirement approaches. Social security, retirement plans, and medical plans are offset by inflation and generally rising incomes. The U.S. Department of Commerce (1975) reported that among persons more than 65 years of age, one in six lives in poverty, compared to one in ten less than 65.

Certain consequences of aging are important variables because they are likely to have direct impact on consuming needs. Digestive and metabolic changes may result in needs for changed diets. Changes in sensory processes, such as eyesight and hearing, may result in requirements for eyeglasses and hearing aids. Physical disabilities may result in needs for medical services, medical products, and in some cases for institutionalization. The death of a spouse may result in income reduction and will require funeral services.

Certain consequences of aging are important variables because they influence the capacity to consume as well as consuming needs. Income is perhaps the most important variable influencing consuming capacity. Not only do persons with low income have less money to buy products and services, but there is evidence that the poor pay higher prices for food, furniture and appliances, and credit (Berry, 1972). Immobility and the necessity of purchasing on credit often limit the poor to shopping at inefficient, uneconomical, and sometimes abusive stores in low income neighborhoods.

The impact of diminished capacity could be expected to have an important impact on consuming processes, because those processes require numerous physical steps and the physical steps require effort, or because any single step requires large energy expenditures. Reduced physical capacity could be expected to have most impact on shopping behaviors.

If Kriauciunas is correct in concluding that diminished energy, with diminished motivation, is responsible for differences in cognitive processing among the aging, it might be expected that reduced physical capacity would have increasing influence on consuming processes as learning costs grow: when the consuming problem is new, when the alternatives are numerous, when the solution requires numerous problem-solving steps. This variable might be particularly important if solving a consuming problem requires developing a new consuming skill, for example, if learning about nutrition were required to cope with changing dietary needs.

Changes in the family living situation could be expected to alter consuming capacity as well as consuming needs. The death of a spouse may result in income reduction and also leaves the surviving partner with additional consuming tasks and new consuming skills to learn. When an aging person begins living with grown children or enters an institution, the effects on consuming needs and consuming capacity are great.

These, then, represent important variables in assessing the influence of aging on communication aspects of consuming processes. The variables are understood to influence consuming processes both directly and indirectly by influencing consuming needs and consuming resources.

This chapter proposes a decision process model to examine influences of aging on communication behaviors associated with the consuming process. There have been numerous decision process models: for general decision processes (Gagne, 1959; Brim et al., 1962), heirarchical psychological effects (Colley, 1961), general consuming processes (Howard and Sheth, 1967), and the like. Among these categories, the model to be presented belongs to the latter class and to a subclass identified by Hansen (1972) as "problem-solving" models, so named because of the emphasis on evaluation of alternatives rather than on information processing. Unlike other general consuming models and like psychological effects models, the present model deals principally with communication behavior. Unlike the heirarchical psychological models, the communication behaviors may involve interpersonal and mass communication as well as intrapersonal communication, and no specific heirarchy or sequence of behaviors is assumed.

In the model, four communication functions are discussed. They are described below.

Recognizing Need Sets

All consuming behavior sequences are assumed to begin with the recognition of some consuming need or need set. Hansen (1972) theorized that environmental stimuli, cognitive stimuli, and primary (physiological) motives combine to stimulate the reticular arousal system, which, in turn, triggers salient response alternatives in the cortex. Hansen describes the process as a sequence of choices among alternative behavior options, including the alternative not to continue the sequence.

Some consuming needs, for example, the bodily need for protein, are never directly experienced by consumers. They learn such needs from external sources and deal with them without directly experiencing the solution to the need, other than perhaps some general feeling of well-being that may or may not be the result of the satisfaction of the need. Such consideration raises an interesting question: Do modifications in sensory processes among the aged influence the recognition of consuming needs?

There is evidence that family consuming processes are specialized (Kenkel, 1961) and become increasingly specialized over time (Granbois, 1962). Experience suggests that even need recognition is subject to specialization, that for certain consuming needs, one family member routinely bears responsibility for noticing when certain products are needed. Such responsibility is probably fixed over time in interpersonal communication processes. The death of a spouse may influence this communication routine, and the survivor is faced with the problem of learning to routinely recognize the needs that the spouse had been responsible for. Conversely, an aging person who moves in with grown children or into an institution is deprived of a role that may be minor, but that deprivation, with others, may contribute to the phenomenon called "disengagement."

In each of the following consuming behaviors, there is the likelihood that the behaviors, associated with specific need sets, are matters of specialized responsibility for aging consumers with similar consequences, for example, in the death of a spouse or in moving in with grown children.

Deciding what Needs to Satisfy

Communication behavior associated with consuming includes deciding among satisfying alternative needs, especially under conditions of economic stress. Granbois (1962) found that joint decision-making declines over the life cycle. This may not apply to all the communication behaviors in consuming, but logic suggests that this communication decision is more frequently a matter of interpersonal negotiation under conditions of economic stress.

What are the rules used by aging consumers to decide among alternatives? The available literature reveals no answers. This communication behavior may be of special importance in understanding apparent consuming "failure," such as the fact that the elderly are often taken in by health fraud instead of seeking competent medical help (Wolgamot, 1967).

Developing and Using Criteria
for Translating Needs into Products and Services

This communication behavior involves learning to associate need satisfaction with characteristics of products and services. Experience with products and services, interpersonal communication, and mass media would appear to influence such criteria. Presumably, persons consult external information sources more often when criteria must be formed, and consumer researchers have, in general, assumed a powerful role for interpersonal influence (Katona and Mueller, 1954; Summers and King, 1969). However, such generalizations may be less true of the aging than of other groups. Several studies have found that more experienced consumers rely more on past experience and less on external information sources (Cox, 1967; Feldman, Sidney, and Spencer, 1966). The consumer is assumed to use such criteria in evaluating and selecting among alternative products and services.

At some point in a completed consuming process, the consumer translates an intention to satisfy a need into a decision to purchase. By that time the consumer has developed or applied criteria for judging costs. Most decision processing models assume that costs are weighed against the need satisfying potential of the product or service. In a survey of marketing literature, Schiffman (1971) found no indication of any systematic effort to explain either the consumer motivation or the buying behavior of the aging. The literature research for this chapter examined consumer behavior sources, marketing sources, and major gerontological journals with the same result.

Other experiences with products and services, for example in preparing and using them, is assumed to add to consuming criteria and to contribute to evaluating specific product or service alternatives.

Learning to Find and Acquire Products and Services

Consuming sequences involve some communication behaviors directed toward finding and acquiring products and services. When the consuming sequence involves finding new alternatives or changed conditions of sale (sale prices), external sources of information such as mass media, interpersonal sources, and shopping become increasingly important. For repetitive purchases and stable conditions of sale, or in circumstances in which consumers cannot seek alternatives (as is often the case with the urban poor), one would expect less information seeking from external sources.

FUTURE TRENDS

A review of research on aging reveals not just a growing knowledge base but a developing social commitment and a massive and complex effort to execute that commitment. Much of the literature represents the process of examining the effects of aging and discovering that many of the effects are problems: physical problems such as ill health and loss of energy, psychological problems such as "disengagement," social problems such as loss of work roles in retirement, and economic problems such as reduction in income.

Other research reflects the process of discovering the monitoring the extent of such problems among the aging. The contributions of economic research have been notable in providing information on income distribution and manpower, purchase patterns, and use of time and money. Economists and home economists have provided information about housing, food and nutrition, health, clothing, and transportation.

Among the research traditions that have dealt with consumer behavior, the business economists (especially marketing) have dealt least with consuming problems associated with aging. Shiffman (1971) commented on the paucity of marketing research dealing with buyer behavior and consumer motivation of the aging, a paucity that still continues. A review of the literature revealed no cases in which the decision process models and cognitive processing models developed in the last two decades have been applied to consuming problems associated with aging.

The consumer behavior literature and the gerontological literature have few studies dealing with the interaction of aging effects on consumer needs or on consumer behavior, with several notable exceptions (Palmore, 1971; Sherman and Brittan, 1973). Such problem-defining research appears especially important to understanding the influence of aging on consuming.

Much research has been generated by the development and evaluation of public programs for the aging and reflects information needs in the administration and coordination of programs: needs assessments, studies of organizational problems, evaluation studies, and research to discover means for extending resources.

SUMMARY AND RECOMMENDATIONS

Understanding the impact of aging on consuming needs and consuming resources and the impact of these on consuming processes is important in developing public and business systems to meet the consuming needs of the aging. There are important questions to be answered about the impact of various consequences of aging, singly and interactively, on consuming. Income, immobility, diminished physical capacity, and changes in living environment appear to have most potential for constraining consuming processes.

Consuming tends to become increasingly specialized over time, with increasing dependence on past experience and decreasing dependence on other sources. This generalization may not hold true when consumers must meet new needs or when important conditions of sale change frequently. Loss of consuming roles or changes in consuming roles may contribute to "disengagement."

There are questions to be answered about consuming processes. Do modifications in sensory processes influence need recognition? What influence do important constraints such as financial stress have on criteria for determining what needs to satisfy? What role do external sources play in need assessment, in decisions to satisfy needs, and in the development and use of criteria for evaluating alternatives?

Two concluding observations seem warranted. Because the effects of aging differ among the aging and because these variables appear to have major roles in consuming processes, it is important to consider them in designing research. They have often been ignored.

Consuming behavior sequences are both complex and dynamic. The last decade has seen important progress in developing theoretical models for dealing with both problems. Several cognitive processing models appear to offer promise (see, for example, Hansen, 1972) for improving understanding of consuming behavior, and the application of these to consuming processes of the aging appear valuable to improving the understanding of those processes.

LITERATURE CITED

Administration on Aging. 1974. Fact Sheet. Research and Development in Aging. Current Projects Funded. No. 4. Washington, D.C.

Berry, L. L. 1972. The low income marketing system: An overview. J. Retail. 48: 44–61.

Brim, O. G., D. G. Glass, D. E. Lavin, and N. Goodman. 1962. Personality and Decision Processes. Stanford University Press, Stanford, Calif.

Colley, R. H. 1961. Defining advertising goals for measured advertising results. Assn. of National Advertisers, New York.

Cowgill, D. O., and L. D. Holmes. 1972. Aging and Modernization. Appleton-Century-Crofts, New York.

Cox, D. F. 1967. The influence of cognitive needs and styles on information handling in making product evaluations. In D. F. Cox (ed.), Risk Taking and Information Handling in Consumer Behavior. Harvard University, Boston.

Feldman, S. P., and M. C. Spencer. 1965. The effect of personal influence in the selection of consumer services. In P. O. Bennet (ed.), Marketing and Economic Development. Proceedings of the Fall Conference of the American Marketing Assn., Chicago.

Gagne, R. M. 1959. Problem solving and thinking. Annual Review of Psychology.

Granbois, D. H. 1962. A study of the family decision making process in the purchase of major household goods. Unpublished doctoral dissertation, Indiana University, Bloomington.

Hansen, Flemming. 1972. Consumer Choice Behavior: A Cognitive Theory, pp. 145–146. The Free Press, New York.

Howard, J. A., and J. N. Sheth. 1967. Theory of buyer behavior. In R. Moyer (ed.), Changing Marketing Systems, pp. 253–269. American Marketing Association, Chicago.

Katona, G., and E. Mueller. 1954. A study of purchase decision. In L. H. Clark (ed.), Consumer Behavior, Vol. 1. New York University Press, New York.

Kenkel, W. F. 1961. Decision-making and the life cycle: Husband-wife interaction in decision-making and decision choices. J. Soc. Psych. 54: 255–262.

Kriauciunas, R. 1968. Short-term memory and age. J. Amer. Geriat. Soc. 16: 83–93.

Kutner, B. 1956. Five Hundred over Sixty: A Community Survey on Aging. Russell Sage Foundation, New York.

Newman, S. 1975. Housing adjustments of older people: A report from the first phase. Institute for Social Research, Ann Arbor, Mich.

Palmore, E. P. 1971. Variables related to needs among the aged poor. J. Gerontol. 26: 524–531.

Schiffman, L. G. 1971. Sources of information for the elderly. J. Advert. Res. October: 33–37.

Schramm, W. 1969. Aging and mass communication. In M. Riley, M. J.

Riley, and M. Johnson (eds.), Aging and Society, Vol. Two: Aging and the Professions, pp. 352–375. Russell Sage Foundation, New York.

Sherman, E. M., and M. R. Brittan. 1973. Contemporary food gatherers: A study of food shopping habits of an elderly urban population. The Gerontologist 13: 358–364.

Summers, J. O., and C. W. King. 1969. Interpersonal communication and new product attitude. Presented at the Fall Conference of the American Marketing Association, Cincinnati.

U.S. Department of Commerce. 1975. Reported in U.S. News and World Report. Feb. 10, 1975.

Wolfbein, S. L. 1963. Changing patterns of working life. Month. Labor Rev. 88: 820–823.

Wolgamot, E. H. 1967. Conference on consumer problems of the aging. J. Home Econ. 59: 677–678.

chapter 8

Communication Considerations in the Health Care of the Aging

Carole O. Bettinghaus, M.A.
Erwin P. Bettinghaus, Ph.D.

Most Americans take communication for granted. The average American spends from 6 to 8 hours a day in direct communication with others, or engages in indirect communication activities through the use of mass media. We can flick the switch of our television set and be instantly connected with London, Rome, or Tokyo. We can pick up a telephone and "dial direct" to millions of people across the United States.

Many take advantage of the ability to communicate or to receive communication with little thought of the way in which communication governs our lives. Communication is used so casually that few are aware that the great advances in communications technology are the product of this century, with their greatest development taking place since the end of World War II.

The revolution in communication that characterizes our society today has forced changes in the way in which health care is delivered. For all of recorded history until the twentieth century, health care depended on interpersonal communication between a physician and a patient. One hundred years ago, a person who was sick had to locate a physician and then discover some way of either getting the physician to visit him or find a way of getting to where the physician was. There were no telephone books to assist in the search for a physician. There were no automobiles or telephones to assist the physician and the patient in communicating with each other.

The changes that improved transportation and improved communication in the field of general health care are well known. There are, however, special considerations that must be made when looking at the communication revolution and the specific effect it has had on the health care of the aging.

This chapter recognizes the fact that everyone is "aging" and that aging begins with birth. Following the definitions presented in the first chapter, however, we shall concentrate our attention on persons in the population who are 65 years of age or older. We shall use the term "health care" in its broadest sense, i.e., to refer to the entire network of individuals and institutions responsible for the prevention and alleviation of illness and maintenance of normal health and functioning within our society. Included in our analysis will be communication considerations relevant to health care which stem from 1) physiological changes in the aging person, 2) environmental changes for the aging person, and 3) social-psychological problems for the aging person in need of health care.

PHYSIOLOGICAL CHANGES AND COMMUNICATION IN THE AGING

Other chapters in this volume will deal with the *nature* of physiological changes that may occur to the aging person. This section will be concerned with the *effects* that such changes might have on the aging person's ability to communicate and to be communicated with.

Hearing Changes

There are many diseases that can cause a significant loss of hearing. Because of the lack of antibiotics in earlier periods, the present aged population may exhibit hearing loss at a greater rate than populations growing up since the advent of antibiotics. Bloom et al. (1971) mention otosclerosis, stroke, Meniere's disease, mastoiditis, otitis media, and nerve damage from trauma or drugs, as some of the conditions or diseases that can cause significant hearing loss in the aging person. Most of these conditions are not correctable or are correctable only with great difficulty, and these provide serious health care problems for the individual and the health care provider.

The modern health care facility, either acute care facility or long-term care facility, normally employs a complex staff of professional and para-professional health care providers. The facility is normally organized in a way that requires a number of different persons to communicate with each patient. The physician, the nurse, the dietician, the X-ray technician, the orderly, and the laboratory technician may all need to communicate with any given patient. In a large facility, not only one physician but many different physicians may need to communicate with the patient.

When that patient is aged and has a hearing impairment, a strain may well be placed on the relationship between the health care professional and the patient. The patient who has developed a long-term relationship with a personal physician benefits from the physician's knowledge of and adjustment to the disability. The physician, in such a situation, makes an accommodation in ways that are understandable and acceptable to the patient. That same patient, when placed in a complex health care facility, will lose that benefit. Some of the health care personnel on the hospital ward may not realize the patient has a hearing disability. Other staff who realize the impairment may not accommodate for it in a manner that is comfortable for the patient, and the patient-provider relationship will deteriorate.

The health care professional in a long-term care facility may find that the task of communicating with the aged, hearing-impaired person can be made easier because there is opportunity to adjust to the patient over time. When there is time to find out whether the patient has general loss of hearing over a wide range, or whether the loss is in a specific range, the health care professional can adjust. In the acute care facility, the patient is normally not in the facility for sufficient time to enable adequate adjustments to be made.

Further complicating the communication problems that may arise with the hearing-impaired person are attitudes commonly held toward the very old. It is all too common to have staff members of the health care facility treat aged patients as if they were senile. Bloom et al. (1971) suggest that the hearing-impaired person may seem to be inattentive, display a strained facial expression, or even answer questions inappropriately. Those symptoms, of course, are ones commonly associated with senility. Because of such symptoms, it is all too common for health care providers to treat patients as though they were senile. Treating a person with a hearing impairment as if he or she were senile can make it very difficult to maintain an effective relationship between the health care professional and the aging patient.

It is difficult for the person with normal hearing to realize how much of what we know about the world comes from hearing. We are constantly being bombarded with sounds, and especially with speech sounds. Most of our institutions have been designed in such a way that the majority of information transmission within the institution is dependent on hearing. The health care system is no different. In fact, the typical hospital depends *more* on passage of information through the aural mode than many other institutions. The patient is *told* about medication, is *told* when to awaken, when to eat, how to bathe, and many other commonplaces. For the average patient, the system works well. For the hearing-impaired patient, the system may not work well. Yet few health care facilities have made formal provisions for alternative ways of passing along information to the patient who is unable to receive and process aural messages. In fact, there seem to be no studies of alternative ways of communication with the aging, hearing-impaired person within a health care facility. (We except the work of the audiology unit that attempts therapy for the patient.)

A final consideration in looking at hearing changes in the aged relates to the use of the electronic media. Use of television and radio to gain information is widespread. The aging person makes use of those media to find out what is going on within his community or to obtain information about product use through advertisements and public service announcements. The person with a hearing impairment is effectively cut off from one of the major sources of information within the society. The problem is far worse for the person whose hearing impairment has come late in life than for the person who has been deaf from a very early age. For the latter, programs exist to teach sign language within a school setting and on an intensive basis. No such programs exist generally for the aging person whose hearing impairment occurred late in life.

If a person has been able to learn sign language or has learned to lip read, television can become a useful information source. Most large communities and many smaller communities present at least one news broadcast a day solely for the deaf person, or at least a broadcast with a simultaneous split screen presentation of a sign language "translation" of the spoken message.

Given sign language, the hearing-impaired person is not completely shut off from the electronic media. For the aging person, however, the problem is normally very serious. Used to receiving steady, important information from the television set and the radio, then suddenly unable to hear clearly, the aging person may reflect the loss through deterioration of health.

Vision Changes

Changes in hearing can produce serious communication problems for the health care of the aging person. Equally serious are the communication problems produced by changes in vision. While many persons experience gradual changes in visual acuity throughout their lifetime, these changes can normally be handled by changes in the lens prescription. In such circumstances, communication problems exist mainly for the person who is unable to afford new glasses or who fails to recognize that some change is needed in the lens.

More serious effects are caused by those diseases responsible for serious loss of vision. Diseases responsible for producing most late developing visual problems in the aging person are glaucoma, cataracts, and hemianopia. While treatment exists for each of these diseases, the treatment course is lengthy, and complete restoration is not always possible.

Rather than concentrate on treatment aspects of the visually-impaired aging person, we shall focus our attention on communication effects related to the health care of the visually-impaired aging person. One of the more serious problems is the difficulty that the health care professional may encounter in even simple communication with the aging person who has suddenly developed visual problems. Such persons may be distrusting, worried about newly experienced awkwardness, fearful of any person who cannot be seen, and concentrating more attention on visual health than on any other health care problem. Under conditions of such personal stress, it is extremely difficult for the patient to concentrate on messages that may be sent by the health care professional.

One can speculate that the more complete the vision loss is for a person, the more difficult communication is likely to be. In similar fashion, although there are apparently no studies available, it seems reasonable to conclude that communication will be more difficult with the person who has very recently undergone a serious change in vision in contrast to the person who comes under the care of a professional only after a period of time has elapsed since the onset of visual impairment.

Although many of the difficulties in communicating with the visually-impaired person seem obvious, we suspect that many of the most standard practices of the health care professional fail to take account of the aging person who may be visually impaired. For example, the hospital attendant may leave the "call" switch in a position that is easily found only by a fully sighted person. Similarly, the busy pharmacist may hand over a prescription to the elderly patient, assuming that the directions can be read. If the patient's eyesight has suddenly deteriorated and the patient has no one available to read the directions, there is a communication problem. The cited examples are relatively simple, but it is easy to construct more complex, and more serious communication problems that could occur between the health care professional and the aging person who is visually handicapped.

A second problem resulting from visual impairment in the aging person is the dependence that most people place on their eyes as a primary means of gaining information about their environment. We read the newspapers to find out what to buy. We read the labels on the cans to find out what to eat. We use our eyes to move easily around the home and to make trips away from home. Most news comes to us through the medium of television, and although we could listen to the radio, habit leads us to local and national television news at specified periods of the day. The aging person with lessened mobility is likely to spend much time with television. If there is some serious impairment of vision of recent onset, the aging person will have serious problems in obtaining necessary information about the environment. While any of these could be related to the health of the person, some specific problems have very serious consequences for the health care of the aging person.

We depend heavily on sight for shaving and other personal grooming, taking medicine, finding food products on the shelf, reading directions, driving, eating, and many other activities. The aging person whose loss of vision is recent may "make mistakes" in any of these activities that can lead to injury or death. The person who is blind from birth has had many years to learn to cope with the problems of obtaining information from the environment. The person whose vision impairment is newly acquired may find it extremely difficult to cope with even simple activities requiring sight.

One final communication situation needs to be examined. In today's society, much of what a person knows about health care comes through the daily newspaper, the weekly news magazine, specialized books, direct mail advertising, and other written public service sources. Correct or incorrect, those sources supply information to many Americans. When the aging person loses the ability to read, the effect is that of shutting off an information tap. Such a person is very likely to resort to obtaining information from friends and neighbors—not extremely competent sources in most cases.

Physical Mobility Changes

Changes in the ability of people to move about physically may occur to anyone, at any age. An automobile accident or a home or job related accident can cause anyone to lose physical mobility. The aging person, however, has the risks attendant with accidents compounded by brittle bones and a number of diseases and other health conditions that do not normally afflict younger persons. Thus, arthritis, stroke, multiple sclerosis, cardiac damage, and Parkinsonianism are only a few of the conditions that may lead to severe limitations in physical mobility on the part of the aging person.

There are a number of communication problems that exist because of physical mobility problems. One of the more serious is the difficulty a person might have in communicating directly with the health care professional. Arthritis may so affect the hands or arms that the person finds it impossible to use the phone. All communication with a health care professional may have to pass through a third party, i.e., wife, husband, or child, or the patient may have to find some way of being transported to a facility where direct communication with the health care provider is possible.

In similar fashion, physical mobility problems may make it difficult for the aging person to follow instructions or suggestions given in a message sent by a health care provider. Told to follow a diet, the aging person who cannot get to a grocery store may find that third parties do not follow instructions and do not obtain products that are required.

Finally, a sudden loss of physical mobility in the aging person may also result in severe emotional stress. The emotional stress may, in turn, result in strained relations with other people in the home or the health care facility, and once again damage communication between the parties. Communication attempts by the physically handicapped may show defensiveness, fear, or irritability. If a receiver does not understand the cause for such reactions and accomodate to them, communication may be permanently damaged.

In this section, we have looked briefly at communication problems that may be associated with hearing changes, vision changes, and changes in the physical mobility of the aging person. In examining the literature in this area, we found several excellent studies (cf. Bloom et al., 1971; Travis, 1966) that detailed the nature of these changes as they might occur in the aging person. Nowhere did we find studies that attempted to assess what health care providers ought to do when faced with patients exhibiting such phenomena. It may well be the case that some hospitals have developed effective training programs to improve communication skills for those who have to treat the aging person who has suffered recent hearing, vision, or mobility changes. We could not locate reports of such attempts nor any surveys of health care facility practices in this important area. While there are a number of texts relating to communication in nurse-patient relationships (cf. Hein, 1973; Travelbee, 1971; Lewis, 1969), none specifically mention the problems outlined above. Furthermore, there are no data to indicate how influential such texts are in the training of health care providers or, more importantly, in the later behavior of health care professionals.

ENVIRONMENTAL CHANGES AND COMMUNICATION PROBLEMS

The mass media sometimes highlight the case of the person who dies at a very advanced age in the same house in which they were born, or at least in the same house in which they lived all their adult life. Somehow, it is pleasant to many of us to contemplate such stability of environment. The reason the mass media feature such situations, however, is because they are rare, and hence newsworthy. Most people change their environment several times during their lifetime, and many of those changes come after the age of 65. The individual moves to a retirement community, or the couple moves from a house to an apartment. There may be a move to live near or with a son or daughter. At some point, the older person may decide to move to a minimal care facility, and eventually into a nursing home or an extended care facility.

There are certainly large numbers of people who make such changes with little stress and few problems, but there are an even larger number of people who have severe reactions to such changes in the environment. The communication problems associated with changes in the environment of the aging person may be substantial and are the focus of this section of the chapter.

Changes in Living Arrangements

In our society, the "magic" age for retirement is 65, the same age we have selected to concentrate on for this volume's examination of the aging person. Many persons suddenly change their geographic environment at that point in their life, either by moving to a new environment within the community or to a new community.

Associated with such changes in geography are likely to be other changes that may affect the health care of the person. If a person moves from his lifelong community to an entirely new environment, the long-familiar physician will be left behind. The person must search for a new physician or new medical environment to accompany the change in environment. The potential communication problems are obvious. From dealing with someone to whom the aging person may have talked for many years, the older person must learn the speaking habits and personal turn of phrase of a new physician, learn how to obtain the attention and comprehension of the physician and the physician's office staff, learn how to interpret the humor and/or gravity of statements the new physician makes, and perhaps even learn how to communicate with bus drivers or taxi drivers in order to find the new physician's office.

Most neighborhoods have developed subtle habits of "watching out" for residents of the block. If a resident fails to appear for several days, a friend or neighbor will make a check to see whether something may have happened to an elderly person who lives alone. Some neighborhoods develop informal or formal telephone networks so that older residents are called daily to see whether the person is in need of any assistance. Such communication devices tend to tie the residents of the community together and to provide emotional strengths to the residents. Such communication measures within a neighborhood, however, are ordinarily extended only to long-time residents of the neighborhood. The newcomer is not treated in similar fashion until after friendships are established. The older person who has experienced a closely knit neighborhood in which close communication exists between neighbors probably will experience real difficulties upon moving into a new neighborhood where he or she is treated as a stranger. For the person who expected to get information about physicians, health care facilities, exercise opportunities, and other health care related activities, the movement to a new neighborhood may prove to be a communication nightmare. Obviously, if the aging person who moves into a new neighborhood also has pressing needs for health care, these problems are intensified.

Other problems can arise with a change in physical geography on the part of the aging person. Drug stores will be new, grocery stores unfamiliar, special services such as hairdressers, tailors, and laundry services must be located and, for some, a new church must be located. In each case, communication skills will have to be employed. For the person whose emotional stability may have been somewhat upset by the drastic change in environment, communication may be difficult.

Similar and related problems may arise for many aging persons who do not move to a different location. These persons hold fast in the old neighborhood, and the familiar environment moves away from them. Often, with deteriorating structures, persons of different ethnic background or socioeconomic status become the new neighbors. Businesses that were once friendly neighborhood groceries, druggists, or cleaning establishments are replaced with sporting goods stores, auto parts stores, and resale shops. Most serious is the move of the familiar physician to the shiny new office on the outskirts of town, near the suburb to which all the old neighbors have removed themselves. Sometimes the old person in such circumstances will even find that the familiar church follows the majority of its congregation to a new location on the periphery of a city, where parking is easier for those same old neighbors.

For these older persons, the businesses, friends, and professions that supported their physical and mental health are simply no longer available for communication. When the problem is compounded by the aging person's inability to be physically mobile, the problem is almost insurmountable. For many such elderly, however, it is not the physical handicap that incapacitates them, but a psychological inability to move outside of their dwelling, caused by fear of the unknown or rejection of the unfamiliar in the homes of their new neighbors or in the new shops or churches on the nearby thoroughfare.

Changes in Family Environment

Lawton (1970) suggests that a perfect environment might be one in which environmental stress "never exceeds the individual's capacity to respond competently." Perhaps the most serious environmental change that can occur to the average older person is to have a sudden change in the "people environment," e.g., a change in the people closest to someone. The loss of a spouse can lead to serious communication problems for the aging person, and can drastically affect the health care of the person.

In many families, a spouse serves as a "pre-screening" person between an aging person and the health care professional. The spouse is frequently told of symptoms and may function as a second memory, frequently reminding the person to mention past occurrences to the physician. The spouse makes the telephone calls to the physician or keeps track of health care appointments or of a schedule of exercise, medication, or diet. The spouse may even be the person to attempt to tell the health care professional what the health problem is for the patient. This is not to indicate a one-sided relationship necessarily. In many marriages of long-standing reciprocity in such caring and supportive functions has become habitual. When there is a sudden loss of a spouse, those functions must either pass to other third parties, or be learned by the aging person, with the self, rather than a spouse as recipient of the behavior.

Another way of viewing this is to say that the spouse frequently serves as the "enforcer" of health care prescriptions and practices. The spouse may be the one who is given instructions by the health care professional as to the time to take drugs, to exercise, or to engage in rehabilitative activities. In the home, the spouse is frequently the person who ensures compliance with health care prescriptions by persuading the patient to take medicine or do exercises. Through the communication activities of the spouse, the aging patient may gain specific support for engaging in difficult therapy, as well as general social support encouraging the patient that the effort is worthwhile. The loss of a spouse may result in the consequent loss of those communication sources most responsible for continuous health care messages.

A second type of change in family environment is the situation in which the aging person moves into a home in which the locus of control rests with a relative. It could be a brother or sister, or a son, daughter, or nephew. Most frequently in our society the move is that of a parent into the home of a son or daughter. Such a move may seriously disrupt the communication patterns the aging person is accustomed to using with a consequent effect on the person's health.

In many of these situations, the problem arises from the drastic change in role that takes place in a very short period of time. Before the move occurs, the aging person is master of the home, or in the case of a husband and wife, there is a long agreed upon set of roles to play. Simple communication situations, such as how to decide what to watch on TV, have been handled with the ease of years of practice. Suddenly, the person is thrust into a situation in which someone else comes first, in which even simple behaviors are questioned, and in which arguments arise over relatively minor problems. The aging person has to learn a new set of role behaviors. Communication with old friends or other family members may be disrupted because such persons are uncomfortable with telephoning or visiting the residence of the third party. The aging person has to learn all over again how to engage in interpersonal communiation. They may feel rejected when other family members communicate successfully around them, appearing to exclude them. They may become fearful of over-communicating or causing controversy. The resulting stress of such a situation may result in health care problems for the aging person, problems that stem rather directly from the communication situations with which the older person is unable to cope adequately.

Both the loss of a spouse or the move of the household of a relative will cause environmental strains to be set in motion. It should be noted, however, that it is not simply the death of a spouse or moving to a new household that causes problems. For many single persons or those who lost the spouse at a much earlier time, the death or move of a familiar and salient other person will create disruption of communication and force relearning of old communication patterns. These authors would argue strongly that the requirement for learning new patterns of communication is perhaps as important as any physical change in the environment.

Changes in the Age Environment

As a person becomes older, the probability increases that the health care providers will be much younger. Increasing difference in age between the health care provider and the aging person provides an environment that can lead to increased communication problems. Two such problems are the differences in language between provider and aging person, and the change in status differential between aging person and provider.

We know that language changes over time, although that change is normally slow enough to permit all persons living at any given time within a society to be able to communicate with each other. For example, although an aged midwesterner may manage to decipher the slang and accent of a young person from the East coast, he could not decipher Chancerian English or the English forms yet to come in the year 2100. The problem, however, arises with the development of new idioms and slang expressions. New idiomatic expressions and new meanings for slang expressions arise and are used all the time. Frequently, the words used are words with other meanings. For example, the slang use of the word "pot" refers to maurijuana. It is quite probable that the aged person could be mystified by television or radio or ordinary conversation in which the sentence, "He was busted for pot" was used.

While ordinary use of slang does change and can cause communication problems, a more important consideration is the use of new technical terms by a health care provider. Accustomed to using such terms with younger patients and with peers, the provider may not realize that the older patient simply does not understand. The resentment that may rise by what seems like condescending treatment then makes further communication even more difficult. The health care provider may find that services are refused or instructions ignored because of language problems between patient and provider. The older person may feel the health professional is "uppitty" or "high fallutin." It may even be that the elderly patient is completely cooperative but simply not able to understand the language or idiom of the health care provider.

Everyone carries a set of perceived status differences about the people with whom we work and interact. We communicate somewhat differently with our boss than with our subordinate. We are usually deferential to those much older than we are. There are special role relationships played with members of the opposite sex, with our children, and with friends and neighbors. Many of the status differences between ourselves and other people, whether perceived or not, are expressed in the ways we communicate with one another. The patterns become so habitual that we do not even think about the slightly different ways we use to approach people of different status.

A second change in communication patterns for the aging person can be caused by newly perceived status differences for the person in an age-heterogeneous environment. Because of special knowledge and skill, the health care provider is in a position to give directive advice to the aging person. However, the patient may be accustomed to receiving deference and giving directive advice and instructions in other age-heterogeneous environments. The new relationship suddenly places the patient in a status-subordinate position when faced with much younger health care providers. Accustomed to being treated deferentially in communication situations, the aging individual may not know how to cope with a sudden change in role relationships. Furthermore, if the health care provider is not very skillful, the natural tendency is to either "bully" or "talk down" to the patient. Either course will further exacerbate the situation. When there are broad differences in age between the patient and the provider, communication problems can lead to failures in health care delivery.

Lawton (1970) suggests that the highly competent person—competent in terms of being able to care for self—can be successfully placed in an age-heterogeneous environment. He suggests that the person of less competency will perhaps do better in a more age-homogeneous environment. Obviously, one cannot hire people on the basis of age to take care of others of specified ages, but an analysis of the needs of patients may result in more effective assignment of personnel.

Change to the Hospital or Nursing Home

In a major review of the literature dealing with the institutionalization of the aging person, Kasl (1972) suggests that both involuntary relocation and institutionalization can have major health consequences for the aging person. The overall hypothesis advanced is that major changes are always traumatic for anyone, and could lead directly to the development of subsequent illness. For the elderly, however, movement to a hospital or nursing home represents a very major change in environment, and may result in significant health care problems.

Potential problems in communication accompany a move to a health care institution. The elderly person has to learn the rules and regulations of the new institution, as well as the names of different attendants, and how best to communicate with those people. If the institution is a long-term care facility, there will be other patients with whom to interact, and new patterns of interaction must be learned. Studies by Sheldon (1954), Niebanck and Pope (1965), and Kleemeier (1963), suggest that the aging prefer to live alone but near to their children and people their own age. Placing the aging person in an institutional setting thus forces him into an undesired situation, and health care may be difficult to carry out under those circumstances.

Blenker (1967) reports on a number of studies suggesting that the aging person does less well in the institutional setting in terms of survival. In particular, she suggests that the first few months within the institution are the most difficult period, with the highest percentage of deaths coming during that time. However, others have suggested various interpretations, based upon comparison of death rates for those persons on institutional waiting lists with those newly admitted to the institution (cf. Costello and Tanaka, 1961; Kasl, 1972; and Lieberman, 1961). Depending upon interpretation, it has been suggested that 1) those who are residents have higher death rates, 2) there is no difference between the two groups, or 3) those who are waiting to enter the institution have higher death rates. This controversy remains to be resolved by further research, perhaps research that uses a true control group, rather than a waiting list group.

As Kasl (1972) indicates however, the persons who have applied and are awaiting the move to an institution may be under great anticipatory stress, compared with persons the same age who have not yet anticipated institutionalization. Thus, the mere anticipation of major moves or relocations may create communication problems with elderly persons.

One could suggest that better attempts to communicate interpersonally with the aging person who is forced to relocate involuntarily may have some positive effect on the health care outcomes for such persons. Novick (1967) reports on the relocation of 125 institutionalized elderly from an older building to a newer building. Communication was undertaken with the residents to counteract their fear of the unknown and to assure them that familiar belongings and interactive relationships would be maintained in the new setting. Under these conditions, the post-relocation death rate was lower than the rate at the old hospital. Such research needs to be carried out using a concurrent control group, however, in order to control for the effect of history and the difference in physical setting.

We have looked at four different types of environmental change that might lead to communication problems for the aging person. While we have attempted to detail only four possible types of change, it should be noted that the communication problems used as examples may be expected to occur with *any* major environmental change for the aging person. The older person with significant personal competency can learn new communication patterns as easily as they were learned when the person was younger. The retarded older adult or those with a reduced level of personal competency cannot cope with changed environments as easily, and may be expected to have difficulties in learning new communication patterns within the new environment.

SOCIAL-PSYCHOLOGICAL PROBLEMS AND COMMUNICATION IN THE AGING

Mankind uses communication as one of the primary processes for maintaining personal stability. When we need reassurance about a proposed course of action, we talk to another person. When we feel temporarily despondent, we seek out people or messages that might raise our spirits. When we worry about whether we made a correct decision, we try to find someone who will tell us that we did the right thing. When we need information, we turn to the newspaper, radio, or television to satisfy our needs for constantly accelerating information needs. All of these communication behaviors are not only normal, but actually required in order for us to be able to maintain our personal stable orientation to the world around us.

When these normal patterns of communication are seriously disturbed, the personal stability of persons is also likely to become disturbed. Attempts to improve health care for a person are made more difficult when he is seriously disturbed, or unable to decide what course of action to follow. Attempts to provide normal health care are hampered when a person has had normal patterns of communication disrupted. At the same time, such disruptions may result in serious psychological damage. This section briefly examines several social psychological theories associated with communication situations, and attempts to relate them to the aging person.

Cognitive Balance and Communication

Among the more productive social psychological theories of recent years has been that variously labeled as balance theory, consistency theory, congruity, or dissonance theory. Very complete discussions of these various positions are given in literature reviews by Zajonc (1969) and McGuire (1969). For purposes of this chapter, the various terminological differences are not as important as understanding the basic propositions inherent in all the various positions and their relationship to the health care of the aging person.

Underlying the various theoretical positions is the notion that people strive to maintain some cognitive consistency with respect to their reactions toward the world. A person does not perceive the world as a series of completely unrelated stimuli. When processing an incoming message or other type of stimulus, a person utilizes what has been learned in the past as a set of screening devices against which to process the new message. Balance theories postulate that there are psychological mechanisms operating to *minimize any inconsistencies* among the messages that are to be processed.

Several kinds of communication situations seem to relate to the possible pressures to restore balance to a person's cognitive states. One of the most common are the responses that might occur to the presence of competing messages. Imagine a situation in which an aging person was told by his physician that his arthritis could not be "cured," but perhaps might be helped by taking aspirin on a regular basis. When the person goes home, his next door neighbor tells him, "Aspirin never helped me. I finally started wearing this copper bracelet, and I feel much better." The presence of such competing messages places the aging person in a dissonant position, and balance theories predict that a person will try to minimize the effect of the competing messages by finding some comfortable middle ground. He might wear the bracelet *and* take aspirin. Or he might stop going to the physician and only wear the bracelet, while swapping tales of ache and pain with the neighbor. Or he might stop seeing the next door neighbor, while asking for repeated reassurance from his doctor that taking aspirin is the best decision. Any of these actions should reduce the dissonance the person feels as the result of the attention paid to competing messages.

While the various consistency theories all predict that there will be cognitive pressures to restore balance whenever imbalance has occurred, there are differences between theories in predicting exactly what outcomes will occur in certain situations. None of the studies available has ever used an aging population as a test group, and one can only speculate that serious psychological and physical health problems might arise for the older person who is exposed to competing messages. We utilized the example of the person receiving just two competing messages. But the average aging person with a health problem is faced with many potentially competing messages. The health care provider, the relative, the friend, and the advertising available from the mass media may all send the aging person competing messages. Whereas the normal, healthy person is able to sort out competing messages and react to them in ways that are consistent with previously established frames of reference, the aging person may be less able to cope with competing messages.

Even though the older person is less able to cope with competing messages, consistency theory would predict that the older person will still attempt to balance the messages received in some fashion. Attempting to predict, however, what methods he might use is difficult. The older person may simply attempt to reject any message that is sent, preferring to remain "behind the times," or even repress vital health care information entirely rather than to attempt to cope with new ideas and new concepts. Shutting off the flow of messages, however, makes health care extremely difficult, because many of the messages ignored by the aging person are ones transmitted by the health care professional. Perhaps one facet of the disengagement theory of aging, the active withdrawal of cathexis of objects and persons may be explained by a simple mechanism such as rejection or repression of competing messages.

Cognitive consistency theories would seem a fertile field to use in attempting to make predictions about the ways in which the older person will react to communication. These authors have, however, been unable to find any experimental studies that attempted to study communication to the older person from the standpoint of cognitive consistency theory. Such studies seem clearly called for.

Dependency, Locus of Control, and Communication

As a person becomes older, the dependency relationship to other people changes. As a child, the relationship is one of subordinancy to a set of parents. The parents speak for the child in many situations, particularly those related to health care. In visits to a physician's office, the parents tell the physician what is wrong with the child (sometimes to the dismay of the physician who would prefer to interact with the patient directly). As a person grows older, dependency on the parents grows less, so that when the child is an adult the dependency on parents is gone, as is the parental locus of control. The person speaks for himself or herself in health care situations. While it is true that in some cultures the husband takes over the communication role for his wife in visits to a health care provider, the normal mode of operation in our society is for the adult to operate independently in health care situations.

The picture changes again with the aging person. As the person becomes older, there is a tendency to fall once again into a dependency relationship. This may happen with the daughter in whose home the person is living, or it may be with professional health care providers in a nursing home situation. It could be the dependency of an aged husband on a somewhat younger wife. In such situations, however, the tendency is for communication control to revert to the situation that the child is in. The daughter tells the physician what is wrong with her mother. The nurse in the nursing home speaks for the aged woman who is visited by a physician. The tendency is for the more dominant person in whom rests the locus of control to take over the communication role.

There are two dangers associated with the tendency for communication to be exercised by the dominant member of a dyad. The first danger is that the actual health state of the aging person may never be accurately determined. If the physician or other health care professional relies on what is being said by the independent person, a totally false picture may be gained. The second danger is that once the aging person allows a dependency relation to begin, the progress toward total dependency may be greatly accelerated, and the person's overall health may suffer.

While a number of studies have commented on the general problem of communication conducted when a dependency relationship exists, (cf. Ericson, 1973; Rogers, 1973; and Watzlavik, Beavin, Jackson, 1967) there seem to be no studies examining the phenomena as it might occur in a health care facility with the aging person. Such studies, carefully conducted, might be able to identify relationships between communication patterns and the general health of the older person.

Attitudes toward the Aging Person and Communication

Attitudes toward old age vary widely from culture to culture. In some cultures, the older person is given great deference and treated as having acquired greater wisdom with greater age. The older person is taken into account in the family plans of sons and daughters. In other cultures, attitudes toward the older person are far more negative. The question is, "What will we do with Momma?" And the question is sometimes even asked when Momma is present.

The general American culture tends toward the consideration of the older person as a problem, not as an opportunity. Attitudes of the general non-elderly population are not particularly favorable toward the aging, with the major exception of the old who have been able to maintain the physical or mental characteristics of younger persons. Those attitudes cannot help but be reflected in the communication patterns adopted with the older person.

Quite frequently, communication situations are reported in which people will be talking about the older patient as if he were not even in the same room. While that could happen with any seriously ill person, the probability is greater that it will happen with the older person. Negative attitudes lead to decreased status, and often the status of a person will be lowered to little more than an object. One might expect that the health care provider would approach the aging person with the same attitudes any patient or potential patient is approached. But if the general attitudes of a culture toward the aging person are negative, there is strong reason to believe that negative attitudes will exist toward the older person in need of health care that would not be evidenced for younger patients.

One can readily see how such attitudes come about. Care of the aging patient is frequently a losing proposition. While one might talk about a "cure" for the 40-year-old, care for the 80-year-old may be purely custodial, with no hope of eventual recovery of vigorous health. In such situations, positive attitudes and positive communication efforts are hardly to be expected, especially in a culture that emphasizes observable success, progress, and productivity.

Several reactions are possible, given negative attitudes of the health care provider toward the older person. There could be an attempt to completely avoid communication with the older person, essentially treating the person more as an object than as an individual. Obviously, one might expect the older person to respond with silence, thus effectively concealing potential health care problems or information. Another possible reaction, given negative reactions, would be communication patterns in which the older person is treated with scorn and contempt. Again, this is not a healthy situation. Or one might expect the older person to be treated in terms of communication patterns as a child might be treated. The older person will be "talked down to," and health care concerns of the older person will be minimized. This will be especially so if the older person has not been successful in learning to talk in health care terms.

This examination of social psychological theories and communication as it might relate to the aging person has been relatively brief. The literature would suggest the possibility of many fruitful studies using these theoretical frameworks as a base for investigation.

RESEARCH QUESTIONS NEEDING ANSWERS

It should be obvious to the reader than many of the communication problems described above could also be described as "potential problems." While research on younger age groups, especially college students, suggests that older populations with less educational attainment would also have similar problems, there is simply very little research that actually looks at communication patterns and problems with an aging population. Thus, one general conclusion that may be made is that further research is needed in each of the areas discussed. In each area there are some specific research questions that can be identified; they are listed below.

How should health care providers best approach the vision- or hearing-impaired elderly patient in terms of interpersonal communication in order to increase their quality of health care or health care outcomes?

What are the patterns of communication adopted by older persons who have lost a spouse, lost a familiar neighborhood, or been relocated in a relative's home or institution; and how do these patterns affect the quality of health care or health care outcomes for such persons?

What patterns of communication would be maximally beneficial in minimizing stress to the older person who is forced to undergo a major change in environment, thereby maximizing health outcomes or quality of health care?

Can the findings of balance theory and cognitive dissonance be replicated on samples of institutionalized and non-institutionalized elderly in order to tailor health care strategies for greater health care benefit to the elderly?

What types of general information processing are utilized by older people, upon which health care strategies and health care outcomes may depend?

What types of communication behavior by health care providers would best operate to change their attitudes toward the elderly, thereby increasing the quality of health care and the health care outcomes for this group?

FUTURE TRENDS

It is difficult to predict the future. It is far more difficult to make predictions about the future when data about the past are scanty. Therefore, our comments about the future of communication research and theory as it applies to the health care of the aging can only be our own. The data available say little or nothing of help to us.

There are very few studies in which communication is linked to health care. Yet communication variables have been found to be useful in explaining a number of phenomena, and the number of people interested in communication has continued to grow at an accelerating pace. We expect that the growth of interest in communication will continue to grow, and that as interest in our aging population increases, attempts will be made to link communication variables to aging phenomena.

Three areas seem of particular interest. We expect that there will be increased efforts to study the communication patterns used by the aging in interpersonal situations. As the population of older Americans increases, finding the most effective methods of communiation with that population will become more and more important. Studies of interpersonal networks have become popular in recent years, and we will expect such studies to be particularly useful in changing the practices of health care professionals and institutions.

The second area to explore are the relationships that might exist between media exposure and usage by the older person and heatlh. There are already a number of studies that look at media exposure of the aging to both print and electronic media. A very natural extension of such studies would be to look at media exposure or other communication variables as correlates to personal health or acceptance of health care.

Finally, as the elderly grow in numbers they have begun to organize into interest groups, pressure groups, and political entities, such as the Association of Retired Persons and the Grey Panthers. These organizational efforts will multiply their visibility to the public beyond their actual numbers. Over time, some of the cultural negativism toward the aging may be reversed: as politicians find that the elderly vote in significant numbers, even after their "productive years" are past; and as programs for the education of elderly adults come on the scene, research into the information processing mechanisms of the elderly will accelerate. Undoubtedly the fallout from such research will also be useful to health care providers.

We are sure that other areas of study that link communication to the health care of the aging will emerge in the next few years. What is more surprising is that such studies have not already been conducted.

SUMMARY

A tempting way to answer the question as to what communication considerations should be made when examining the health care of the aging would be to say, "We do not know." The lack of specific studies certainly tempts that type of answer. The answer we prefer to give is, "We do not know, but here are some variables that might be important."

We have attempted to examine three major areas that seem related both to communication and to health care. Most easily identified are those physiological changes in the aging that affect both communication and health care. These include hearing changes, vision changes, and various types of changes in physiological mobility.

The second type of variable are those associated with changes in interpersonal environment for the aging person. Changes in the neighborhood, moves to a retirement home, urban renewal programs all may lead to rather traumatic changes for the older person. In turn, such changes may mean the necessity of changes in communication patterns for the older person if health is to be maintained. Other kinds of environmental changes that must be considered include loss of a spouse, forced relocation to the home of a child or other relative, and institutionalization.

Finally, we provided a brief look at social psychological theories that might usefully tie communication effects to health care. Of particular importance would seem to be studies of the various cognitive consistency mechanisms as they apply to an aging population.

RECOMMENDATIONS

Some of the phenomena discussed here are not easily changed by the adoption of a concrete recommendation. We feel sure that no great breakthroughs are possible in the cure or prevention of hearing and sight loss in the elderly, and that the functional decrements brought on by chronic disease in the elderly will not easily be lessened. However, as more and more states adopt legislation mandating that public buildings be accessible to the handicapped, there will be a fallout boom for those elderly who are mobility handicapped. Ramps, elevators, escalators, and wider doors cannot help but be helpful in allowing older people to move out of their homes to communicate with the world about them. As the technology of equipment for public buildings improves, there may be more widely available products for installation in private residences. Besides supporting such projects we would also support public transportation systems and special "dial-a-ride" transportation systems that have come into being in many communities.

While long-term health care institutions abound and flourish, our culture remains one in which only certain classes of people are denied the freedom of normal human traffic and social intercourse within the supportive institution of the family. Those classes include the criminal, the insane, the extremely disabled, and the elderly.

To alleviate the occurrence of traumatic institutionalization for the elderly we would recommend that, whenever possible, health care be brought to the aged persons, keeping them in familiar surroundings to as great an extent as possible. New methods of health care delivery to the aged, such as home health care, day care, and respite care that includes special services in the home like "meals-on-wheels" should be encouraged. Respite care allows persons to be institutionalized for short temporary periods so that other family members may go on vacations, take seasonal employment, or themselves be hospitalized in acute care facilities. Because such institutionalization is not irreversible, we feel it will be less traumatic, just as summer camp is not forever for the home-sick child and can, therefore, become a pleasant change of pace.

Day care allows other members of the family to work or just catch up with their friends or hobbies, while the older person is able to return to familiar surroundings in the evenings, having had access to therapy, exercise, counseling, health care testing, and monitoring of their condition during the day.

One of us is currently associated with a research and demonstration project in home health care for the chronically ill, including many who are elderly. This strategy of health care promises much in maintaining normal or familiar surroundings for the elderly patient, thus avoiding adjustment to unfamiliar communication patterns and allowing the older persons to maintain their status through independence and internal locus of control.

It is not enough that health care providers make new forms of health care available, such as alternatives to institutionalization. Methods for financing these health care services must also be found through third party payers and governmental programs such as Medicare and Medicaid, so that they become viable choices for the elderly person unable to pay for them from private resources.

At the same time, we must realize that other less drastic adjustments in communication will be necessary when an elderly person enrolls for such a service. The respite care patient will have all the adjustments to new surroundings and absence of family that a fledgling camper has, but the adjustments are temporary. The day care patient will have to learn to communicate with health care personnel and will make new friends among the patients, just as the student must learn the ways of a teacher and the friendships of classmates, but can return to a supportive family each evening. In the case of the home care patient, the old habits of communicating with guests in the home may persist, but will need to be replaced with patterns that allow a limited loss of locus of control to the health care provider who comes across the threshold.

Finally, we recommend measures that indicate a positive attitude, honored status, and preferential treatment for the elderly, such as reduced recreational and transportation fares, tax breaks for elderly home owners, reduced drug rates, and normal-appearing positive image roles in the mass media for elderly. There is no minority to which the majority could so reasonably be expected to apply the golden rule as the elderly. The amazing thing is that it has been so slow in happening. Men cannot become women, whites cannot become blacks, and adults cannot become children, but everyone may become old.

LITERATURE CITED

Blenkner, M. 1967. Environmental change and the aging individual. The Geontologist 7: 102–105.
Bloom, M., E. Duchon, G. Frires, H. Hanson, G. Hurd, and V. South. 1971. Interviewing the ill aged. The Gerontologist 11: 292–299.
Costello, J. P., and G. M. Tanaka. 1961. Mortality and morbidity in long-term institutional care of the aged. J. Amer. Geriatric Soc. 9: 959.
Ericson, P. 1973. Relational Communication: Complementarity and Sym-

etry and their Relation to Dominance-Submission. Unpublished doctoral dissertation, Michigan State University.

Hein, E. C. 1973. Communication in Nursing Practice. Brown, Boston.

Kasl, S. 1972. Physical and mental health effects of involuntary relocation and institutionalization on the elderly: A review. Amer. J. Public Health 62: 377–384.

Kleemeier, R. W. 1963. Attitudes toward special settings for the aged. *In* R. H. Williams et al. Processes of Aging. Vol. II., pp. 101–121. Atherton Press, New York.

Lawton, M. P. 1970. Assessment, integration, and environments for older people. The Gerontologist 10: 38–45.

Lewis, G. 1969. Nurse-Patient Communication. C. Brown, Dubuque, Iowa.

Lieberman, M. A. 1961. Relationship of mortality rates to entrance to a home for the aged. Geriatrics 16: 515.

McGuire, W. J. 1969. The nature of attitudes and attitude change. *In* G. Lindzey and E. Aronson (eds.), Handbook of Social Psychology. Vol. 3, pp. 136–314. Addison Wesley, Reading, Mass.

Niebanck, P. L., and J. B. Pope. 1965. The elderly in older urban areas. Institute of Environmental Studies, University of Pennsylvania, Philadelphia.

Novick, L. J. 1967. Easing the stress of moving day. Hospital 41: 64–74.

Rogers, E. 1973. Dyadic Systems and Transactional Communication in a Family Context. Unpublished doctoral dissertation, Michigan State University.

Sheldon, J. H. 1954. The social philosophy of old age. Lancet 2: 151.

Travelbee, J. 1971. Interpersonal Aspects of Nursing. F. A. Davis, Philadelphia.

Travis, G. 1966. Chronic disease and disability: A social worker's guide. University of California Press, Berkeley.

Watzlavik, P., J. Beavin, and D. Jackson. 1967. Pragmatics of Human Communication. W. W. Norton, New York.

Zajonc, R. B. 1969. Cognitive theories in social psychology. *In* G. Lindzey and E. Aronson (eds.), Handbook of Social Psychology. Vol. 1, 320–411. Addison Wesley, Reading, Mass.

SUGGESTED READINGS

Aaronson, B. S. 1964. Personality stereotypes of chronological age. Gerontologist No. 3, Pt. 11, 15, abstract.

Aaronson, B. S. 1966. Personality stereotypes of aging. J. Gerontol. 21: 458–462.

Adams, D. 1969. Analysis of a life satisfaction index. J. Gerontol. 24: 470–474.

Aldridge, G. J. 1953. Old age as a social problem. J. Public Law 2: 333–339.

Anderson, N. N. 1967. The significance of age categories for older persons. The Gerontologist 7: 164–167.

Bebard, E. M. 1967. Unmet needs versus perceived needs: The effect of inadequate communication. *In* ANA Regional Clinical Conferences, pp. 71–77. Appleton-Century-Crofts, New York.

Bekker, L. D., and C. Taylor. 1966. Attitudes toward the aged in a multi-generational sample. J. Gerontol. 21: 115–118.

Bell, T. 1967. Social involvement and feeling old among residents in houses for the aged. J. Gerontol. 22: 17–22.

Blau, Z. S. 1961. Structural constraints on friendships in old age. Amer. Sociol. Rev. 26: 429–439.

Brim, O. G., Jr. 1966. Socialization through the life cycle. *In* O. G. Brim, Jr., and S. Wheeler, Socialization after Childhood. John Wiley and Sons, New York.

Buhler, C. 1968. The course of human life as a psychological problem. Human Devel. 11: 184–200.

Burgess, E. W. 1960. Aging in Western Societies. University of Chicago Press, Chicago.

Burgess, E. W., R. Cavan, R. Havighurst, and H. Goldhamer. 1949. Personal Adjustment in Old Age. Science Research Associates, Chicago.

Cameron, P. 1971. The generation gap: Beliefs about adult stability-of-life. J. Gerontol. 26: 81.

Clark, M., and B. G. Anderson. 1967. Culture and Aging. Charles C Thomas, Springfield, Ill.

Ederman, L. E. 1966. Attitudes of adult children toward parents and parents' problems. Geriatrics 21: 217–222.

Eisdorfer, C., and J. Altorcchi. 1961. A comparison of attitudes toward old age and mental illness. J. Gerontol. 16: 340–343.

Eisdorfer, C., and F. Wilkie. 1967. Attitudes toward older people: A semantic analysis. Paper presented at the meeting of the Gerontological Society, St. Petersburg, Florida.

Ginzberg, R. 1952. The negative attitude toward the elderly. Geriatrics 7: 297–302.

Hanson, R. C., and M. G. Beech. 1963. Communicating health arguments across cultures. Nursing Res. 12: 237–241.

Havighurst, R. J. 1949. Old age: An American problem. J. Gerontol. 4: 298–304.

Heller, J. R. 1969. What does the patient understand as comprehensive health care? Arch. Phys. Med. Rehab. 50: 563–565.

Jones, R. W. 1974. Communication problems of the client in a nursing home or rehabilitation center. *In* S. M. Schneeweiss and S. W. Davis (eds.), Nursing Home Administration, pp. 127–143. University Park Press, Baltimore.

Kaplan, H. B., and A. D. Pokorny. 1970. Aging and self-attitude: A conditional relationship. Aging Human Devel. 1: 241–250.

Kariel, P. E. 1961. The dynamics of behavior in relation to health. Nursing Outlook 10: 402–405.

Kastenbaum, R. (ed.). 1965. Old age as a social issue. J. Soc. Issues Vol. 21.

Kent, D. P. 1965. Aging: fact and fancy. The Gerontologist 5: 51–56.

Kerchoff, A. C. 1964. Husband-wife expectations and reactions to retirement. J. Gerontol. 19: 510–516.

Lane, B. 1964. Attitudes of youth toward the aged. J. Marriage and Family 26: 299–231.

Linden, M. E. 1957. Effects of social attitudes on the mental health of the aging. Geriatrics 12: 109–115.

Lowenthal, M. F., and D. Boler. 1965. Voluntary vs. involuntary social withdrawal. J. Gerontol. 20: 363–371.

Maddox, G. 1970. Adaptation to retirement. The Gerontologist 10: 14–18.

Maddox, G., and C. Eisdorfer. 1962. Some correlates of activity and morale among the aged. Social Forces 4: 254–260.

Mohammad, M. F. B. 1964. Patients' understanding of written health information. Nursing Res. 13: 100–103.

Riley, M. W., A. Foner, B. Hess, and M. L. Toby. 1969. Socialization for the middle and later years. *In* D. A. Goslin, (ed.), Handbook of Socialization Theory and Research. Rand McNally, Chicago.

Shanas, E. 1962. The Health of Older People. Harvard University Press, Cambridge.

Tobin, S., and B. L. Neugarten. 1961. Life satisfaction and social interaction in the aging. J. Gerontol. 16: 344–346.

Townsend, P. 1963. The family life of old people. Penguin Books, Baltimore.

Tuckman, J., and I. Lorge. 1953. When aging begins and stereotypes about aging. J. Gerontol. 8: 489–492.

Williams, R., and C. Wirth. 1965. Lives through the Years. Atherton Press, New York.

chapter 9

Speech and Language Functioning among the Aging

John M. Hutchinson, Ph.D.
Daniel S. Beasley, Ph.D.

... language as it exists is always the posses-
sion of individuals. Vocabularies are individual vocabularies, and ways of speaking are
always the ways of indivduals. A man's
speech is peculiar to him, as inseparable
from him, as his own shadow. It has grown
with him, and most of it will die with him;
like his shadow, it is to a degree made anew
every day (p. 22).

Charlton Laird, *The Miracle of Language*

The growth, fluctuation, and individuality of human communication
reflected in these words is of particular significance in any consideration of
speech and language functioning among aging persons. In the first place,
there are characteristic changes in manner and style of speaking that
permit listeners to identify older persons. Moreover, physiological alterations that accompany the aging process produce predictable changes in the
acoustic parameters of speech, providing additional cues in detecting older
talkers. Finally, aging persons are particularly susceptible to neurological
degeneration and disease that interrupt normal language functioning and
the peripheral execution of speech events. In short, the aging person
exhibits differences in oral communication either as a result of the normal
aging process, neurological disease, or both. This chapter explores these
communicative correlates of aging and suggests new directions for increasing the understanding of the speech and language differences observed in
the geriatric population.

A MODEL OF HUMAN COMMUNICATION

To provide a measure of continuity to this discussion of oral communication changes characteristic of aging persons, a model that delineates several hypothetical levels of language encoding will be offered. However, before presenting this model, two important terms must be defined so that a full appreciation of the model may be gained.

Language: A language is a system of symbols which, when arranged in a particular order, may be used to communicate thoughts, desires, ideas, and emotions among persons for whom the symbols have meaning. Any oral language encompasses three fundamental components. 1) *Syntax* concerns the language-specific rules for combining constituent elements to form grammatical sentences. 2) *Semantics* refers to the meaning of constituent elements in a language. 3) *Phonology* concerns the structure of the sound system within a given language. It refers to the rules for combining phonemes (smallest sound units within a language that signal a semantic difference) to produce appropriate words.

Speech: Speech refers to the audible expression of language and involves the generation of sound through the interactive participation of three physiological systems: respiratory, phonatory, and articulatory. First, the respiratory system initiates the driving force required in speech production. This driving force usually takes the form of an egressive flow of air through the human vocal tract. Second, this air flow can generate either vibration of the vocal folds in the larynx or it can become turbulent at some point in the vocal tract. The vibration and/or turbulence serve as the sound sources for human speech. Third, the articulatory system typically involves supralaryngeal modulation of the sound source by means of complex vocal tract constrictions and occlusions to produce distinctive acoustic signals (phones) that may be classified into phonemic families within a given language.

With these terms properly defined, the aforementioned model of human communication can now be elaborated. This model was originally developed by Noll (1972) and is neurologically based. It involves four levels of language encoding (Figure 1).

Level I–Ideation

Level I of communication is of the highest order and refers to the basic generation of an idea, thought, or desire. It is fundamentally a process of intellectualization or conceptualization and is largely a function of cortical operations.

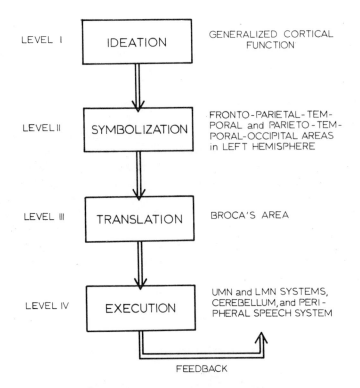

LEVEL I

IDEATION

GENERALIZED CORTICAL
FUNCTION

LEVEL II

SYMBOLIZATION

FRONTO-PARIETAL-TEM-
PORAL and PARIETO-TEM-
PORAL-OCCIPITAL AREAS
in LEFT HEMISPHERE

LEVEL III

TRANSLATION

BROCA'S AREA

LEVEL IV

EXECUTION

UMN and LMN SYSTEMS,
CEREBELLUM, and PERI-
PHERAL SPEECH SYSTEM

FEEDBACK

Figure 1. Noll's (1972) hierarchical model of human communication.

Luria (1966) has described some of the intellectual functions associated with various areas of the cerebral cortex. For example, the temporal lobe appears important for digressive reasoning that requires verbal associations and for the performance of intellectual functions involving a series or sequence of operations. The occipital and occipitoparietal regions are important for problem solving requiring the identification of visual signs and symbols. The sensorimotor region of the brain (postcentral and precentral regions, collectively) is important for *understanding* which, according to Luria, encompasses tasks requiring complex conceptual systems. Finally, the frontal lobe is employed in analyzing systematically the essential aspects of a problem. In addition, the hierarchical organization of the intellectual operations necessary for problem-solving functions appears localized primarily in the frontal lobe.

Level II—Symbolization

The second level of language encoding involves a process of casting the generated thought, idea, desire, etc., into the symbolic representation of a speaker's native language. In particular, it involves retrieval of constituent elements with appropriate semantic representations and the organization of these elements into proper syntactic relationships according to the rules of the language.

There is considerable controversy over the exact neurological structures responsible for the symbolization process, but most authorities agree that lesions in the fronto-parietal-temporal and parieto-temporal-occipital regions in the dominant hemisphere will produce an identifiable impairment of symbolization (Figure 2). Pribram (1971) has observed that if the lesion extends in an anterior direction, the disfunction tends to be more expressive. A posterior excursion of the lesion produces a more profound disturbance characterized by confusion as well as expressive difficulties. Pribram noted further that a posterior-inferior extension of the lesion, toward the occipital lobe, results in associated visual impairments and a posterior-superior involvement generally produces problems with semantic function.

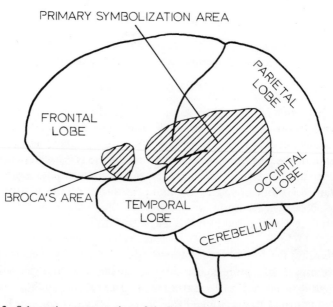

Figure 2. Schematic representation of the human brain showing the primary symbolization area and Broca's area.

Level III–Translation

This third level of oral language expression involves translation of the symbolic code into appropriate motor programs for execution by the peripheral speech mechanism. It involves what Luria (1966) has called the "kinetic organization of the motor act" (p. 196).

With regard to speech function, most authorities agree that this programming function is executed in Broca's area of the brain or the base of the third frontal convolution in the dominant (usually left) hemisphere. A lesion in this area produces a disorder commonly termed oral apraxia, which is characterized by inconsistent and unpredictable articulatory errors.

Level IV–Execution

The fourth and final level of encoding involves execution of the articulatory motor program by the peripheral speech mechanism through proper coordination of the respiratory, phonatory, and articulatory systems. This execution process involves the upper and lower motor neuron systems, the cerebellum, peripheral muscular apparatus, and articulatory structures. Any pathology that disturbs the integrity of these neurological systems and/or peripheral structures produces one of a variety of execution disorders.

Feedback

A final very important component of the speech production process involves sensory feedback from the respiratory, laryngeal, and articulatory systems to subcortical and cortical regions in the central nervous system. The exact role of peripheral feedback during speech production is unclear. However, recent deafferentation research (e.g., Taub and Berman, 1968) and oral anesthesia investigations (Hutchinson and Putnam, 1974; Hutchinson and Ringel, 1975; Putnam, 1973; and Scott and Ringel, 1971) have provided evidence that, while sensory feedback is not vital for the triggering and ongoing execution of speech events, it is important for precision and refinement of certain peripheral vocal tract gestures.

SPEECH AND LANGUAGE CHANGES
ASSOCIATED WITH THE NORMAL AGING PROCESS

With this model of speech and language function as background, it is appropriate to review the literature describing speech and language changes as a function of the normal aging process. These alterations will be described with reference to each component of this encoding model.

Alterations in Ideational Function

There is no question that some aspects of intellectual function deteriorate with age. It is beyond the scope of this chapter to review the relevant data regarding alterations in the intellectual profile of geriatric persons. Suffice it to say, as a general statement, it would appear that tasks requiring abstract intelligence, such as analogies, become increasingly difficult for older persons, but those tasks that reflect accumulated experience, such as vocabulary, may be less affected (Jones, 1959). It would also appear that not all older persons show a typical decline in intellectual behavior. Those with superior intelligence generally retain their elevated status, partially because they may develop better strategies for learning new things and retaining those things that were previously learned.

The observed reductions in intellectual function among older persons may be the result of three factors. 1) Deteriorative changes in the central nervous system are well documented. There is approximately an 11 percent decrease in brain weight between 25 and 96 years of age (Appel and Appel, 1942). This is accompanied by a decrease in neuronal density, particularly in the superior temporal gyrus, precentral gyrus, and area straita (Brody, 1955). 2) A loss in motivation to perform well on measures of intellectual function must also be considered. As Jones (1959) has pointed out, motivation and ability are highly interrelated; people tend to do things that they do well and resist performing tasks that reflect their weaknesses. Hence, a loss in mental ability as a result of central nervous system deterioration may result in a reduced motivation to engage in intellectual activities. 3) A third factor related to the observed decrement in intellectual performance as a function of age may be a lack of practice in performing some of the skills tapped by certain intelligence batteries. This consideration would appear particularly appropriate for those whose educational level is relatively low.

The effect of this deterioration in intellectual function upon communcation is rather obvious. The content and complexity of the message will be affected; though, except in the case of substantial organic deterioration, the extent may be relatively minor.

Alterations in Symbolization Function

Except in the case of relatively severe organic pathology, symbolization skills would appear to be spared the typical changes associated with the aging brain. However, little experimental effort has been devoted to the study of subtle symbolization changes that may exist among geriatric patients. Halpern, Darley, and Brown (1973) examined the syntactic capabilities of 10 patients with diffuse intellectual impairments (primarily degeneration in eight of the ten patients). The subjects had a mean age of 58 years, with five subjects over 60 years. The results confirmed little impairment of grammatical inflection or additions, substitutions, and deletions of syntactic words. These subjects did evidence some inadequacy in responses to definitions, reading comprehension, and arithmetic skills. Obviously, the subjects in this experimental sample were much more severely impaired than most aging persons. However, it may be hypothesized that the language impairments of older persons may be qualitatively similar to but less extensive than the profile of impairments observed in these 10 patients.

Alterations in Translation Function

As in the case of symbolization function, little experimental work has been completed to determine the existence of subtle apractic disturbances in aging persons. It would appear that the typical degenerative changes in the brain do not seriously impair programming functions. Some support for this position can be drawn from the study cited previously by Halpern, Darley, and Brown (1973). In patients with isolated apraxias of speech, fluency was markedly impaired. Clearly the hesitations, repetitions, and reduced responses characteristic of this group were indicative of the search and struggle for proper motor programs. However, patients with generalized degenerative intellectual impairments evidenced normal or near normal fluency scores. Again, qualitative comparison of these patients to the aging population in general is hazardous. Further research is needed to determine the tenability of such an hypothesis.

Alterations in Execution

A large body of experimental evidence is available to describe peripheral alterations among older talkers. Investigators have dealt primarily with acoustic and perceptual aspects of speech production with little direct attention to peripheral physiologic changes associated with the aging process. Nevertheless, these acoustic and perceptual data permit some speculations regarding changes in vocal tract structure and function in the geriatric population.

One of the earliest research efforts aimed at quantifying some of the acoustic changes in speech production as a function of aging was that of Mysak (1959). Three groups of subjects were required to read a short paragraph from which measures of vocal fundamental frequency, range of fundamental frequency, phonation/time ratio (percentage of total speaking time involved in voicing), and words per minute were obtained. There was a progressive increment in fundamental frequency from about age 50 to age 85. There was also a tendency toward greater pitch variability with increasing age. Phonation/time ratios decreased as a function of age as did the overall speaking rate. The pitch changes were interpreted as evidence of a combined influence of physiological and socioemotional factors, although the exact mechanisms whereby these factors would effect pitch were not elaborated. Changes in speaking rate and phonation/time ratio were assumed to be the result of a general slowing of neuromuscular activity as a function of advancing age.

In a parallel study, McGlone and Hollien (1963) extended Mysak's research strategy to a sample of aging women. Two groups of 10 subjects with mean ages of 72.6 years and 85 years, respectively, were recorded during oral reading. Measures of fundamental frequency and range of fundamental frequency were obtained. In contrast to Mysak's results, there was no significant change in fundamental frequency from young adulthood to advancing age. Similar results were reported by Charlip (1968). Moreover, there was a slight decrease in pitch variability with age in this group of women. In an effort to explain the discrepancy between the data for females and those for males in Mysak's study, McGlone and Hollien suggested that anatomical changes in the female larynx are not as extensive during puberty and therefore degenerative changes may not be as profound in later life.

The two studies reported previously were concerned with a relatively restricted number of age groups. In an effort to provide data regarding fundamental frequency throughout adult life, Hollien and Shipp (1972) sampled the speech of 25 talkers in each of seven decades ranging from 20 to 89 years of age. The results demonstrated a slight decrement in mean fundamental frequency from 20 to 50 years of age. However, beyond that age, in accordance with the results of Mysak (1959), there was a steady increase in fundamental frequency. Hollien and Shipp observed that the larynegeal structures of older persons evidence decreasing tissue elasticity and the vocal folds may have reduced thickness as a result of muscle atrophy. Accordingly, the notable increase in pitch among older persons may be largely a function of these physiologic changes.

Further evidence concerning fundamental frequency characteristics as a function of age was reported by Endres, Bambach, and Flösser (1970). Their research involved a longitudenal investigation of six adult subjects over a 13- to 15-year period. Though they reported data for only one subject, it was their general observation that people experience a reduced fundamental frequency and decreased fundamental frequency range as a function of age. These results are difficult to interpret, however, because there was only a limited sample of subjects and complete age data were not given.

Limited research has been reported concerning acoustic variables other than fundamental frequency. Perhaps the most complete study to date is that of Ryan (1972). He obtained recordings of 20 normal-hearing subjects with no vocal pathology in each of four age groups: 40 to 49, 50 to 59, 60 to 69, and 70 to 79. From these recordings he obtained average vocal intensity, words per minute, and words per minute per sentence for both oral reading and impromptu speech. There was a slight increase in average vocal intensity as a function of age, but no statistically significant increment was observed until the 70-year-old group was compared with the younger groups. Similarly, there was a progressive decrement in speaking rate with increased age, but the only significant differences were observed between the oldest and youngest groups for impromptu speaking. The oral reading task resulted in significantly slower rates for the oldest group when compared with all other groups. These data supported the general conclusions presented earlier by Mysak (1959).

In interpreting these findings, Ryan made several interesting speculations. He suggested that the general increase in vocal intensity may have reflected a reduction in feedback from peripheral sensory receptors. As a result, increased vocal effort may have been adopted as a compensatory strategy for coping with the generally reduced feedback load. Similarly, it was suggested that a reduced speaking rate might also have been adopted by older talkers as a coping mechanism to accommodate increased ranges of articulator movement, thereby preserving an acceptable level of feedback. Such an hypothesis assumes greater credence in light of the observation that as many as 25 percent of the nerve cells in the brain, spinal cord, and peripheral ganglia may be lost by the eighth or ninth decade of life (Gardner, 1969).

As mentioned previously, few research efforts have been aimed at measuring directly the physiologic correlates of speech production in geriatric subjects. Ptacek et al. (1966) provided some preliminary data by examining maximum performances of a group of geriatric adults for several physiologic and acoustic variables. Specifically, they examined pitch range, oral diadochokinesis (rapid, repetitive movements of the articulators), maximum vowel intensity, maximum vowel duration, maximum intraoral air pressure, and vital capacity. It was found that for all dependent variables, reduced maximum performances were recorded for both geriatric males and geriatric females. These data are certainly a valuable contribution to the literature, but their significance is difficult to discern in the absence of similar measures obtained during typical speech production.

In summary, the research to date permits several general conclusions with regard to characteristic alterations in speech execution as a function of age. First, geriatric males generally exhibit an increase in vocal fundamental frequency, but no consistent changes have been observed for geriatic females. Second, the range of fundamental frequency is reduced in older speakers. Third, vocal intensity is slightly higher for older persons who have normal hearing. Fourth, measures of speech rate reflect reductions in the speed of utterance for geriatric subjects. Fifth, measures of maximum physiologic performance as related to the speech system are generally reduced as a function of age.

Perceptual Studies of Aging

There is a growing body of research evidence pertaining to the perception of age as related to acoustic parameters of speech production. This literature warrants some review because of the insights it permits concerning the process of aging.

In general, this experimental evidence has indicated that subjects can reliably differentiate "old" and "young" simply on the basis of listening to the speech. For example, Ptacek and Sander (1966) asked 10 listeners to differentiate young (less than 35 years of age) and old (more than 65 years of age) subjects. Recordings of a sustained vowel and a reading passage played both forward and backward for each subject were presented to the listeners. They showed a striking ability to differentiate older and younger subjects with 99 percent accuracy in judging the forward speech samples. The listeners indicated that rate of speech, pitch, voice quality, loudness, and fluency were among the most important cues permitting correct identification.

The research of Ptacek and Sander (1966) involved only a binary decision of "young" versus "old," and the question arose as to whether or not listeners could accurately identify speakers with reference to a much broader age continuum. In an effort to answer this question, Shipp and Hollien (1969) obtained recordings of 175 adult males equally divided into seven age groups ranging from 20 to 90 years old. They then conducted three perceptual experiments with three different groups of listeners. One group was asked to assign each speech sample to one of three categories, "old," "young," and "neither old nor young." The second group of listeners assigned a rating of two through eight to each speech sample corresponding to the perceived decade of life. The final group was asked to make a direct age estimation. The results for the first two listening groups revealed that values for both scaling tasks were directly related to chronological age. Furthermore, the third listening group evidenced an excellent ability to estimate age on a 70-year continuum. There was a correlation of +0.88 between mean perceived age and actual chronological age. Shipp and Hollien conclude:

> Our findings quantify an empirical impression that most people are able to estimate a talker's age from his voice, perhaps as a result of their constant confrontation with this task throughout their lives, i.e., when answering a telephone, listening to a radio, or overhearing the speech of an unseen talker (p. 709).

Given this high reliability in making direct age estimations, it is logical that there exists a hierarchy of acoustic cues that permits this judgment accuracy. Such an hypothesis led Ryan and Burk (1974) to investigate the primary perceptual and acoustic attributes that contribute to accurate estimates of a talker's age.

In the first of two experiments, Ryan and Burk reasoned that some subjects will elicit a highly consistent and reliable set of age estimates, regardless of the actual chronological age of the talker. Therefore, the first experiment was designed to identify only those talkers whose mean estimated age was judged accurately with a standard deviation of 6 years or less. Recordings for the 40 subjects who met these criteria were then presented to 18 trained speech pathologists who judged the presence or absence of 10 voice characteristics. In addition, five acoustic measures were obtained for each of the 40 samples (mean intensity level, words per minute, mean fundamental frequency, and standard deviation of fundamental frequency). The perceptual and acoustic data were then combined to form a pool of predictor variables for a stepwise multiple regression analysis in which actual chronological age served as the criterion. The results revealed that six of the predictor variables accounted for a multiple correlation of 0.96. Those variables were: 1) laryngeal air loss, 2) laryngeal tension, 3) voice tremor, 4) imprecise consonants, 5) slow articulation rate, and 6) mean fundamental frequency.

In reviewing these findings, Ryan and Burk (1974) noted that three of the most important predictors of age were related to laryngeal function. They suggested that aging may result in "an alteration in the fine control of vocal fold vibratory activity" (p. 190). It was also argued that some of the changes in speech function may have reflected the effects of age on higher neurological centers (e.g., upper motor neuron channels, cerebellum, etc.) that are responsible for control of peripheral structures.

SPEECH AND LANGUAGE CHANGES ASSOCIATED WITH NEUROLOGICAL DISEASE

It is beyond the scope of this chapter to provide an extensive review of speech and language pathologies associated with specific disturbances of the central nervous system. However, as mentioned previously, aging persons are particularly susceptible to such nervous system disorders and, hence, a brief overview of these problems seems warranted. Again, these disorders will be discussed with reference to the previously described model of language functioning developed by Noll (1972). Where possible, transcripts from the senior author's clinical files, which are representative examples of the various disorders, will be provided.

Disorders of Ideation

Disorders of ideation generally result from relatively severe diffuse central nervous system pathology. Such disorders often result from cerebral arteriosclerosis, brain atrophy, toxic reactions, Alzheimer's disease, Pick's disease, and so on. Clinically, patients with widespread disruption of brain function will evidence impairments of calculation, comprehension, learning potential, judgment, memory, and personal orientation—all of which are dependent upon cortical structures and associated pathways affected by the disease. Emotional responses are frequently elicited and may be inappropriate to the situation. As Busse (1959) has noted:

> The type and severity of the symptoms are not necessarily directly proportionate to the extent of the physiological disturbance, as they are often influenced by psychological patterns of long standing and the particular psychological state of the patient at the time the disorder develops (p. 367).

Following is an actual transcript of the language behavior of a 75-year-old female patient with intellectual deterioration:

Clinician: How do you feel today?
Patient: Upside down. (Prolonged laughter)
Clinician: (Showing the patient a picture) Can you tell me what you see in the picture?
Patient: Ah, it's a little girl with things on her rings and I don't know what that is up there. She's looking at me. Poor little . . . What's your name, honey?

Clinician: (Showing the patient five printed words) Can you read any of these words?
Patient: Huh?
Clinician: (Pointing to the word "man") What's this word here?
Patient: There ain't none in here. (Prolonged laughter) Am I sitting on one?
Clinician: Mrs. J., can you tell me what a robin is?
Patient: A robin . . . Dear me, I don't know what a robin means. I don't understand that . . . Oh yes, in the morning they are always singing. I remember that, but the rest of it I can't need. I don't need it.

Disorders of Symbolization

Aphasia, the term typically applied to problems of symbolization, is a very broad concept because the nature of these symbolic disturbances can be highly variable. The variability becomes quite apparent when considering the numerous attempts to classify aphasic involvements and the extensive terminology developed to describe specific problems. The most common pathology resulting in aphasic disturbances is a cerebral vascular accident primarily involving the middle cerebral artery, which nurtures the cortical areas largely responsible for symbolic functions. Of course, head traumas such as missile penetration can also result in symbolic disorders. In this chapter, only oral language disturbances are discussed. However, it must be recognized that many other breakdowns such as sensory recognition problems (agnosias), writing problems (agraphia), arithmetic difficulties (acalculia), reading disturbances (alexia), personality changes, and so on, accompany this disorder.

One common linguistic problem concerns a disturbance in *semantic* functioning. Many patients cannot comprehend the full meaning or significance of certain words. Related to this is the problem of *anomia,* in which the patient has difficulty evoking an appropriate word to express his or her thoughts. *Syntactic* breakdowns are also commonly observed among aphasic patients. Typically, there is omission of many function words (articles, conjunctions, prepositions, pronouns) as well as inflections indicating tense and number. Often, this speech is telegraphic in nature because only substantive words may be preserved. Following is a transcript of a 79-year-old male who was tested 2 years following a cerebral vascular accident. He exhibits both semantic and syntatic disturbances:

Clinician: (Showing the patient a picture) Tell me what you see in the picture.
Patient: Well, no . . . can't say.
Clinician: How about a little help? (Pointing to a man in the picture) What is this?

Patient: That's man.
Clinician: Good. (Pointing to a picture of a girl) What is this?
Patient: Girl . . . Running . . . father.
Clinican: Good. Mr. M., what does "leather" mean?
Patient: Oh . . . cow . . . uh . . . can't say.
Clinician: Can you tell me where we get leather?
Patient: Cow . . . uh . . . uh . . . horse.
Clinician: Good. What do we use leather for?
Patient: (Points to his shoes) Uh . . . feet . . . leather.

In cases of severe aphasic involvement, the patient may display *jargon* that consists of generally unintelligible sound combinations, though some normal inflection patterns may be preserved. Another rather severe disturbance is *paraphasia,* which may be defined as the substitution of an inappropriate sound sequence in the place of an appropriate utterance. Related to paraphasia is the development of *neologisms,* in which the patient develops a completely new word, the meaning of which may or may not be obvious. Following is an example of a 22-year-old who suffered an embolism following a war wound to the heart. Paraphasia and neologisms are apparent:

Clinican: Tell me what happened.
Patient: I won into the umy the sikty eight munch. An I won to O.C.S.
             March sixty nahn. Then I went ovoo to Nam an I wa oht in the
             firld and I got saht in the haht.
Clinician: Where else did you get shot?
Patient: In my owite ahm.
Clinician: Then what happened?
Patient: I was newin at this time and I suht twenty rounds won I was
             hot.

Often, patients with more global aphasic involvements will evidence a loss in the use of propositional language. This is a high level, creative language designed with a specific communicative intent. Non-propositional language is automatic and may involve expletives, cliches, or highly over-learned verbal sequences (counting, reciting the days of the week, reciting prayers, etc.).

Disorders of Translation

As mentioned earlier, lesions in Broca's area of the brain have been associated with the disorder of apraxia, which is characterized by an inability to program properly the motor adjustments required for speech. Johns and Darley (1970) described apraxia in the following way:

> . . . variability of phonemic production; unrelated and additive substi-
> tutions, repetitions, and blocks; groping through repeated efforts

toward right production; disturbances of prosody; and perseverative and anticipatory errors, more evident in tasks of reading and repeating then in spontaneous conversation—are alterations of volitional articulation which fit well within the generic term *apraxia* (p. 582).

The following sample, from the speech of a 65-year-old, post-stroke patient illustrates an apractic problem:

Clinician: Say the word "crysanthemums."
Patient: C . . . cr . . . uh . . . cay. I can't say it. I know what it means.
Clinician: Sure. I know you know what it means. It's just tough to get it out sometimes. Watch my mouth as I say "crysanthemums."
Patient: Cuhsansemums, crysansemems, crysanthemums . . . There I got it.

Disorders of Execution

A wide variety of neurological impairments may result in disturbances of control over the peripheral respiratory, phonatory, and articulatory movements required for speech. The generic term for these disturbances is *dysarthria,* which Darley, Aronson, and Brown (1969a) defined as "a group of speech disorders resulting from disturbances in muscular control over the speech mechanism due to damage of the central or peripheral nervous system. It designates problems in oral communication due to paralysis, weakness, or incoordination of the speech musculature" (p. 246).

These same investigators (Darley, Aronson, and Brown, 1969a; 1969b) conducted a perceptual evaluation of 212 patients with a variety of rather discrete neurologic involvements. They were able to identify unique speech patterns for six different types of dysarthria.

Flaccid Dysarthria Patients with lower motor neuron lesions (e.g., bulbar palsy, myasthenia gravis, Möbius syndrome) were classified as flaccid dysarthrics. The major identifying symptoms of this group were hypernasality, imprecise consonants, breathy voice, and monopitch. These characteristics are consistent with a neurologic involvement producing weakness and hyporeflexia.

Spastic Dysarthria A wide variety of problems such as infant cerebral palsy, multiple strokes, tumors, encephalitis, etc., can produce an upper motor neuron lesion involving damage to the pyramidal and extrapyramidal systems. Darley, Aronson, and Brown (1969a) discovered the following major speech deviations in patients with upper motor neuron lesions: imprecise consonants, monopitch, reduced stress, harsh voice, monoloudness, low pitch, slow rate, hypernasality, strained-strangled voice quality, and short phrases. These characteristics, subsumed under the term spastic dysarthria, fit well within the general pattern of spasticity, hyper-reflexia, and loss of skilled movement typical of upper motor neuron lesions.

Mixed Dysarthria Certain neurological conditions such as amyotrophic lateral sclerosis can result in a progressive degeneration of both the upper and lower motor neuron systems. The result is often a mixed dysarthric condition with characteristics of both flaccid and spastic dysarthria.

Ataxic Dysarthria Darley, Aronson, and Brown (1969a) noted that the cerebellum serves a regulatory function involving control of timing, range, force, and direction of peripheral movements. It was reasoned that cerebellar lesions would, therefore, affect these dimensions of speech production, and their perceptual research confirmed this hypothesis. They termed such speech disorders ataxic dysarthria and identified five major deviations characteristic of patients with cerebellar problems, including imprecise consonants, stress disturbances, irregular articulatory breakdown, distorted vowels, and harsh voice.

Hypokinetic Dysarthria In examining the symptoms of certain extrapyramidal lesions, Darley, Aronson, and Brown (1969a) observed a characteristic pattern of slowness, limited range of movement, and limited force of muscular contraction. The common disorder resulting in this symptom pattern is Parkinsonism, and perceptual analysis of the speech of patients with this disease revealed the following dimensions: monopitch, reduced stress, monoloudness, imprecise consonants, inappropriate silences, short rushes of speech, harsh and breathy voice. This pattern of speech deviations was termed hypokinetic dysarthria.

Hyperkinetic Dysarthria Extrapyramidal lesions can also result in movement disorders characterized by excessive speed, extensive movement ranges, and exaggerated muscle contraction. Patients with the disorder of dystonia exhibit some of these general symptoms. Muscle contractions are extensive; prolonged distorted limb and body postures are often observed. However, the movements are generally slow. Primary speech deviations characteristic of dystonia patients include imprecise consonants, distorted vowels, harsh voice, irregular articulatory breakdown, strained-strangled voice, monopitch, and monoloudness. This type of speech disorder may be termed a slow hyperkinetic dysarthria.

Another group of patients with choreas, which is also a disease primarily involving the extrapyramidal system, were observed to have very quick, irregular limb and body movements, often excessive in range with exaggerated contraction. Speech dimensions characteristic of this group were observed to be imprecise consonants, prolonged intervals, variable rate, monopitch, harsh voice, inappropriate silences, distorted vowels, and excess variations in loudness. This form of dysarthria may be termed quick hyperkinetic dysarthria (Darley, Aronson, and Brown, 1969b).

FUTURE TRENDS

After reviewing the normal degenerative processes, as well as the disease conditions that affect language and speech functioning of our geriatric population, it becomes quite obvious that a great deal more research is necessary. This research is particularly critical with reference to the normal aging process.

When speaking of the "normal" aging process, it becomes immediately apparent that there is no set of standard neurological changes that can be anticipated. There is certainly no one-to-one relationship between chronological and biological age. Many persons begin to exhibit substantial neurological change by the sixth and seventh decades of life, whereas others evidence few degenerative symptoms. Given the complexity and elegance of language functioning, it would appear that measures of expressive and receptive function may provide a sensitive index of the general level of biological activity. Therefore, future investigations should be aimed at defining "normal" functioning with cognizance of the frequent disparity between chronological age and biological activity.

There is a very limited understanding of possible subclinical language disturbances that may exist among older persons. It is quite possible that routine day-to-day communication by many older persons is not affected by the aging process. However, subtle syntactic, semantic, and/or programming problems may exist and future research efforts might focus on the development of diagnostic procedures designed to reveal these minor problems. Such tests might provide some predictive information concerning the nature of future deteriorations for a given person. Moreover, the discovery of subtle deficits may lead to the development of clinical intervention procedures that could help the patient to maintain a high level of functioning for as long as possible.

In addition, much more information is necessary to specify completely the language execution deviations characteristic of older persons. Whereas there is a growing body of evidence concerning acoustic and perceptual correlates of the aging voice, little attention has been directed to evaluation of physiologic function. Accordingly, future efforts might be directed toward the gathering of data concerning such parameters as aerodynamic functioning during speech, muscle activity characteristics, and vocal fold vibratory patterns as a function of age. Specification of the role of afferent information in speech production changes among aging persons is also necessary. Some preliminary published data by McDonald and Aungst (1967) concerning oral form perception evidenced decreased oral perceptual skills among aging persons. However, our knowledge is certainly limited in this area, and additional research is warranted.

SUMMARY

Most aging persons suffer a markedly reduced interpersonal communication network as the result of a loss of peers through death and the dispersion of family members. Unfortunately, at this critical time, their potential ability to broaden this network may be reduced by deteriorations in communication skill, not the least of which are deviations in oral language function. In this chapter, disturbances in ideation, symbolization, translation, and execution associated with "normal" degenerative processes have been presented. In addition, communicative disorders arising from neurological disease were reviewed. Our knowledge regarding oral language behavior in the geriatric population is definitely limited and much more research is necessary. Hopefully, this growing body of knowledge will permit a better understanding of the communication problems of older persons and will improve our ability to ensure that aging persons are provided a full and meaningful life.

ACKNOWLEDGMENTS

The authors would like to thank Dr. J. Douglas Noll, Department of Audiology and Speech Sciences, Purdue University; Dr. William J. Ryan, Audie Murphy Memorial Veterans Hospital, San Antonio; and Dr. Larry V. Sant, Department of Speech Pathology and Audiology, Idaho State University, for their assistance in the preparation of the manuscript. Thanks are also extended to Mrs. Diane Hutchinson for her secretarial efforts.

LITERATURE CITED

Appel, F. W., and E. M. Appel. 1942. Intracranial variation in the weight of the human brain. Human Biol. 14: 48–68.
Brody, H. 1955. Organization of the cerebral cortex. III. A study of aging in the human cerebral cortex. J. Comp. Neurol. 102: 511–556.
Busse, E. W. 1959. Psychopathology. In J. E. Birren (ed.), Handbook of Aging and the Individual, pp. 364–399. University of Chicago Press, Chicago.

Charlip, W. S. 1968. The aging female voice: Selected fundamental frequency characteristics and listener judgments. Unpublished doctoral dissertation. Purdue University, West Lafayette, Ind.

Darley, F. L., A. E. Aronson, and J. R. Brown. 1969a. Differential diagnostic patterns of dysarthria. J. Speech and Hearing Res. 12: 246–269.

Darley, F. L., A. E. Aronson, and J. R. Brown. 1969b. Clusters of deviant speech dimensions in the dysarthrias. J. Speech and Hearing Res. 12: 462–496.

Endres, W., W. Bambach, and G. Flösser. 1970. Voice spectrograms as a function of age, voice disguise, and voice imitation. J. Acoust. Soc. Amer. 49: 1842–1848.

Gardner, E. 1969. Fundamentals of Neurology. 5th Ed. W. B. Saunders, Philadelphia.

Halpern, H., F. L. Darley, and J. R. Brown. 1973. Differential language and neurologic characteristics in cerebral involvement. J. Speech and Hearing Dis. 38: 162–173.

Hollien, H., and T. Shipp. 1972. Speaking fundamental frequency and chronologic age in males. J. Speech and Hearing Res. 15: 155–159.

Hutchinson, J. M., and A. H. B. Putnam. 1974. Aerodynamic aspects of sensory deprived speech. J. Acoust. Soc. Amer. 56: 1612–1617.

Hutchinson, J. M., and R. L. Ringel. 1975. The effect of oral sensory deprivation on stuttering behavior. J. Commun. Dis. 8: 249–258.

Johns, D. F., and F. L. Darley. 1970. Phonemic variability in apraxia of speech. J. Speech and Hearing Res. 13: 556–583.

Jones, H. E. 1959. Intelligence and problem solving. In J. E. Birren (ed.), Handbook of Aging and the Individual, pp. 700–738. University of Chicago Press, Chicago.

Laird, C. 1962. The Miracle of Language. Fawcett Publ., Greenwich, Conn.

Luria, A. R. 1966. Higher Cortical Functions in Man. Basic Books, Consultants Bureau, New York.

McDonald, E. T., and L. F. Aungst. 1967. Studies in oral sensorimotor function. In J. F. Bosma (ed.), Symposium on Oral Sensation and Perception, pp. 202–220. Charles C Thomas, Springfield, Ill.

McGlone, R. E., and H. Hollien. 1963. Vocal pitch characteristics of aged women. J. Speech and Hearing Res. 6: 164–170.

Mysak, E. D. 1959. Pitch and duration characteristics of older males. J. Speech and Hearing Res. 2: 46–54.

Noll, J. D. 1972. Personal communication.

Putnam, A. H. B. 1973. Articulation with reduced sensory control: A cineradiographic study. Unpublished doctoral dissertation, Purdue University, West Lafayette, Ind.

Pribram, K. H. 1971. Languages of the Brain. Prentice-Hall, Englewood Cliffs, N.J.

Ptacek, P. H., and E. K. Sander. 1966. Age recognition from voice. J. Speech and Hearing Res. 9: 273–277.

Ptacek, P. H., E. K. Sander, W. H. Maloney, and C. R. Jackson. 1966. Phonatory and related changes with advanced age. J. Speech and Hearing Res. 9: 353–360.

Ryan, W. J. 1972. Acoustic aspects of the aging voice. J. Gerontol. 27: 265–268.

Ryan, W. J., and K. W. Burk. 1974. Perceptual and acoustic correlates of aging in the speech of males. J. Commun. Dis. 7: 181–192.

Scott, C. M., and R. L. Ringel. 1971. Articulation without oral sensory control. J. Speech and Hearing Res. 14: 804–818.

Shipp, T., and H. Hollien. 1969. Perception of the aging male voice. J. Speech and Hearing Res. 12: 703–710.

Taub, E., and A. J. Berman. 1968. Movement and learning in the absence of feedback. *In* S. J. Freedman (ed.), The Neuropsychology of Spatially Oriented Behavior, pp. 173–192. Dorsey Press, Homewood, Ill.

SUGGESTED READINGS

Canter, G. J. 1972. Changes in communication associated with aging. *In* Proceedings of the Conference: Orofacial Function: Clinical Research in Dentistry and Speech Pathology. ASHA Reports 7, pp. 26–32. American Speech and Hearing Assn., Washington, D.C.

Darley, F. L., A. E. Aronson, and J. R. Brown. 1969a. Differential diagnostic patterns of dysarthria. J. Speech and Hearing Res. 12: 246–269.

Darley, F. L., A. E. Aronson, and J. R. Brown. 1969b. Clusters of deviant speech dimensions in the dysarthrias. J. Speech and Hearing Res. 12: 462–496.

Eisenson, J. 1973. Adult Aphasia. Appleton-Century-Crofts, New York.

Halpern, H., F. L. Darley, and J. R. Brown. 1973. Differential language and neurologic characteristics in cerebral involvement. J. Speech and Hearing Dis. 38: 162–173.

Johns, D. F., and F. L. Darley. 1970. Phonemic variability in apraxia of speech. J. Speech and Hearing Res. 13: 556–583.

Luria, A. R. 1966. Higher Cortical Functions in Man. Basic Books, Consultants Bureau, New York.

Ryan, W. J., and K. W. Burk. 1974. Perceptual and acoustic correlates of aging in the speech of males. J. Commun. Dis. 7: 181–192.

chapter 10
Hearing Disorders in the Aging:
Effects upon Communication

Herbert J. Oyer, Ph.D.
Yash Pal Kapur, M.D.
Leo V. Deal, Ph.D.

Of all the sensory problems that afflict the older person, hearing impairment can be most devastating to the communication process. Surveys of hearing function have shown that, in the main, handicapping hearing loss is more frequently seen among men than among women at all age levels. It is a known fact that hearing loss in the population increases with increasing age. Estimates show that it is approximately 10 times as great in the older age group than it is among those in early adulthood.

OVERVIEW

When hearing loss occurs, it begins to interfere with social efficiency. The extent of the interference is in relation to the severity of the hearing loss that is sustained. If the hearing loss becomes severe the older person might well be forced out of oral communication situations, particularly if amplification through a hearing aid is not available, or does not seem to help.

Hearing loss in older persons is referred to as presbyacusis, and the deterioration causing presbyacusis may be a result of lesions in various parts of the auditory pathway. Presbyacusis is more or less taken for granted among older people here in the United States; however, it has been shown that in some primitive societies it does not exist. The lack of its appearance in some primitive societies has been attributed to the relatively low noise level in which people live, as well as to the differences that exist in the general diet and health.

With increased life span, it can well be expected that hearing loss will also increase substantially. With increased hearing loss together with the increased complexity of our society, it can also be expected that the problems attending hearing loss will also increase.

Data from the National Health Survey (National Center for Health Statistics, 1962–1963) show that the ratio of persons with hearing loss in both ears increases from 3.5 per 1,000 persons less than 17 years of age to 133.0 per 1,000 persons 65 years of age or older. Eighty percent of the persons sustaining hearing loss in two ears were 45 years of age or older. However, 55 percent of this group were 65 years of age or older.

As Senator Church pointed out (United States Congress, Senate, 1968) in his opening statement to the Subcommittee on Consumer Interests (a unit of the Senate Special Committee on Aging dealing with Hearing Loss, Hearing Aids, and the Elderly), the elderly are in greatest need of trained counsel and are three times more likely to have significant hearing loss than younger people. The Subcommittee directed its attention to three basic areas: 1) improvement of delivery of services to older people sustaining hearing loss, 2) sales of hearing aids to older persons, and 3) effects of increasing noise on future generations of older Americans.

The point made here is that the United States government has shown an interest in the extent of hearing loss among older persons. Furthermore, it has provided in various ways assistance to older persons in the support of programs of rehabilitation.

In a recent study made in Scotland by Milne and Lauder (1975), it was shown that the 487 older people studied showed increases in hearing loss in each frequency with increasing age, with hearing loss being greater for men than for women.

The terms employed by those dealing with the hearing handicapped to describe the extent to which hearing is defective are: 1) mild hearing loss, 2) moderate hearing loss, 3) severe hearing loss, and 4) deafness. The term *deaf* usually refers to a person who has been born deaf or has become deaf before the onset of language. The term *deafened* refers to a person who has lost her/his hearing after the development of language.

The older person who is deaf faces needs that are somewhat different from those older people who have become hard of hearing. In effect, their problems are compounded by the fact that they are deaf, for they do not have general access to the broadcast media and telephone communication as do other people. Their comfort and even their safety might be at stake because of not being able to hear someone's knock at the door or perhaps other kinds of warning signals—the blowing of an automobile horn, the shout of a person, or the barking of a dog.

In the chapter on Aging and Deafness in the 1971 Whitehouse Conference on Aging, it is pointed out that the deaf older person, unlike those who have become deaf, probably has not had the opportunity for educational, occupational, and social development. Since the disability is an invisible one, they are not readily taken care of by society as are those older people who have highly visible problems. The older deaf person, because of the communication problems associated with deafness, often cannot engage in the social, recreational, and other kinds of opportunities that are available to others. Their time is often spent in lonely, boring, and unproductive situations. Their ability to communicate and understand the very benefits that society provides for them is often impaired. Additionally, they have not had the opportunity, in most cases, to discuss problems that face older people and, therefore, are ill-equipped to meet those problems often handled quite well by those who have made adequate preparation for them.

THE WORLD OF SOUNDS

Sounds are all around us, and the lives of older people are so filled with sounds that most of them are probably taken for granted. There are the sounds of the television, the radio, traffic noise, dishes clattering, people talking, the telephone ringing, etc. Sometimes we begin to feel that our environment is so noisy that we would like to live in a world without sound. As pleasant as that might seem at times, we would find a noiseless world a very depressing one.

We hear any sound that reaches the ear above the threshold of hearing. Whether we listen to it is another matter. Because we are constantly bombarded with sounds, we tend to ignore those sounds that have little importance to us. In other words, we listen only to those sounds that have meaning or importance to us at the time. The humming of electric lights, the ticking of a clock, or even the sounds of our own bodies are generally ignored. We hear them, but do not necessarily listen to them unless they are brought to our attention or for some reason become important to us.

Yet, it is these sounds, as unimportant as they may seem, that keep us in touch with the world around us. We rely on sounds more than might be imagined. Have you ever stepped off a curb without looking both ways and yet felt safe in doing so? Without realizing it, we depend heavily upon the hearing of sounds. Touch, taste, smell, and movement are senses that give us information about things happening immediately around us; but sight and hearing give us information about things farther away. When these senses are diminished or lost, as is the case with many older persons, they might begin to feel out of contact with the environment. This seems to be especially true with the sense of hearing. It is possible to simulate a loss of sight by closing our eyes and thus gain some small appreciation of the problems of the blind. It is rare, however, that we can block out sound enough to simulate deafness. The sense of hearing is a continuous monitoring system that keeps us in contact with what is happening around us.

When an older person loses his hearing and can no longer hear these background sounds, he may begin to feel removed from the ongoing world. If he cannot hear his own body sounds, he may even feel out of contact with himself. Under such circumstances, the person may begin to question what is happening around him and to him; he may become suspicious of other people and of what they are saying "about him."

Sound, therefore, is important for self-protection and for identification with the environment. But sound has one other very important effect. It is essential for the normal acquisition and development of spoken language; for spoken language is learned by hearing others speak. A child must also compare his own speech sounds to the models he has heard. After speech is learned, kinesthetic feedback probably plays a major role in speech production; but the sense of hearing continues to be very important in monitoring spoken language.

The effects of hearing loss on language acquisition are obvious. The child who is born deaf must receive years of intensive training in order to produce spoken language. Even after years of training, the deaf may not approach normal speech. If speech has been learned before a hearing loss occurs, the effects on speech production will not be so great; nevertheless, the loss of the auditory monitoring system will probably have some effect on how speech is produced. Even though a person may not lose his hearing until he becomes older, speech production may still be affected. Although hearing loss related to the aging process is usually gradual, there can be definite effects upon the person's speech. At first, there may be few if any noticeable effects because the kinesthetic system may be the primary monitor; but gradually the precision of phonation and articulation may become affected. Qualitative aspects of speech such as nasal resonance may also be affected. But more important than the production of speech is the reception of speech.

An older person who sustains hearing loss may misunderstand what is said. When a person begins to recognize that he is not understanding what others say to him, he may try to guess the content of the message. If he guesses wrong, communication breaks down. The speaker may try to repeat the message; but he may resent having to do so. Additionally, the hearing-impaired older person may feel insulted or embarrassed because the speaker is repeating. Sometimes a hearing-impaired person may even begin to feel that people are talking behind his back or plotting against him. As a result of this ineffective communication, a hearing-impaired older person may feel out of contact with others in the environment; in fact, he may withdraw from interpersonal contacts.

In cases of presbyacusis, it often helps if the speaker increases the loudness of his voice to bring speech sounds above the hearing-imparied person's threshold of hearing. It is not unusual for older persons to ask a speaker to repeat the message; however, if the speaker repeats too loudly, the listener may say, "Well, you don't have to shout!" This common situation is probably the result of a condition called *recruitment*. Recruitment is an abnormal increase in loudness. Although it takes a louder sound to reach the person's threshold of hearing, once the threshold is passed, the sound may be perceived as loudly as though there were no hearing loss at all.

The pitch of sound is a factor in the hearing of older persons as well. Usually in presbyacusis, hearing is affected more in the high frequencies. While some sounds and words may be received and understood with little difficulty, other high frequency sounds, such as s, z, f, v, sh, and th, may present considerable difficulty.

The duration of sounds may also be a factor in the understanding of speech by older people. If loudness and pitch of speech are interfering with its comprehension, the hearing-impaired older person may need more time to sort out the information. Therefore, by speaking at a slightly slower rate one might help them to be more successful in comprehending spoken language.

MEDICAL ASPECTS OF HEARING DISORDERS IN THE AGING

Hearing, the sensory function that permits an organism to respond to the sound stimulus, is a means of contact between the organism and its environment. There are basically two systems: 1) the *peripheral*, which relays the sound, and 2) the *central*, or the brain with its neural pathways. The peripheral system is involved with the reception and perception of sound. The central system is involved with integration and with language, and the capacity to use auditory as well as visual symbols meaningfully. Efficient speech demands not only a good peripheral function but a good function of the central auditory pathways and the auditory centers in the brain.

Peripheral Auditory System: Anatomy and Physiology

The ear, the organ of peripheral hearing and equilibrium, is divided into the external, middle, and inner ear. Each of these is described below.

External Ear The external ear is composed of the auricle and the external auditory canal. The auricle is a fold of skin containing a cartilaginous framework and is fixed in position by muscles and ligaments. The cartilage of the auricle is continuous with that of the external canal. The auricle is not really important for hearing.

The external auditory canal in adults measures about 2.5 to 3.5 cm. The outer one third of the canal is formed in its outer one third by an extension of the cartilage of the auricle and in its inner two thirds by bone that is part of the temporal bone which houses the middle and inner ears. The bony external canal ends at the ear drum. The skin lining the outer third of the canal bears stiff hairs and secretes wax that, as a rule, protects the ear and keeps the ear canal and ear drum from drying out.

Middle Ear The middle ear includes the ear drum and the air-filled cavity behind it as well as its contents. The ear drum is composed of three layers, the outer layer of skin, an inner layer of the mucosal lining of the middle ear, and, except in its superior part, layers of fibrous tissue. The fibrous tissue gives the ear drum its shape and its tensile strength. The most prominent landmark in the ear drum is the handle of malleus, one of the three tiny bones in the middle ear. In the anterior and inferior part of the membrane is seen a light reflex. This light reflex is seen only during an examination of the drum and is the result of the reflection of the examination light from the wall of the middle ear. The middle ear space measures about 15 mm from above downwards and from side to side. The space is very narrow from side to side and is wider above and below. The inner or medial wall of the middle ear has two windows through which it communicates with the inner ear. The superiorly placed window is the oval window. The window below is the round window. There are three bones in the middle ear; they are called ossicles and form a chain from the ear drum to the inner wall of the middle ear. The largest bone that forms part of the ear drum is called the malleus, or "hammer." This connects with the middle bone, the incus or "anvil," which in turn is connected with the third bone, the stapes or "stirrup," which fits into the oval window and connects the middle ear with the inner ear.

This chain of small bones acts as a system of levers gaining an advantage in the force of the mechanical impulse transmitted from the ear drum to the inner ear fluid system.

Inner Ear The inner ear is called the labyrinth because of the complexity of its shape. It houses the sense organs involved with hearing and balance and is completely formed at birth. The inner ear consists of two parts, the osseous, or bony labyrinth, and a series of cavities filled with clear watery fluid. Lying in these cavities are a corresponding series of delicate fluid-filled membraneous canals and sacs and their supporting structures. These constitute the membraneous labyrinth.

The entire system is filled with fluid, that within the membraneous canal being endolymph and that between the membraneous and osseous canals being perilymph. The part of the inner ear concerned with hearing is called the cochlea. Its shape resembles a snail shell of two and a half turns. The canal within it is little over 35 mm long and ends blindly at the apex. The canal is divided into upper (vestibular) and lower (tympanic) parts. The vestibular part communicates with the oval window, and the tympanic part communicates with the round window. The division into these two parts is completed by a fibrous membrane, the basilar membraneous tube, which contains the sensory cells and their supporting structures known as the organ of Corti. This is rather a complicated structure. It is divided into an inner and outer portion by a tunnel composed of two rows of rods. These rods are called the inner and outer pillars of Corti. On the inner side of the inner pillar is a single row of hair cells referred to as the inner hair cells. On the outer side of the outer pillars are the outer hair cells. They form three or four rows. The hair cells are so called because of the cilia or tiny hair cells that project from their upper ends. A semi-solid structure called the tectorial membrane lies on the superior surface of the organ of Corti. The Reissner's membrane separates the space containing the organ of Corti (cochlear duct) from the scala vestibule. The basilar membrane separates the cochlear duct from the scala tympani.

The hair cells receive the termination of fibers of the auditory part of the eighth cranial nerve. The mechanical vibrations of the basilar membrane and the organ of Corti generate electric potentials (cochlear microphonics). These correspond in form and frequency to the mechanical activity in the inner ear. It is believed that the hair cells of the organ of Corti generate the cochlear microphonics. The high frequencies are associated with the base of the cochlea, and the low frequencies are associated with the apex of the cochlea.

Nerve impulses are set up in the auditory nerve as a result of cochlear microphonics. The auditory nerve fiber passes upward toward the lower part of the brain and enters the brain stem in the region of two cochlear nuclei, dorsal and ventral.

TYPES AND CAUSES OF HEARING LOSS IN THE ELDERLY

Hearing loss is of two general types, a conductive type and a sensorineural type. There may be an element of both types in a patient, and then the loss is called mixed.

Any impairment of the conduction of the sound impulse through the external ear canal, ear drum, or middle ear space can cause a conductive type of hearing loss. Any interference with the perception of the sound stimulus by the organ of Corti, auditory nerve from the organ of Corti to its connection to the brain stem, causes a sensorineural type of hearing loss.

The association of hearing loss with advancing age is proverbial. The main types of hearing disorders seen in the aging, inner ear or sensorineural impairment and central deafness or dysfunction, are described below.

Sensorineural Hearing Loss

Hearing impairment associated with advancing age, as stated at the outset of this chapter, is called presbyacusis. The auditory system, like all systems on the body, exhibits senescent changes with the passage of time. The time of onset and the rate of progression vary widely. The durability of the auditory mechanism, like other body systems, is determined in part by genetic factors and the physical stress to which it is subjected. Environmental factors such as noise and diet appear to play a role, and it is frequently difficult to distinguish between hereditary deafness and presbyacusis. The impairment in presbyacusis appears to involve mainly the high frequencies, i.e., over 2,000 Hz. Schuknecht (1974) describes three major types of presbyacusis.

Sensory Presbyacusis Sensory presbyacusis results from atrophy of the organ of Corti at the basal end of the cochlea and is manifested by abrupt high tone loss that begins in middle age. The condition progresses slowly, and the communication handicap is limited because the speech frequencies are not affected. The etiological factor appears to be caused by the aging process, as is seen by an accumulation of "wear and tear" pigment.

Neural Presbyacusis Neural presbyacusis may begin at any age, but its effect on hearing is manifested late in life. The degenerative changes seem to be controlled by genetic factors. There is loss of neuronal propulation in the cochlea. The end organ is not affected. This results in a characteristic loss of speech discrimination, which is relatively more severe than the hearing loss of pure tones. The progressive loss of speech discrimination in the presence of stable pure tone thresholds is termed phonemic regression (Gaeth, 1948). There may be associated degenerative changes in the central nervous system, such as other motor and sensory deficits. The communication problem is mainly in the understanding of speech and, because of the loss, poor speech discrimination patients with neural presbyacusis find amplification by hearing aids to be of limited value.

Strial Presbyacusis This type affects several members of a family. The onset of hearing loss is insidious, mainly in the third to sixth decades of life, and progresses slowly. The audiometric pattern is a flat hearing loss with good speech discrimination scores. These patients use hearing aids

with great benefit. It is called strial presbyacusis because of the pathologi-
cal changes seen in the striae vascularis, a set of blood vessels in the wall of
the cochlea. The tissue of the striae vascularis shows high metabolic
activity, and metabolic disorders are thought to affect the glucose metab-
olism which may be essential for cochlear function. Decreased blood
supply because of arteriosclerotic changes in the blood supply of the
cochlea may affect the metabolic activity in the stria vascularis and result
in atrophy of this area.

Central Deafness

Central deafness is caused by a lesion within the central auditory system in
the brain.

REHABILITATING THE OLDER PERSON WITH A HEARING LOSS

Because hearing loss interferes with communication, the principal purpose
of a rehabilitative program is to help the older person become a more
effective communicator. Some older persons are interested in programs of
aural rehabilitation, whereas others are not. Frequently, it is a concerned
spouse or other relative who brings the older person to an audiology clinic
for evaluation and rehabilitation. It has been observed by these authors
that the older person is not always eager to engage in such a program.
When this is the case, an attempt is made to show what the program might
do for them and proceed from that point. There seems to be a natural
"tuning out" phenomenon that occurs with some older people. Some do
not appear to be nearly as interested in hearing what is going on as the
younger ones around them are in having them hear what goes on.

Any program of rehabilition should be built upon diagnostic
findings. As mentioned earlier, the older person is frequently afflicted with
presbyacusis; when this occurs the perception of speech becomes impaired.
Additionally, the older person sometimes suffers a reduced capacity for
understanding spoken language. A number of years ago in the study made
of the speech discrimination skills of older people, Gaeth (1948) determined that some older people have great difficulty in discriminating the
elements of speech despite the fact that one would not predict this
problem on the basis of their pure tone audiometric test results. He found
that this "phonemic regression" was more frequently observed in persons
more than 50 years of age than in younger people. However, he also found
that many older persons with hearing losses did not have this difficulty.

The hearing aid has been of real help to many older people; unfortunately, a hearing aid does not always work very well for the older person

who is suffering from presbyacusis. The hearing aid simply makes sounds louder and does not necessarily assist the person in distinguishing or discriminating among speech elements. Therefore, other means of rehabilitation must be undertaken frequently to assist the older person who is having difficulty in aural communication. This is not to say that older persons do not benefit at all by a hearing aid, for many do receive substantial help from hearing aids. If, indeed, they do have a hearing aid or are counseled to buy one, there should be a period of hearing aid orientation in which they are helped to become thoroughly familiar with the operation of the aid for the various situations in which they will have to communicate.

One of the familiar approaches to be used in the hearing rehabilitation process is that of lipreading. Most people rely upon lipreading even though they do not have a hearing loss. Lipreading training for people with hearing loss must aim toward providing older persons with added information that they do not get simply from hearing alone. Not all people are good lipreaders even after training; however, even a little improvement can be quite valuable to the older person. Actually, the lipreading, or speech-reading as it is sometimes called, is an important supplement to the communication situation. Lipreading lessons can be interesting, particularly when they are focused upon the experiences and interests of the older person. Some sounds are harder to see, whereas other sounds are relatively easy to see. Many good practice books are available as aids in learning to lipread.

Another approach in rehabilitation is that of auditory training. The purpose of auditory training is to assist the person in utilizing residual hearing to the fullest extent. It is important that older persons understand the basic principles involved in the auditory training task. They should be informed of the reasons for doing the tasks through simple and clear explanations of the objectives set for them.

In a recent study, Alpiner (1973) states that the major reasons why older persons reject help in aural rehabilitation is apparently the lack of motivation. In general, the underlying attitudes were that there was no problem and, consequently, no necessity for an aural rehabilitation program. Also, there seemed to be a sense of hopelessness on the part of the older person and a suggestion that perhaps time would be better spent on younger people who have hearing problems.

As Harless and Rupp point out (1972), one of the major problems that confronts the older person is the cost involved in aural rehabilitation services. In some instances this is offered free, in others at a nominal cost.

taxes to finance education, which falls hardest on retirees living on fixed incomes that are steadily eroded by inflation.

In addition to the 80 percent living in their own homes, another 15 percent live in rooms. The remaining 5 percent live in institutions, with half of this group having chronic or complete disability.

Living arrangements for some older persons involve migration to warmer climates such as are found in the southeast and southwest. However, only about 10 percent move anywhere, and not more than one tenth of these move to another state. These proportions will rise, but migration is unlikely to affect most older persons in the near future.

IMPLICATIONS FOR EDUCATORS

From the above, it is clear that more elderly persons are living longer and with increased leisure, most are economically deprived, and most live in their own homes. These facts need to be borne in mind by educators.

"It is always in season for old men to learn," said Aeschylus, who lived and wrote until he was 81. The general theme of the recommendations from the first White House Conference on Aging, held in 1961, was that continuing education in a variety of settings be readily available to the elderly. The delegates also stressed the need for training in practical as well as academic subjects. Such recommendations were again urged at the second White House Conference on Aging, held in 1971.

Since the first White House Conference, a major development was the passage in 1966 of the Adult Education Act, creating the Adult Basic Education Program. The Federal government finances 90 percent of the program; the states fund 10 percent of the program and also administer it, mainly in the public schools. All persons 16 and over are eligible for instruction in subjects through the 12th grade level, including the three Rs, and speech and verbal comprehension.

The potential usefulness of such a program is attested by the fact that two thirds of Americans over 65 have had no schooling beyond the eighth grade, and one out of five cannot read or write competently. Yet it is well documented that age is inversely related to participation in continuing education: the older the person, the less likely to be engaged in any organized continuing education activity (Peterson, 1974). The United States Office of Education reported that in 1972 only 2.4 percent of persons 65 and older participated in adult education (Academy for Educational Development, 1974).

Apathy on the part of the aging only partly explains their present lack of participation in adult education programs. No unit of the federal government provides guidance or leadership in that field, and only a few state departments of education have a section devoted exclusively to adult education. Nor have leadership and stimulation come from most universities.

Some recent studies, however, offer data to suggest that an informal setting may be conducive to greater participation by the elderly in education. Only 7 percent of the aging respondents in a major study mentioned school as the place of their most recent instruction. Far higher proportions of the respondents mentioned the facilities of community, religious, and business organizations.

Among several encouraging developments in recent years are the growing number and scope of community colleges whose budgets provide for community services and continuing education. Television, mobile learning laboratories, and other modern techniques are also reaching the elderly in nursing homes or isolated areas.

Unfortunately, most continuing education is geared largely to educated middle and upper class groups. One way to increase the participation of the less affluent may be to provide practical courses concerned with daily living—instruction, for example, in consumer problems, employment opportunities, and leisure-time activities. In 1970, the President's Task Force on Education recommended that the Department of Education and the Administration on Aging work together to set up a new program to conduct research and offer local communities technical assistance on "education for continued living" (National Retired Teachers Association, 1971).

Even so cursory a review of the general situation of older persons in America does not suggest a reassuring profile. Although years have been added to their life expectancy, the added years for many persons are lived in actual or near poverty. While relatively few require total health care, for many persons the needed care is substandard. While many might benefit from continuing education, few find such programs readily available or sufficiently appealing. What can be drawn from, especially, this last point?

Howard McClusky (1971), longtime leader in the field of continuing education, points out:

> When we search the world of scholarship for "hard data" related to the education of older people, we emerge from our inquiry with several substantial impressions. First, such data on the education of older persons is extremely limited: obviously, this is a domain much neglected by educational research. Second, with respect to the amount of formal education attained, older persons are extremely disadvantaged. Third, rates of participation by the aging in activities designed for the education of adults are very low, in fact the lowest for all age segments

of the population. Fourth, the ability of older people to learn continues at a high functional level well into the later years, age, therefore, in itself, being no barrier to learning.

In brief, then, older people are for the most part seriously deficient in formal education, generally nonparticipant in educational activities, but at the same time capable of an educational response far greater than that offered by existing opportunities and presumably expected by the society (p. 9).

Older persons are usually good—often among the best—students, tending to have high motivation, clear goals, and good work-study habits. They do well and contribute much to the regular student body. Older students add a priceless dimension: seasoning. The possible physiologically related decrement in intellectual acrobatics is usually offset by increments of sagacity—wisdom, if you will. And their relationships with young students can be mutually productive and rewarding. Indeed, the young and the old can often communicate with relative ease and understanding. (There may be something to the old saw about grandparents and grandchildren getting along well: they have a common enemy!).

But the communication gap is not with these older persons who tend to be self-actualizing; they are among the 3 percent who identify and make use of offered educational programs. Rather, concern needs to be directed toward the other 97 percent, at least some of whom represent a viable educational constituency.

Among the reasons for difficulty in communicating with older persons these three may be primary:

1. The aging in the United States, in spite of a few conspicuous exceptions, no longer occupy the respected position characteristically held by the aging in most past and a few contemporary societies.
2. They have the dubious status of "retired" with no recognized function in our society.
3. They are not provided by our society with any sanctioned pattern of activities by which the transition from middle age to old age might be mediated.

The first reason will not easily or soon be resolved. The youth-oriented nature of American society is too strongly based in the frontier tradition, in which youth and vitality were highly valued. There is a strong reluctance to age, even gracefully. This is reflected in a common finding among interviewers: when older persons are asked the age when they believe people are old, it is usually about 10 years older than the respondent.

The second and third reasons, related to dubious retirement status and activity patterns, may be more amenable to change. For example, many current retirees were brought up during the early 1900s, with a Puritan background and the concomitant view that leisure is idleness and idleness is sinful. For some, a kind of residual guilt inhibits their full enjoyment of leisure.

Increasingly, this concept of leisure being sinful is yielding to healthier attitudes in which leisure is valued as productive, creative, or plain restful. Associated with this development is likely to be a more flexible view of retirement as an integral part of the life continuum, rather than an isolated and set-apart period of decline.

It needs to be recognized that aging is a continuous process rather than a series of steps or phases, and that older people share with all people basic needs and desires, although these may differ in degree and expression at different ages. Apart from a guaranteed minimum income, the ordinary person needs the assurance that he will be helped when he finds himself in unusual difficulty, whether physical, emotional, or social. Furthermore, he requires the stability that comes from moving in a reasonably familiar world, that is, a world in which he is not exposed to unknown risks and where he knows and is preprared to meet the everyday social expectations. Related to these, he must feel he is contributing something of recognized value to others. These are the basic components of a contented life for older people as well as for others.

Experiences that threaten the security of older people have become closely associated with aging in American society. The older person's efforts to meet his continuing needs and desires are often modified by the social limitations of his retirement role. These factors, perhaps more than the simple passing of time, contribute to older adults being a group apart.

What this means for those who communicate and work with older persons is clear. Older persons need and want to be considered very much like others. And, because of social restrictions, they need special consideration as well. Persons are needed, then, who can be helped to communicate and work more effectively with people generally and with older persons particularly.

WORKING WITH OLDER PEOPLE

We are here assuming that some form of training in human relations is required for effective work with people and that, in addition, work with older people poses special demands. The specifics of the special training will be related to the worker's particular area of service: education, medicine, audiology, social work, recreation, and the other professions and disciplines concerned with effective communication with older persons.

It is not appropriate here to consider training needs in the various fields concerned with older persons, except to note that much is basic in all fields; for example, it might generally be accepted that one could not work with optimum effectiveness in any program for older people without some appreciation of the physical, intellectual, social, and emotional effects and implications of the aging process.

In this discussion of preparation for effective work with older persons, we shall continue to consider some of the implications for adult and lifelong education. Potentially, because of such factors as increasing leisure time, older persons can be among the major "consumers" of education. This requires substantial commitment to the concept of lifelong education, and rests on the willingness and ability of educators and institutions to change, adapt, innovate, and communicate. The track record to date, particularly in colleges and universities, has not been impressive. Lip service, rather than implementation, has been the rule. However, interest in and pressure for development of viable programs of lifelong education have been mounting during the past few years, and a growing number of institutions is becoming more than superficially responsive.

With educational institutions beginning to accept the appropriateness of increasing responsibility concerning problems and opportunities in aging, their role in the preparation of workers to develop and carry out programs for older persons becomes of first importance. The shortage of trained persons in all fields for work with older persons is steadily increasing as more services are developed for growing numbers of older persons. Efforts to meet this expanding need are being made by universities and other agencies, but often on a sporadic and expedient basis. Many universities offer workshops, institutes, or one or two courses entirely concerned with aging, usually in schools of social work and medicine and occasionally in such departments as education, sociology, and psychology. Most universities offer courses in which there is some concern with aging. A few have a particular department or division with a major program in aging.

Along with the pressing need for universities and colleges to develop course offerings in aging, there must be increased concern with comprehensive training programs. Individual courses are important, but the magnitude of the problem and the continuing growth of inquiry and knowledge in gerontology demand more organized attention. Training programs in gerontology, as distinct from single courses, exist in a relatively small number of universities. Whether or not the degree is offered in gerontology does not seem crucial. In some universities, perhaps an existing department or school can best develop and coordinate this kind of program. In other institutions, an interdepartmental arrangement may be most suitable. Whatever the administrative and organizational framework, the need for well integrated and functional training programs, premised upon sound intra and interdepartmental communication, is with us; largely, this need is not being met.

In this connection, a most promising development was the establishment in 1974 of the Association for Gerontology in Higher Education (AGHE), an association in which membership is by institution and each institution is entitled to one vote. From an ad hoc group of a few interested colleges and universities, AGHE has grown in 2 years to a participating membership of over 70 institutions. The Association's purposes are summarized in its prospectus (1975):

> To unite in a common organization educational institutions which provide for professional education and training, research, and technical assistance in the field of gerontology and to provide a network of communication among such institutions; to promote and encourage the proper education and training of individuals preparing for careers in the field of gerontology and to increase the awareness of the general public to the need for such education and training; and to provide a forum which will enable its membership to exchange ideas and knowledge which will serve to advance the field of gerontology in higher education.

Role of Continuing Education

The potential role of education, specifically of continuing education, is crucial for future developments in preparing for work with older people. More programs for older people will need to be developed as an integral part of continuing education emphasis. Leaders for these programs must be trained, and it is not a task that can be carried more appropriately under auspices other than those of continuing education.

The skills and attitudes characteristic of continuing education work in other areas are, in fact, especially relevant to work with older people: enabling persons as individuals and as members of groups to grow in interest and productiveness; helping persons to become more effective and comfortable within themselves and in their relationships with others; tapping and fostering latent or laid-aside abilities; opening new or untried gates to knowledge and know-how; establishing a social and emotional climate that motivates the person to explore and try to meet his needs for security, status, and independence.

These are some of the goals of continuing education, and they have particular significance for work with older persons. Using oneself in ways that enable people to move toward such goals is essentially learned behavior—given such fundamentals as liking for and faith in people, and ability to relate to and communicate with others.

Basic Principles

At this stage, it is impracticable to try to reduce the problem of training to specifics: such and such a course or program is needed, for example. The range of variables such as needs, purposes, facilities, and personnel is too vast. But at least some underlying concepts and principles can be identified. It is becoming increasingly clear that in all education of professional and related personnel there should be emphasis upon broad general principles and understanding underlying the professional field as opposed to preoccupation with technical skills.

It is not necessary to underline the particular relevance of these concepts for continuing education. Translating them into programs cannot be thought of in terms of any one approach or set of approaches. The requirements might involve many of the disciplines and professional fields concerned with problems and opportunities in aging; the framework might well be that of continuing education. On the foundation of sound training in a particular discipline or professional field, heightened awareness of the effects and implications of aging needs to be a goal. There is some incorporation of this within graduate education in several fields, but much of it is carried on in sporadic and uneven fashion. A great deal more will need to be done at the level of formal education.

However, for some time to come much training for work with older people will probably take place after the period of full-time education. Hence, the growing significance of institutes, workshops, and evening courses. Through these media, training programs focused on helping workers become more aware of and able to cope with material and nonmaterial needs of the aging and premised on the concepts mentioned earlier could be among the most important educational services.

The specific subject matter for these training programs is beyond the scope of this chapter and would, as already mentioned, be conditioned by factors such as needs, purposes, facilities, and personnel. Broadly speaking, it might be recognized that such programs should be offered to persons who genuinely like and want to work more effectively with older people. Related to the frustrations and intolerances faced by many older people in our society is their expectation of being exploited, rebuffed, or ignored. This tends to make work with them a demanding experience requiring special understanding, patience, and skill in establishing effective communication and in fostering a helping relationship, whether it be with the older person as an individual or as a member of a group. On these bases, knowledge and know-how with respect to older people can be approached with more assurance.

Knowledge might well begin with the interpretation of aging as a normal and continuing life process, rather than as a succession of biological, psychological, and social difficulties. It needs to be concerned with the implications of aging in our culture in terms of social and emotional adjustment and with respect to the special needs, aspirations, and frustrations of older people. There should be consideration of available resources for meeting such needs. The program should enable the worker to understand aging as a process rather than as a condition and to see problems stemming from this process in the larger context of American society rather than as distinct entities.

A training program's concern with know-how needs to be intimately bound up with its concern with knowledge. Know-how is not simply a matter of techniques, although these are important. In genuinely effective work with people of any age group, techniques must emerge from helping attitudes, such as basic respect for the inherent dignity and worth of each person, nonjudgmental acceptance of persons whose behavior and beliefs may be different or deviant, and appreciation of human behavior as adjustment-seeking; and such attitudes must be communicated clearly.

Know-how, in work with people in groups, rests primarily on the ability of the worker to help individuals *become* a group. This requires an investment, an identification of self with the purposes of the group, which initially may be especially difficult for older people. The worker's role here in enabling the group's members to "find their feet" socially and emotionally, to become free to communicate and relate with others, is of cardinal importance and requires all his skill and understanding in human relations.

The worker, then, needs the kind of training program that will support and build upon an already solid basis of understanding and acceptance of people, with a particular interest in work with older people. He needs help in using himself effectively with older people, in recognizing their needs, desires, and limitations, in enabling them to become more satisfied with their personal lot and more able in their social relationships.

These are fundamentals in work with all people, and perhaps especially with older people. Specific ways through which these are implemented, such as discussion forums, arts and crafts, and courses, are important but subsidiary. They are the avenues of expression, but the dynamics of enabling people to move and grow are the motivating forces without which these avenues will not be traveled with optimum benefit.

FUTURE TRENDS

Some educational implications have been identified in this chapter, and the crucial importance of preparation for working effectively with older people considered. If we accept as a premise the emerging commitment of educational institutions to the concept of lifelong education, where, then, are we headed?

Developing educational trends are encouraging in that they seem to be moving more surely and dynamically in both traditional and nontraditional directions. Perhaps a major milestone is the gradual achieving of academic as well as societal respectability on the part of gerontological studies and programs. Educational institutions at every level are becoming involved in offering programs concerned with aging and retirement, as are other agencies such as libraries, museums, churches, park and recreation departments, business firms, labor unions, and voluntary and community organizations. A clear inference is the heightened need for these institutions and agencies to communicate such developments effectively, both to their publics and to their organizational colleagues.

Acting for the Administration on Aging, the Adult Education Association of the United States recently summarized findings from questionnaires returned by 3,500 agencies reporting learning opportunities for older persons. DeCrow (1975), who carried out the study, reported that 58 percent of these agencies had begun new activities within the preceding 12 months:

> Overwhelmingly, the learning opportunities are practical in intent, relatively simple in content, and surprisingly similar in all the many disparate kinds of agencies reporting. This similarity . . . shows the natural tendency everywhere to start first with the most apparent needs of the most available parts of the new audience and to serve them by the easiest adjustments of already operational adult education programs. Nonetheless, we see also many examples of innovative programs and serious planning in some agencies for more powerful involvement and more meaningful services in the future . . .
>
> Hobbies and recreation, consumer education, health related subjects, home and family life, personal development—these are the popular subjects in almost every agency serving the older population. Some senior citizens are enrolled in academic programs, ranging from basic education and literacy through the most esoteric and advanced studies imaginable . . . Some are learning through training for voluntary personal or community service. A few, very few, are learning small appliance repair or other skills with a view of paid employment . . . In general, despite some unique special interests, the learning needs of older adults are diverse and not much different from those of the rest

of us. One highly observable trend is an almost frenzied outburst of preretirement programs, a sudden recognition of the importance of planning ahead (p. 6).

The Academy for Educational Development (1974) conducted a comparable study of 300 colleges, universities, and community colleges to determine the available educational opportunities for older Americans. Special attention was given to programs that help older people remain active and involved in their communities. On the basis of this study, the Academy estimated that less than one fourth of all colleges and universities in the United States were offering special courses or services for older people. At the same time, the Academy noted that the interest of postsecondary institutions in older people is increasing, with some already embarked on creative experiments. Burgeoning strength and extension of the concept of lifelong education was identified by the Academy (1974) as a primary influence in this growth:

> Because of the recent trend toward lifelong learning . . . a small but growing number of colleges are creating special education programs for older people. These programs range from free or reduced tuition in regular undergraduate, graduate, or continuing education courses, to classes and other services created specifically for the needs of the elderly. Within this last category, the Academy has identified some principal characteristics, many of which overlap, but all of which suggest considerations for future program planners:
>
> Courses on a residential or on-campus basis
> Outreach courses in convenient off-campus locations
> Peer group instruction in localities that have large pools of well-educated retired professionals
> Comprehensive educational programs in geographic areas that have high concentrations of older citizens
> Preretirement planning before the often traumatic transition into a new lifestyle
> Educational vacations on college campuses
> Consortia of institutions to maximize resources
> Supplementary services, such as health, transportation, or counseling
> Mass media instruction and information (TV, radio, newspapers, and magazines)—public and commercial—tailored especially for an older audience
> Manpower training for personnel working with the aged
> New careers and retraining for older people

The "new careers" approach, offering counseling, preparation, and/or placement in a paid or volunteer position, is one of the most interesting yet least explored areas. Many older people do not want to retire only to leisure. They want to keep active and involved. And if ways can be found to direct them into meaningful and useful roles, society can profit greatly from their valuable skills and experience (pp. vi–vii).

It is clear that the nation's institutions of higher education have space to accommodate older people and resources with which to help them become more involved, and thus welcome and needed, in their communities. It seems equally clear that bringing older people and educational resources together is a major trend of the future, an ultimate affirmation of the principle of lifelong education.

SUMMARY

While the number and proportion of older persons in America have been growing, their social situation has been deteriorating. In a youth-oriented society, with concomitant emphasis on economic productivity, their status and influence have steadily diminished. Yet, a prevailing stereotype of older people as unhappy, ailing, withdrawn, and reactionary is incompatible with the facts. Although many older persons are economically deprived, the majority report themselves as reasonably satisfied with life—including retirement—and interested in being active and involved. For a growing number of these persons, education could help to move interest toward fulfillment.

Once considered an experience usually concluded in the teens or, for some, in the early twenties, education is increasingly regarded as continuing throughout the lifespan. The relevance of educational opportunities for older persons is evident. Because of factors such as available leisure, older persons can be among the major "consumers" of education. To date, however, relatively few older persons have found continuing education programs readily available or sufficiently appealing. Their participation in programs offered in more informal settings such as community, religious, and business organizations tends to be higher but still involves the minority.

A growing body of data reinforces the conviction that age, in itself, is no barrier to learning, and that many older persons could be drawn into formal and/or informal educational programs that are relevant, absorbing, and accessible.

Working with older people in educational and other programs requires commitment and preparation. For such work, persons are needed who can be helped to function and communicate more effectively with people generally and with older persons particularly. In the educational field, this rests in part on the willingness and ability of educators and institutions to change. Although slow in gaining momentum, interest in and pressure for development of viable programs of lifelong education have been mounting.

Developing educational trends are moving progressively in both traditional and nontraditional directions, with gerontological studies and programs achieving academic and societal respectability. While many learning opportunities for older persons tend to be retreads of already operational adult education programs, an increasing number of innovative and experimental efforts is surfacing. Clearly, alignment of educational resources with older people's interests and needs is with us. Its continuing development in the immediate years ahead will give meaning and implementation to the concept of lifelong education.

RECOMMENDATIONS

Perhaps an essential recommendation with respect to lifelong education and the aging is simplistic: for those institutions not yet involved, get under way with planning and development; for those already under way, keep testing the limits and plumbing the possibilities. For all institutions and organizations, involve older people in planning, development, and implementation. They are our constituency and can become helpful and productive in their and our interests.

There will always be need for the kinds of "standard" courses and programs usually developed for older persons. Hopefully, there will be broadening use of innovative, experimental, nontraditional experiences. These are emerging across the country, but tend to be limited by inadequate funding. More money is usually a routine and sometimes an irresponsible recommendation, but in this instance it is crucial. A modest fraction of the budgetary allocations required for educational programs at earlier years, would extend the possibility of comparable progress across the life continuum.

Such progress will be accelerated as more gerontological programs move beyond disparate course offerings toward the development of multidisciplinary centers in which an institution's resources—scholarly, fiscal, and spatial—can be brought together in the academic and societal interests and needs of older persons.

Along with the growth of innovative educational experiences, it is necessary for knowledge of these to become available to other experimenters. At present, such programs are being established with little or no knowledge of comparable developments elsewhere. Particularly in view of limited resources and the urgent need for viable programs, knowledge gained in one project needs analysis and circulation to others. Although a few nation-wide studies have been carried out by educational organizations, there is no agency or association, educational and/or governmental, to collect, assess, and disseminate information about experimental projects on a continuing basis. Such an agency should be established.

A few existing programs in several areas of the country have become known as highly effective in fulfilling their mission. It would be useful for these to be studied intensively to determine, for example, why and in what ways they are successful, and the extent to which these factors might be applicable to other settings.

A final recommendation is essentially a premise: namely that productive formal and informal educational programs involving older people in teaching-learning situations best develop within a frame of reference characterized by effective communication, creativity, and concern. This frame of reference should guide working relations between and among educational institutions, and particularly between the institutions and the older population they seek to serve.

These are minimal needs, but their addressing and resolution are fundamental to forward movement. The realization of effective and lifelong learning and living is a right and a hope, expressed poignantly by McClusky (1974):

> In brief, then, what we have been proposing is that the last of life at its best should be a guide for education at all the earlier stages of life leading thereto. When, as, and if this thesis is effectively internalized and implemented it will produce a transformation of the goals, processes, and programs of the entire educational enterprise, both formal and informal, from the beginning to the end of life (pp. 353–354).

LITERATURE CITED

Academy for Educational Development. 1974. Never Too Old to Learn, pp. vi–vii, 9–19. Academy for Educational Development, New York.

Association for Gerontology in Higher Education. 1975. Prospectus, p. 4. AGHE.

DeCrow, R. 1975. New Learning for Older Americans: An Overview of National Effort, p. 6. Adult Education Association of the United States, Washington, D.C.

McClusky, H. Y. 1971. Education: Background and Issues, p. 9. White House Conference on Aging, U.S. Government Printing Office, Washington, D.C.

McClusky, H. Y. 1974. Education for aging: the scope of the field and perspectives for the future. In S. Grabowski and W. D. Mason (eds.), Learning for Aging, pp. 353–354. Adult Education Association of the United States, Washington, D.C.

National Retired Teachers Association-American Association of Retired Persons. 1971. The 1971 White House Conference on Aging, The End of a Beginning? pp. 47–48. NRTA-AARP, Washington, D.C.

Peterson, D. A. 1974. The role of gerontology in adult education. *In* S. Grabowski and W. D. Mason (eds.), Learning for Aging, p. 48. Adult Education Association of the United States, Washington, D.C.

U.S. Department of Health, Education, and Welfare. 1961. Education for Aging. Reports and Guidelines from the White House Conference on Aging. U.S. Government Printing Office, Washington, D.C.

SUGGESTED READINGS

Academy for Educational Development. 1974. Never Too Old to Learn. Academy for Educational Development, New York.

Andrews, E. 1972. A Survey of Educational and Informational Needs of Older People Living in the Schoolcraft College District. Institute of Gerontology, University of Michigan, Ann Arbor.

Birren, J. E., and D. S. Woodruff. 1973. A life-span perspective for education. NYU Ed. Quart. 4: 25–31.

DeCrow, R. 1975. New Learning for Older Americans: An Overview of National Effort. Adult Education Association of the United States, Washington, D.C.

Eklund, L. 1969. Aging and the field of education. *In* M. W. Riley, J. W. Riley, and M. Johnson (eds.), Aging and Society, Volume II: Aging and the Professions, pp. 324–351. Russell Sage Foundation, New York.

Grabowski, S., and W. D. Mason (eds.). 1974. Learning for Aging. Adult Education Association of the United States, Washington, D.C.

Hendrickson, A. (ed.). 1973. A Manual on Planning Educational Programs for Older Adults. Department of Adult Education, Florida State University, Tallahassee.

Hesburgh, T., P. Miller, and C. Wharton. 1973. Patterns for Lifelong Learning. Jossey-Bass, San Francisco.

Heyman, D. 1975. Community and Junior Colleges: Education and Training for Work with the Elderly. Center for the Study of Aging and Human Development, Duke University, Durham, N.C.

Hiemstra, R. P. 1972. Continuing education for the aged: a survey of needs and interests of older people. Adult Education 22: 100–109.

Hixson, L. E. 1969. Non-threatening education for older adults. Adult Leadership 18: 84–85.

Houghton, V., and K. Richardson (eds.). 1974. Recurrent Education: A Plea for Lifelong Education. Ward Lock Educational Association for Recurrent Education, London.

Hunter, W. W. 1973. Preparation for Retirement. Institute of Gerontology, University of Michigan, Ann Arbor.

Jacobs, H. L. 1970. Education for aging. *In* A. M. Hoffman (ed.), Daily Needs and Interests of Older People, pp. 380–398. Charles C Thomas, Springfield, Ill.

Jacobs, H. L., W. D. Mason, and E. Kauffman. 1970. Education for Aging: A Review of Recent Literature. Adult Education Association of the United States, Washington, D.C.

Kauffman, E. 1969. The Older Adult as a University Student. Council on Aging, University of Kentucky, Lexington.

Korim, A. 1974. Older Americans and Community Colleges: A Guide for Program Implementation. American Association of Community and Junior Colleges, Washington, D.C.

Londoner, C. A. 1971. Survival needs of the aged: Implications for program planning. Aging and Human Development 2: 113–117.

McClusky, H. Y. 1971. Education: Background and Issues. White House Conference on Aging, Washington, D.C.

Michigan State University Task Force on Lifelong Education. 1973. The Lifelong University. Michigan State University, East Lansing.

Peterson, D. A. 1975. Life-span education and gerontology. The Gerontologist 15: 436–441.

Sarvis, R. E. 1973. Educational Needs of the Elderly: Their Relationships to Educational Institutions. Edmonds Community College, Lynnwood, Wash.

Spinetta, J. J., and T. Hickey. 1975. Aging and higher education: The institutional response. The Gerontologist 15: 431–435.

Swack, L. G. 1975. Continuing education and changing needs. Social Work 20: 474–480.

U.S. Department of Health, Education, and Welfare. 1973. A Trainer's Guide to Androgogy: Its Concepts, Experience, and Application. U.S. Government Printing Office, Washington, D.C.

Weg, R. B. 1975. Educational intervention and gerontology: An integration. The Gerontologist 15: 448–451.

Wray, R. P. 1970. Institutions of higher education as a resource for a state-wide continuing education program in gerontology. Adult Leadership 19: 156–158.

chapter 12
Legal and Public Policy Problems in Communication Arising with Aging

Thomas A. Muth, J.D., Ph.D.

Relationships among communication, aging, and law have generally not been the subject of study or analysis. Literature in the fields of gerontology, law, and communication sometimes provides oblique reference to possible interrelationships that may exist, but studies directly addressing the general legal problems in communication arising with aging have not been found.

This is not surprising because few studies of correlations between the processes of communication and aging are found in social and general science literature. Additionally, the body of common law concerning aging persons is not well developed and usually found in isolated circumstances. Furthermore, legal and policy analysis of communication is a relatively new and dynamic field, and the analysis of law from the standpoint of communication theory is just beginning. As a consequence, any attempt to examine the coincidence of the three fields must be necessarily general if not somewhat cavalier.

Indeed, this chapter presents generalized jurisprudential considerations concerning communication and the communication process that are implied in the aging of mature adults in the United States. This chapter is an attempt to relate some general findings in social, behavioral, and general science, in the area of geronotology and communication, to law and public policy, and to raise questions suggesting courses for further research.

OVERVIEW

It is fairly certain that the ability to communicate is one of man's rather unique attributes. It is learned in childhood and seems to change throughout one's life. Changes in communicative ability in later life may alter the attitudes and behaviors of a person or in some circumstances produce dysfunction.

As with all systems, communication tends toward entropy and disorganization (Von Bertalanffy, 1968; Barnlund, 1968). However, intervention by human action continuously restructures communication so that common meanings and ends remain somewhat constant (Reusch and Bateson, 1968). Over time, individual biological systems age and likewise deteriorate, and similar entropy and disorganization in the communicative capabilities of the person arise.

During one's lifetime, there seems to be a tendency to communicate to learn. But as time passes and life ebbs, the goals of communication may change. New information may be less important, old information may suffice. Ultimately, individual communication ceases with death, except for records and intrapersonal memories about the deceased.

Many societies inform the young and seek informed wisdom from the aging. Technologically based societies have concluded that formal education of the young is vital and have imposed it as a legal right and duty. The rise of technology has established a need to process increasing quantities and varied qualities of dynamic information. Change and the rate of change tend to dominate the character of vital information for the society, and old information seems to be of less consequence.

The complexity of contemporary society is resulting in basic changes in institutions legally designated communicate information. Where education formally imparted information to the young for future individual and societal benefit, it is becoming regarded as a continuing and lifelong process. It should be recalled that laws related to education originally sought to ensure basic literacy in societies. Later, it was seen as the duty of education to generally maintain and develop information and to train people for careers to benefit society. The current thrust toward lifelong education may be understood as an effort to ensure that all age groups are sufficiently informed to cope with and share in maintaining the social fabric.

Maintenance of society in the United States has generally fallen to persons in their middle years of life. Such people are generally at the height of productive careers, in tune with the social dynamic, and equipped with the physical ability to process and store substantial new and old information. Persons in middle life are in constant communication with their chronological peers, and their pre-eminence of authority in society depends largely upon knowledge of social inner workings gained through communication with authoritative peers.

As the middle years pass and people come to the end of active careers, new information concerning work occupations becomes less critical. As careers terminate with retirement, the need for work-related information ends and, unless goals attuned to retirement have been identified, the need and purpose for communication become obscure (Loeb, 1973). Indeed, retirement often signals the end of communication with general society. In technologically developed societies such as the United States, retired persons seem to have no functional role. They are thought to need rest, sleep, quiet, and the absence of conflict for the balance of their lives (Cowgill, 1974). Such assumptions ignore the experience in many less technically orientated societies in which aged persons are taken as the principal source of wisdom. The essence of their daily experience lies in decision making for the society. In this capacity they are constantly presented with new information upon which they must make judgments.

In contrast, in the United States, an attitude has developed that relegates older persons to pre-established, nonfunctional roles. This attitude concludes that the end of the middle years of life terminates the potential for contribution of aging persons. They are generally left alone to live out a presumed dotage. They are excluded from communicative exchange when they lose a place to work. They lose old friends through death. And, as travel becomes more difficult with their advancing years, they tend to lose the opportunity to communicate with persons of their chronological age group and with the larger society as a whole. They are made to become dependent on others for transportation when they want to communicate. They may move to a center providing living quarters and special services for aging persons, but usually such facilities are well beyond the finances of most aging persons. Consequently, attitudes and practices in the United States are systematically forcing aging persons into isolation and defenselessness.

The aging become more isolated as their latter years pass, and their potential to affect the society becomes obscure and is perhaps lost. To the extent that they are isolated and without communicative potential, the aging can neither express their individual and group needs nor observations that might benefit the larger society. In their isolation, they cannot establish communities of interest they may have with other aging persons. In remaining outside social groupings based upon mutuality of interests, they tend to become burdens on society.

If, however, the society can guarantee the absence of discrimination in communication based upon age, aging persons might exchange information leading to common bonds with other aging persons in like or similar circumstances. They then may have the potential to identify a mutuality of interests that leads to common defense and self-reliance. If the class of aging persons can communicate with their peers, group actions for resolution of common problems are implied. If aging persons are accorded basic protection for unreasonable discrimination in communications simply because of age, the attitude of society toward aging might change. If the society can encourage and support measures that will enhance communication concerning aging and aging persons, it is likely that a political consensus will develop to avoid destitution and loss for the aging, aging persons, and society as a whole. Given adequate communication, aging persons might resume dialogue among themselves and with the larger society.

AGE AS A LEGAL STANDARD

Age has been used in law as an index to a standard of performance anticipated in people.[1] This generally assumes the context of functional age based on biological development. However, in modern society, formal age based upon chronology has assumed increasing importance (Clark and Anderson, 1967).

Age alone is most frequently used in the interests of justice to vary the application of legal standards as related to children. Recently, both functional and formal age have been considered in the broadcast field to vary standards for programming addressed to children from those applied to adults (Comstock and Rubinstein, 1972).

Children of "tender years" have been accorded considerable deference in common law courts for a century or more. Doctrines such as the "attractive nuisance" in torts, policies on the status of children's testimony, and special criminal standards for youth have established a climate favoring varied consideration for children based upon their age and experience. In this context, both functional and formal age are considered.

Legislation in the Anglo-American system has also established special treatment for persons of younger ages in areas such as labor, contracts, and estates. Today, a considerable body of legislation exists that protects and provides special treatment for persons solely because of their youth.

Correlative law according special status for adults solely because of advanced age is far less developed. It appears that such a status has failed to develop because of fears that age alone is an inadequate index of grounds for protection or disability among older persons.[2] Courts and legislatures seem comfortable in believing that children have less wisdom and information upon which to make rational decisions; however, they have not seen advancing age alone as grounds to generally infer or presume

---

[1] Stanley V. Chicago M. and St. P. Ry. Co. 112, Mo. App. 601, 87 S. W. 112; *Pass v. Pass* 195 GA 155, 23 S. E. 29 697.

[2] This fear is not articulated in a simple summary form. It has arisen through long years of cases and legislative decisions. Perhaps its most cogent expression is found in legal attempts to protect persons about to be declared incompetent. For examples see: 9 *American Law Reports,* 3rd ed., p. 828 8 (a), *Annotation (on Guardianships).*

organizational dysfunctions demanding special protection and consideration (Cain, 1974).

Aging persons have been accorded legal standards that may vary with individual cases, but such variations are generally predicated upon additional facts.[3] Age, coupled with evidence of physical disability, senility, or clear misrepresentations by others, may vary as a standard of law as applied to an aging person, but age alone is rarely presumed or inferred as grounds for special consideration.[4]

In the few circumstances in which advanced age is cited as grounds for special treatment, inuendo remains that the treatment is based upon the inference of disability. In most instances in which advanced age results in special treatment or protection, the aging person is required to demonstrate the inference between age and some other factor. Thus, while the coalition of other factors with age may give rise to exceptions in law for older persons, age alone is virtually not an adequate index to vary the generalized standards applicable.

Special statuses for aging persons generally rely upon legislation and administrative rule. Legislation expressly concerning aging persons has arisen for special purposes or in instances of specific abuse.[5] Thus, in most instances, the special legal status for aging and its relationship to communication must be inferred from facts. Exceptions arise in statutes and in some administrative rules or laws of agencies. However, as a general rule of law, advanced age alone has not produced varied treatment. It may imply only an inference for variation of a general standard.

RESEARCH QUESTIONS NEEDING ANSWERS

Problems requiring research and development in law and public policy relating to communication arising with aging can be examined from several perspectives. First, the paradigm employed here concentrates on four

---

[3] Additional facts such as disability have been relied upon in cases involving aging person's contributory negligence in carrier cases. See: 30 *American Law Reports,* 2nd ed., p. 343 4, *Alighting Passenger-Disability.*

[4] For examples of how age and aging is employed at law to create exemptions and special treatment see: *Flowers* v. *Graves,* 125 So. 659, 660, 220, Ala. 445; *Allen* v. *Pearce,* 28 S.E. 859, 860, 101 Ga. 316; 74 *American Law Reports* and 950, 966 6 Contributory Negligence–Forgetfulness; *Monroe* v. *Shrivers,* 29 Ohio App. 109, 162 N.E. 780, (age as one index to mental capacity to make a will).

[5] For example: 42 USC 3029 Transportation projects for aging persons imply special status; *Old Age Security Law* (CA.) Statutues, 1937, 1078 describes "aging poor"; Minn. Statutues Annotated 525.54 (allowing probate appointment of a guardian), see also 9 *American Law Reports* 781 3 (a) *Incompetent–Guardian–Mental State–Effect of Statutes;* 29 *U.S. Code* 621 et seq. Age Discrimination in Employment.

categories of communication that can concern aging and aging persons. Legal and policy problems related to general communication among aging persons are treated in the initial section. Second, problems implied in law and public policy are considered in the context of general communication by society about aging and aging persons. Third, questions of legal and policy nature concerning communication to aging persons are treated. Fourth, are considerations of the rights and duties associated with communication by and from aging persons to the larger society.

General questions concerning aspects of each category are presented at the beginning of each following section. General discussions of the categories follow each set of questions.

Legal and Policy Problems
Concerning Communication among and between Aging Persons

1. What relationships exist between aging and the need for peer communications?
2. Do conceptual affinities exist among aging persons that arise as a product of aging?
3. Do peer communication interests and affinities based on age underlie grounds for communities of interest?
4. Do such communities of interest have consequence in public policy and law?
5. How might law and public policy be employed to protect individuals and communities of vital interest among aging persons as matters of due process of law and freedom of expression?

People born in the same generation generally share common experiences. As they age, throughout life a general community of interest and affinity based on their common experience also grows (Cutler and Benyston, 1974). As they mature and become older, their numbers dwindle. Many find comfort and strength in peer associations. In recent years, interests based on chronological peer groupings have become politically significant (Cain, 1974). Older persons seek assertion of their interests as a whole, which implies that they have the faculty and facility to communicate among themselves. Such intra-group communication allows them concentration and clear formulation of issues vital to their ultimate interests.[6]

---

[6] Rights, duties, and responsibilities are generally grounded in the vital nature of interests of individual groups. See: "Rights," "Duties," and "Responsibilities," *Blacks Law Dictionary*. St. Paul, Minnesota; West Publishing Co., 1972; also, "Rights" and "Responsibilities" in *Words and Phrases*.

Aside from political necessity, communication among aging persons demands facilitation to ensure individual justice. Complex modern society is technologically based. And communications systems have been developed to a technologically sophisticated level. If individuals are to understand themselves they must have opportunities to compare their lifestyle with other persons similarly situated. Thus, aging persons need the means of peer communications to carry on their lives (Douglas, Cleveland, and Maddox, 1974).

Additionally, cohorts demand the comradery of fellows with similar experiences. There is no substitution for the exchange of lifelong experiences among friends (Loeb, 1973).

Communication among aging persons is critical from several points of view. Peer communications have legal import in proportion to their effect upon vital interests. Certainly, individual expression is basic to the constitutional democratic society in the United States (Emerson, 1966).

At intrapersonal levels, cognition concerning self identity is predicated upon information about one's status. The aging person derives such information from others in varied communication forms (Johnson, 1972). Interpersonal communication with other aging persons by personal visits, mail, or telephone may be one source (Thompson, 1974; Tunstall, 1966); mass information on aging and by aging persons is another (Davis, 1971). Still others involve a variety of models such as small group exchanges, or exchanges between minority subgroupings of the aged. The interests of older poor black persons certainly differ from those of the aging affluent white population in the suburbs. Other subgroupings of aged persons may arise from geographical settings, career interests, and formal social memberships (Douglas, Cleveland, and Maddox, 1974).

Despite the model of communication involved, it is certain that aging persons must communicate among themselves (Maddox, 1964). This need formulates questions concerning methods of communication used and implied for aging persons. Identification of the methods permits examination of legal issues attending communication needs of the aging.

With age, transportation becomes increasingly problematic (Cutler, 1972). Visits, or interpersonal exchanges, that once entailed a short walk may demand reliance on some means of conveyance. As aging proceeds, even transportation becomes difficult. Eventually, most aging persons are dependent wholly on friends, taxis, or mass transit (if it exists) to maintain relatively proximate neighborhood relationships. As mobility declines, many aging persons move to retirement centers to ensure communication with peers. Others are forced to rely on telecommunication systems for basic societal information and exchange (Schramm, 1969). Broadcast media and the telephone (along with newspapers and mail), may become a vital necessity to such persons (Davis, 1971).

The telephone is needed to order medicine, food, laundry, and even clothing. The telephone is frequently the only proximate link to society. It is both an emergency service and an alarm device (Faberow and Moriwaki, 1975). In the technological society, the singular aging person cannot function without telephone equipment service and systems (Thompson, 1974).

Mass media are also critical to aging persons (DeGrazia, 1961; Glick and Levy, 1962; Ripley and Buell, 1954; and Schramm, 1969). They are the primary source for information on policies directly affecting aged persons. They also function as a potential forum for exchange among the elderly. Guest editorials and letters by the aging, broadcasting by aging persons, and unique services such as "call in" radio programs provide forums for communication exchange among the aging (Gaitz and Scott, 1975).

Access to mass and quasi mass communication can ensure the aging an opportunity to communicate with peers. In such fashion, political consensus, mutual defenses against discrimination, and general patterns of self-help may be fostered among the aging (Barron, 1967). All of these services are in one manner or another predicated upon law and legal policy.

The press informs under guarantees in the first amendment against abridgement of the freedom of expression. Broadcasting must deal fairly with important issues of community concern such as aging under the administrative law of the FCC.[7] Telephone systems are public utilities and must serve the convenience and necessity of the whole community without unreasonable discrimination. Rates, installation practices, service policies, and even equipment design may not unreasonably discriminate against any class of citizens.[8] This obviously includes the aging. In fact, it may be argued that carrier utilities, such as telephone companies, are under a duty to provide special care for persons simply because of their age.[9]

Generally, American society must ensure equal protection to communicate for all persons (Cain, 1974a). As persons age, their mere age may give rise to certain societal duties of care. And age, coupled with other

---

[7] Applicability of the Fairness Doctrine . . . op cit.

[8] 47 U.S. Code 202, *Carriers: Discriminations and Preferences.*

[9] This argument would be based upon analogy to the special status required to be accorded blind, sick, very young, crippled, or infirm passengers by common carriers. See: 9 *American Law Reports* 2nd ed., 958 10 (Alighting from motor bus); 56 *American Law Reports* 2nd ed., 1263 5.

factors such as minority status or disability, gives rise to more specific duties.[10] Society may be required to design equipment and to provide systems and services that do not unduly discriminate against persons because of their age. We may have to seek out, ascertain, and assess communication needs among the aging. Even the provision of extraordinary services to older persons to alleviate emergencies and to assist in exchanging critical information may ultimately be seen as necessary to allow social functioning throughout life.

Communication about Aging Persons and about the Subject of Aging in Society

1. What communications about aging are generally accurate?
2. What prejudices or biases toward the aging process and aging persons appear or are implied in societal communications?
3. What interests are affected by such communications?
4. Are legal rights and duties apparent or implied in the interests affected by the communication?
5. How should law and public policy be implemented to address issues concerning rights and duties implied?

Communication about aging and aging persons have legal consequences that depend heavily on the context and their criteria for use. When society communicates about the process of aging there may be effects upon the legal status of aging persons. Where aging persons, individually and collectively, are the subject of societal information exchange, there is risk to them. The communication might misrepresent or omit important aspects that are of vital concern and interest to persons who are acutely subject to the process of aging. Generally, such persons are older citizens, and with the advance of years, age, aging, and the aging process become increasingly more connected with interests (Jansson, 1972).

Chronological age attainment determines qualification and disqualification to many rights and statuses associated with law. In the United States, the right to Social Security and other benefits guranteeed by law arises with chronological age attainment.[11] Furthermore, many privileges are accorded persons merely by virtue of chronological age (Clark and Anderson, 1967). Thus, communication concerning chronological age may affect rights and privileges of aging persons.

---

[10] See for example: *O'Mara* v. *Hudson River Ry. Co.* 38 N.Y. 445, *Missouri Pac. Ry. Co.* 65 Tex 443.

[11] See for example: *Social Security Act of 1935* (as amended) Title 42, U.S. Code.

Additionally, communication may bear upon the functional aging of persons (Cain, 1974a). Communication misrepresenting or omitting information about work habits and customs of aging persons may affect older people and segments of the older population.[12] The misrepresentation may damage a person or a class of aging persons.

Communication about aging and older persons should generally concern law when interests are involved that must be protected as a matter of justice to persons or to benefit the whole society. Such interests may be identified in judicial cases[13] and in legislation concerning communication about aging and aging persons. It also arises in administrative law through rules, regulations, and administrative decisions concerning communication to the aging.[14] The interest may become a legal right to be protected if the context of the communication involves impairment of elements such as economic benefit, reputation, privacy, or the due process of law commonly associated with the Bill of Rights in the Constitution.[15]

They may also demand protection by virtue of specific statutes creating rights by, of, and for aging persons. The presence of rights associated with aging and aging persons implies a correlative duty upon society to communicate about aging persons so as not to damage them individually or as a group (Lewis, 1963). News stories inaccurately depicting important facts concerning abuse of Social Security, Medicare, or Medicade by a beneficiary might damage a person who sustains a loss, or larger classes among older persons who become the subject of program curtailment. Advertising generally implying or depicting aging persons as senile or doting may impair employment, credit, and commercial reputations, or may prejudice privileges and licenses (Ashmore, 1975). It may thus be the subject of administrative regulation. Television and radio programs that unfairly treat issues of vital community importance concerning aging may result in sanctions upon the broadcasters.[16] Pamphlets, publications, by-

---

[12] *Older Americans Act of 1965,* 79 Statutes 219, and amendments. Title III provides examples of services dependent on narrow construction which can easily be lost by the aging.

[13] Principally found in instances such as a defense to contributory negligence, 30 *American Law Reports,* 2nd ed. 343, where special status may arise because of aging in the law applied to carriers, *Little Rock* v. *Ft. St. Railway Co.* v. *Tankersley* 54 Ark. 25, 14 S.W. 1099, or in special applications of the attorney client privilege, 64 *American Law Reports,* 189.

[14] For example see: *Heinz W. Kirschner,* 63 FTC 1290 (1967) affd 153 F2, 751 (9th Cir. 1964) where guillibility and trust are weighed.

[15] U.S. Constitution, Bill of Rights, Amendment V, XIV and the guarantee against abidgment of the freedom of speech of Amendment I.

[16] See: *Applicability of the Fairness Doctrine in the Handling of Controversial Issues of Public Importance,* 29 Federal Register 10415, 10421 (1964).

laws, and communications by individuals, institutions, and organizations impairing vital interests associated with aging persons might be enjoined or otherwise regulated.[17]

Communication about aging and aging persons may also damage individuals and the society in a more general sense. If a society supports, fosters, or acquiesces with inaccurate communication about the aging process and aging persons, a climate of prejudice and bias will prevail (Palmore and Manton, 1973). Aging persons may then suffer because the society is unjust. An unexamined belief that Medicade recipients are somehow less moral than Medicare beneficiaries or that subsidized housing is to be avoided, fails to recognize the general circumstances of the aging. The cost of surviving in old age bears little relationship to average income and savings. The resources for retirement and old age care must be borne by large segments of adult populations. Aged populations are becoming larger; older persons are forced from employment at increasingly earlier ages (Cowgill, 1974). The extentions of their lives, their presence in society, and the resource they offer must be the subject of supportive, accurate, and benevolent communication (Binstock, 1974). The community of aging persons must be examined by a standard according to their age and experience (Brinley, Jovick, and McLaughlin, 1974). Issues are suggested that communication about aging and aging persons should in justice clearly contain good measures of reverence, warmth, benevolence, and understanding.

General attitudes in communication concerning aging should be examined carefully to determine their societal effect upon aging and aging persons. If communications persist that unjustly disfavor older persons, individual suits might be encouraged against offenders or new legislative or rule-making actions might be formulated to protect the aging.

Communication Particularly Addressing Aging Persons

1. What communications are directed to persons primarily because they are aging?
2. What are the goals of such communications?
3. Are the goals involved legitimate and socially desirable?
4. Do the goals, the substance, or the process involved in the communication adversely affect persons simply becuase they are aging or aged?

---

[17] *Facwett Publications Inc.* v. *Morris,* 377 p. 2d 42 (Okla, 1962) Cert den. 376 v. 513 (1963) limited a group libel action to 60 members, however individual members of the group may attempt to enjoin or sue for damages. See also: *FTC* v. *Rhodes Pharmaceutical Co.* 191 F 2d 744 (7th cir., 1951) for FTC injunctive authority.

5. Are adversities involved impairing interests that are vital to aging persons or to society in general; are rights and duties implied or expressed affecting aging persons or the general society?
6. What legal remedies or public policies are implied that might support or facilitate the rights or duties implied?

The law generally presumes that reasonable persons can discern obvious distinctions between truth and falsity.[18] Furthermore, not all inaccurate or colored representations are appropriately classified as misrepresentative and damaging.[19] Puffery in sales and advertising has long been accepted as legal, and considerable latitude must be permitted within editorial matter consistent to freedom of expression (Preston and Johnson, 1972).

However, when communication addresses an audience composed of disabled persons who do not have the normal ability to discern facts, the standard may vary.[20] Justice demands that society not permit unfair advantage to be taken of disadvantaged persons.[21] To the extent that aging has brought disorganization to the human organism and has weakened levels of reasoning considered normal, it may provide index to disability. Such index may alter standards applicable to communications expressly addressing aging persons (Brinley, Jovick, and McLaughlin, 1974).

For example, information carefully calculated to be narrowly within the law might be mailed only to persons 65 and older inducing them to enter contracts or other obligations. Such communication might well be construed as an attempt to take unfair advantage of a class of persons solely because of their age. The implication of age as related to disability and infirmity coupled with the close question of legality of the material mailed might lead a court or regulatory agency to restrain the firm sending the mailing. Without the factor of advanced age of the intended class of recipients, the communication would have been lawful.

The special status of the aging is somewhat implied in some leading cases involving the Federal Trade Commission's regulation of advertising.[22] Products involved in many of these cases appeal to the aging, rural

---

[18] *Carlay* v. *FTC*, 153 F 2d 493 (7th cir, 1946).

[19] *Heinz* v. *Kirchner*, 63 FTC 1282 (1963).

[20] *Aronberg* v. *FTC*, 132 F 2d 165, (7th cir., 1942).

[21] *FTC* v. *Standard Education Society*, 302 U.S. 112, 116.

[22] *SSS Co.* v. *FTC*, 416 F. 2d 226 (6th cir., 1969); *U.S.* v. *J. B. Williams Co.*, 354, F. Supp. 521, (S.D. N.Y., 1973), J. B. Williams Co. (1970–73, Transfer Binder) Trade Reg. Reports Para. 18, 821.

poor. However, neither administrative nor common law generally relies alone on the advanced age of the intended audience as criteria for special treatment (Weirsma and Klausmeirer, 1965). Age is more likely one among other components in reaching particular conclusions.

Some of the reasoning contained in research on age among children as a ground for exceptional treatment might be analogized to older persons (Cain, 1974b; Northcott, 1975). As a result of such research, a series of cases and proposals for legislation have arisen to protect children from particular advertising appeals.[23] The primary ground for protection is the lack of experience of the youth or the young age of the class of persons addressed.

The advanced years of aging citizens might also be taken as grounds for special consideration. Then, appeals directed to persons because of characteristics associated with aging might be better controlled. Persons authoring and implementing advertising and sales appeals to aging persons would be under a higher standard than those dealing with the general public. Certain duties to protect the rights of the aging would be involved. Presumptions in transactions with aging persons might shift from "let the buyer beware" to "let the seller be aware."

Communication by Aging Persons Addressing the General Society

1. What communications by aging persons are addressed generally or to members of the larger society?
2. What means are used by aging persons to communicate with the larger society?
3. Are aging persons succeeding in communicating with the larger society?
4. What interests are involved when aging persons are not communicating with the larger society?
5. Are duties and rights of aging persons affected by the failure and thwarting of communication?
6. What laws and public policies might be implemented to support communication by aging persons to the larger society?

Aging persons must function as citizens. Therefore, they communicate with the larger community. If the aging fail to advise the larger community of their problems, there is little hope for resolution (Markson, 1971). Aging persons will always remain the most reliable source of information about aging and the problems of aging persons (Johnson, 1972). Most

---

[23] *Action for Childrens Television* v. *FCC,* (U.S. C.A., Dist. of Columbia) Case No. 74-2006; U.S. House of Rep. Bill 8613, Intro. by Rep. Wirth, (Colo.).

aging persons retain considerable communicative ability, and if the aging as a whole are determined to preserve and assert legal and political rights, they are under a duty to communicate (Cain, 1974b).

As persons advance in years, they are obliged to communicate their demands and needs to the larger community. Age alone may be grounds for exceptional consideration; however, aging persons must demonstrate that to be the case. Indeed, in older, perhaps pastoral societies, the aging are respected not merely because of the advanced state of their years, but because of the wisdom they impart to the larger community. They communicate information concerning their status and well-being, and they offer seasoned, deliberate judgment on matters of general concern. The respect for their age derives from the wisdom they articulate.

Generally taken, aging persons seem to proceed under a duty, first, to reasonably communicate their demands and needs to the larger society and, second, to provide benefit to the whole community in the form of wise judgments. Fulfillment of this two-fold duty by the aging results in mutuality between the general society and aging persons (Weinberg, 1974). To the extent that the aging fulfill the duty, they may sustain the respect of the society. To the extent that their wisdom and experience are at variance with social problems and conditions, they may lose respect and status. The circumstance of the aging in the United States is in marked contrast to the fabled "tyranny of the old" found in non-technological societies. In developing countries, the aging have retained respect of the society by maintaining dialogue with younger generations.

The maintenance of dialogue with the larger society, however, assumes that social structures can facilitate communication (Beverley, 1975). It assumes that the forums and channels exist, allowing communication from older members of the society to be forthcoming. It assumes that the aging have some means of access to communication facilities. In tribal life, this is accomplished by councils in which elders speak. But such rites of oracle are lost as societies acquire mediated communication technologies and their accompanying efficiencies (Barron, 1967). Education substitutes for experience, and more efficiency is demanded in communication from information sources. Age ceases as a criterion for knowledge as information becomes dynamic. The mere change associated with information handling militates against the aging. They know neither how to address the larger society nor what subjects are current. The societal pace favors rapid growth associated with youth.

Younger persons are educated to process a steady stream of information and to communicate based on that information. With aging, less potential to remain in communication with society occurs (Loeb, 1973).

As retirement approaches, the need to travel, the custom of work-related reading, and on-job conversations cease. Thus, the aging in western society retire to relative isolation. With time, it becomes more difficult for them to write and to see to read, and the aging may turn to telecommunication. They may assume a passive role as a part of a broadcast audience. Eventually, even the telephone becomes too complex for use by many aging persons.

Over time, aging persons lose both faculties and facilities for communication. They often become deaf, blind, or otherwise disabled. They can neither hear, see, or travel to remain in communication with society (Cutler, 1972). They may move into a retirement center or to a nursing home where even the existence of facilities to communicate with society are discouraged. In technological cultures, the aging tend to move into a society of their own and cease to have potential for functioning to support themselves or to benefit the larger society.

The aging have a duty to communicate with society, but there is also strong implication of interest among the aging to provide such communication. This implication may in some circumstances rise to the status of a right; however, it obtains only in a general way.

In the United States, aging persons have few communication facilities or programs designed to support their interest in communicating to the larger society. Indeed, even where rights are clearly defined in statutes, such as with the Social Security program, it is difficult for beneficiaries to quickly communicate their needs to concerned agencies. Where an interest or right is less defined, as for example in addressing groups of aging persons to develop a political consensus, there is virtually no communication facility available. Aging persons are hard-pressed to speak, to be heard, to redress petitions, or to assert individual or group interests at the federal, state, or local level of government. Indeed, any communication dysfunctions appearing generally in the society are greatly amplified for aging persons.

Each day, human communication becomes more dependent upon the mastery of technical devices. Color-tuning a television set, direct-distance telephone dialing, even addressing an envelope demands considerable manipulation of empirical data. Hands that shake, failing memory, poor eyesight and hearing, all associated with the aging, plague the operation of devices and manipulation of numbers.

Many aging persons have ignored music and public broadcasting because the continuous band tuners of radios and UHF television present insurmountable difficulty. And many aging persons express fear of using complex communication equipment such as video tape recorders, intercommunication devices, or voting machines. They simply present too much complexity and new information for the aging person to process.

The aging must be afforded equal rights to communicate. Communication equipment, means, and media must be designed and operated to avoid exclusion of the aging. Special devices and methods must be employed to ensure aging persons a right of communication. If communication carriers, broadcasters, and institutions operating under color of law are reducing the freedom to speak or publish of the elderly, a violation of basic first amendment rights may be worked, and due process of law may be breached.

The recent realization that handicapped persons are being excluded from society by the design of streets, buildings, and the height of telephones suggests an approach to problems of the aging. Simplified dialing, special operator assistance numbers, periodic free clinics for television sets and home lighting might all become part of a public policy for the aging.

It is not difficult to favorably speculate that persons have valuable information to offer society because they have lived through many years of detailed experience (Weinberg, 1974).

They should be encouraged, specially trained, and provided equipment and means to communicate. They may have information of a social and individual nature that is now being lost. Taped oral family histories; oral letters to friends, relatives and editors; video taped statements and programs from retired person's "production centers," all might develop to benefit American society. The aging must be provided guidance and training by younger persons to communicate.

SUMMARY

Jurisprudence and public policy concerning issues arising in communication with aging is examined to consider communication among aging persons, about aging and aging persons, to and by aging persons.

Law and public policy can implement communication among the aging to support individual and group needs. Where communication concerns aging and aging persons in the general society, law and public policy should protect against inaccuracy and encourage presentation of facts about aging. Law and policy should improve the general negative and exclusionary attitude toward aging and aging persons currently prevalent in American society.

Where communication from the larger society addresses the issues of aging or aging persons, the risk of misrepresentation should be considered.

Altered standards for determining what information aging persons perceive in messages they receive requires consideration.

Aging persons should communicate to the larger society. They should be encouraged through law and public policy to communicate. Special consideration in design and method of communication should be undertaken to determine existing and potential uses of communication by aging persons.

RECOMMENDATIONS

Gerontological and communication research should generally address problems of communication related to aging and aging persons. Where implications of legal and political rights and duties are suggested in research on communication and aging, programs should be developed to explore those implications. Where programs of specialized research on communication and aging identify pivotal issues vital to the interests of the aging or the whole society, legislation and administrative programs to support rights, duties, and policies involved should be established.

Justice can be informed through science. The difficult problem of associating the general condition of aging with legal rights can be comprehended if judges, legislators, and policy makers are advised of communication needs among the aging. A major drawback to the development of communication programs for the aging is a lack of general telecommunication policy development at state and local levels. Programs of telecommunication policy education and development should be established for local and state officials and for retired persons. If the aging learn how communication might be employed to assist them in formulating policy, they may substantially contribute to state and local laws and policy in communication. With such contribution, they may resume meaningful participation and contribution to society.

LITERATURE CITED

Ashmore, H. S. 1975. Commerical television's calculated indifference to the old. Center Magazine 8: 18—20.

Barnlund, D. C. 1968. Communication and change. *In* C. E. Jansen and F. E. X. Dance (eds.), Perspectives on Communication, pp. 24—40. Helix Press, Madison, Wisc.

Barron, J. A. 1967. Access to the press: A new first amendment right. Harvard Law Rev. 80: 1641.

Beverley, E. V. 1975. Making the right connections between people and services. Geriatrics 30: 114—119.

Binstock, R. H. 1974. Aging and the future of American politics. Ann. Amer. Acad. Pol. Soc. Sci. 415: 199–212.

Brinley, J. A., T. J. Jovick, and L. M. McLaughlin. 1974. Age, reasoning, and memory in adults. J. Gerontol. 29(2): 182–189.

Cain, L. D. 1974a. The growing importance of legal age in determining the status of the elderly. The Gerontologist 14: 167–174.

Cain, L. D. 1974b. Political factors in the emerging age status of the elderly. Ann. Amer. Acad. Pol. Soc. Sci. 415: 70–79.

Clark, M., and G. B. Anderson. 1967. Culture and Aging: An Anthropological Study of Older Americans. Charles C Thomas, Springfield, Ill.

Comstock, G. A., and E. Rubinstein. 1972. Television and Social Behavior: A Technical Report to the Surgeon General's Scientific Advisory Committee on Television and Social Behavior. U.S. Department of Health, Education and Welfare, Washington, D.C.

Cowgill, D. O. 1974. The aging of populations and societies. Ann. Amer. Acad. Pol. Soc. Sci. 415: 1–18.

Cutler, N. E., and V. L. Benyston. 1974. Age and political alienation: Maturation, generation, and period effects. Ann. Amer. Acad. Pol. Soc. Sci. 415: 160–175.

Cutler, S. J. 1972. The availability of personal transportation, residential location, and life satisfaction among the aged. J. Gerontol. 23: 383–389.

Davis, R. H. 1971. Television and the older adult. J. Broadcasting 15: 153–160.

Davis, R. H., and A. E. Edwards. 1975. Television: A Therapeutic Tool for the Aged. University of Southern California, Los Angeles.

DeGrazia, S. 1961. The uses of time. In R. Kleemeier (ed.), Aging and Leisure, 447–453. Oxford University Press, New York.

Douglas, E., W. Cleveland, and G. L. Maddox. 1974. Political attitudes, age, and aging: A cohort analysis of archival data. J. Gerontol. 29: 666–675.

Emerson, T. I. 1966. Toward a General Theory of the First Amendment. Random House, New York.

Faberow, N. L., and S. Y. Moriwaki. 1975. Self destructive crises in the older person. The Gerontologist 15: 333–337.

Gaitz, C. M., and J. Scott. 1975. Analysis of letters to "Dear Abby" concerning old age. The Gerontologist 15: 47–51.

Glick, I. O., and J. J. Levy. 1962. Living with Television. Aldine Publ., Chicago.

Jansson, B. 1972. Brief Chronology of Development of Federal Policy Pertaining to Social Services. University of Chicago School of Social Service Administration, Center for the Study of Welfare Policy, Chicago.

Johnson, M. 1972. Self-perception of need amongst the elderly: An analysis of illness behavior. Sociol. Rev. 20: 521–531.

Loeb, R. 1973. Disengagement, activity or maturity? Sociol. Soc. Res. 57: 367–382.

Lewis, J. 1963. The individual member's right to recover for a defamation leveled at the group. Univ. Miami Law Rev. 17: 519.

Maddox, G. L. 1964. Self assessment of health status: A longitudinal study of selected elderly subjects. J. Chronic Dis. 17: 449–460.

Markson, E. W. 1971. A hiding place to die. Trans-Action 11: 48–54.

Northcott, H. C. 1975. Too young, too old: Age in the world of television. The Gerontologist 15: 184–186.

Palmore, E., and K. Manton. 1973. Ageism compared to racism and sexism. J. Gerontol. 28: 363–369.

Preston, J., and A. Johnson. 1972. Puffery: A problem the FTC didn't want (and may try to eliminate). Journal. Quart. 49: 558.

Reusch, J., and G. Bateson. 1968. Communication: The Social Matrix of Society. W. W. Norton, New York.

Ripley, J. M., and S. D. Buell. 1954. Characteristics of the Television Audience of Columbus and Franklin County Ohio. Ohio State University, Columbus.

Schramm, W. 1969. Aging and mass communication. In M. Riley, J. Riley, M. Johnson (eds.), Aging and Society, Vol. II: Aging and the Professions. Russel Sage Foundation, New York.

Thompson, M. K. 1974. Old people alone. Modern Geriatrics 4: 262–268.

Tunstall, J. 1966. Old and Alone: A Sociological Study of Old People. Rutledge, Kegan, and Paul, London.

Von Bertalanffy, L. 1968. General Systems Theory. George Brazillier, New York.

Weinberg, J. 1974. What do I say to my mother when I have nothing to say? Geriatrics 29(11): 155–159.

Weirsma, W., and H. J. Klausmeirer. 1965. The effect of age on speed of concept attainment. J. Gerontol. 20: 398–400.

Whittington, S., F. Wilkie, and C. Eisdorfer. 1972. Attitudes of young adults and older people toward concepts related to old age. The Gerontologist 12: 55.

chapter 13

Organized Religion:
Communication Considerations

Carl Wesley Staser, M.S., M.Div.
Helen Taft Staser, B.S.

Organized religion provides a large, continuous family of those who know us, appreciate us, and share our lives. The congregation is a communing and communicating fellowship, a support system concerned with us from birth to death. This chapter shows how organized religion communicates with the elderly and how they are helped by organized religion to communicate effectively with each other and the rest of society.

How can congregations meet specific communication needs of the elderly? Following are examples of activities, programs, and approaches used by organized religion in communication with older people.

COMMUNICATION THROUGH WORSHIP SERVICES

Weekly worship services bring all ages together in an expanded family setting. Every elderly person is a part of the parent or grandparent generation. Their own children or grandchildren may not be present, but the younger people who worship with them are a part of the extended family of the elderly. A sense of belonging exists. All ages together seek satisfactory answers to the "why" questions of human existence. A mood is created for quiet personal meditation and reflection. Life is made more acceptable and challenging by the shared worship experience. The people then scatter with a renewed enthusiasm for living.

COMMUNICATION THROUGH RECOGNITION

Attention to the elderly is given commandment status in some religions: "Honor thy father and thy mother that thy days may be long in the land which the Lord thy God giveth thee."

There are many ways churches can honor or recognize their older members. Those who have been members of the church, or residents of the community for 25, 35, or 50 years or more, can be invited to special programs or services for recognition. Publicity given before and after the event can acknowledge the service they have rendered and continue to give to the church and to the community. If the group seems too large, it can be broken down into manageable segments to be honored on successive occasions.

Churches should look for opportunities to celebrate the past and to recognize those who have contributed. This not only helps the older members feel worthwhile and appreciated but also gives the whole congregation a sense of history, continuity, and belonging.

Variations of this recognition are needed. We live in a highly mobile society. Not everyone has belonged to the same church or lived in the same community for a long period of time. In concentrated retirement areas, persons can be recognized on their birthdays (mention of age should be optional), by the states they come from, by years they have lived in the community, or for the contributions they are presently making to the church or community. Everyone needs to be important to someone for some reason. The church can help identify the reasons and should acknowledge and encourage the participation and contributions that older persons continue to make. Persons tend to live roles that are expected of them. If you expect more of older people, you will get it!! The churches have traditionally recognized the accomplishments and contributions of people at their funerals. Many churches are trying to do an equally good job of recognizing the living.

COMMUNICATION THROUGH THE ELDERLY

We are strong advocates of communicating *through* the elderly, as well as *to* the elderly. Older persons are effective volunteers in virtually every phase of the church program. Some of the most effective volunteers handling telephone assignments are relatively home-bound people, and in some cases totally bedridden. We believe almost *everyone* is capable, and *needs* an opportunity to make a contribution *somewhere*. The job can be tailored to fit the capabilities, interests, and energy level of the person.

Our society needs to find ways to allow and encourage people to make contributions (volunteer and paid) as long as they are willing and able. The continuing use of retired ministers is a bright spot on the national retirement scene. Retired ministers are serving as pastors of churches too small to afford full-time pastoral leadership. They also serve as interim ministers, chaplains, and institutional administrators at hospitals, retirement centers, and children's homes.

COMMUNICATION THROUGH RADIO AND TELEVISION

Radio and television bring a great variety of religious programs to the elderly. These programs are especially of value to the home-bound. Religious programs include weekly worship services, special holiday programs and services, daily devotions or meditations, talks by religious leaders, healing and evangelistic services, and music programs. For some older people, these programs are their only contact with organized religion. For others, the radio and television programs supplement their local church or other religious participation.

COMMUNICATION BY MAIL

Devotional periodicals are mailed to the elderly as are church bulletins, sermons, magazines, newspapers, plus a variety of mimeographed material promoting various church programs.

Denominations publish state and national magazines and newspapers. Some church publications have been specifically designed for the elderly. Especially useful are newsletters that help the elderly find local groups, activities, and programs that meet their needs.

There are so many options open to older people that few are aware of more than a fraction of them. In East Lansing, Michigan, many senior church members help draw together a wide range of options and resources for a quarterly newsletter. Areas covered include adult education and recreation, sports events, entertainment, TV, and radio (that especially addresses the older person, including the hard of hearing), business, legislation, health, books, food tips, special services, volunteer opportunities, and travel. One older person commented, "I have dreaded the thought of retirement. After reading about the exciting things people are doing, I can hardly wait to retire next year." This newsletter is mailed to over 2,000 persons, 55 years of age and older, in the East Lansing area, plus approximately 200 in other communities who have requested it. Sixty seniors from the churches and community at large plan the layout, write or solicit articles, edit contributions, proofread, type, and assemble the final newsletter.

COMMUNICATION BY TELEPHONE

Telephone reassurance programs are operated by many churches. The elderly and home-bound are invited to participate in the program, either to be called or to call others. A phone call each morning at about the same time gives a cheery good morning, starts the day with dialogue, and checks to see that the telephone companion is alright. If the one to be called plans to be away from home, the caller is notified in advance. Otherwise, if the phone call is not answered, someone checks to see if all is well. These calls are looked forward to with anticipation by those being called. We recommend that the callers be persons who have time to visit! Lasting friendships often develop out of these contacts. The callers are given a feeling of responsibility and satisfaction related to worthwhile community service. If the caller were originally a "lonely" person, two needs have been met. Telephone reassurance removes fear of an older person being left unattended when in serious need.

The telephone greatly increases ministers' communication with the elderly. For the minister, it multiplies the number of contacts possible in a given period of time, compared to home visitations. For the elderly, it provides prompt access to a minister. Persons calling for counseling appointments often have their needs met during the phone call. An answering service can relay calls to the minister. Some churches use elderly volunteers in church offices. These volunteers are especially helpful in churches without paid secretarial help. When possible, the church should have at least two lines because some calls last a long time. Emergency calls deserve immediate attention. The telephone is the most effective communication tool when many elderly people need to be reached in some personal way. The human voice dispels loneliness. People can be counseled, advised, and reassured by phone.

Some religious organizations sponsor dial-a-prayer programs. Prayers are pre-recorded, and the caller hears the prayer for the day.

Problems of a serious nature that need an immediate response or listener have led to the development, often with church backing, of "Listening Ear" or "Crisis Intervention" programs. Phones with a well publicized number are manned 24 hours a day. Those operating the service are trained listeners. They also have community referral numbers for those needing specific expertise or aid. Suicide prevention is a major part of these crisis intervention programs. Darkness increases depression, and greatest personal need often occurs when the church offices are closed.

For the home-bound elderly, the telephone is a lifeline. Recognizing the telephone as a necessity, some companies have greatly reduced telephone rates for the elderly. Churches might pay for the telephone costs of those who cannot afford them. This money could come from the Outreach or Missionary portion of church budgets. Relationships with persons in need could lead the churches to develop more extensive support systems for the elderly.

COMMUNICATION THROUGH SMALL GROUPS

Churches have many small groups that provide ongoing opportunities for fellowship, study, and service. What people do when they are together is far less important than the social interaction that takes place as they do it. The people are the program. If the elderly and their needs are kept at the center of program planning, the activities can be designed to meet those needs.

From childhood into adulthood, the size of groups for satisfying experiences increase from a few, two or three, to many, 30 to 40. As the aging process continues beyond middle age, the size of the group needs to diminish. Our capacity to interact with many in groups reaches a peak and then declines. Small groups have an intimacy usually lacking in large groups.

The "friendly workers" may have only six or eight present for their monthly quilting party. They work on quilts for the needy, and share a meal with much visiting. A value may be placed on the quilts produced. It is impossible to place a value on the social interaction and the personal rewards for such work and fellowship sessions.

Some adult Sunday School classes go on for over 50 years. A Bible class organized in 1921 dissolved in 1973 because its original assistant teacher was no longer able to teach the class. Those Sunday morning hours were golden. The old songs were sung. The Bible was studied. Social issues were discussed. A fellowship existed. The monthly dinner meetings provided an additional social outlet that cost little but produced much in friendship and shared happy times.

There are many small groups in churches. Womens' circles, missionary societies, men's clubs, ushers' clubs, visitors' guilds, evening service guilds, Sunday School classes, and church choirs. As we do something of value together, we are happier for having done it.

COMMUNICATION THROUGH
MINISTERIAL VISITING AND COUNSELING

Ministers visit regularly in hospitals. They try to be especially close to individuals and families facing serious health problems and those with special needs. Ministers call at the homes of older people, but this practice is becoming less common. Those who feel the need to talk about a personal problem will often make an appointment to visit the minister in his office.

COMMUNICATION THROUGH LAY VISITING

Some elderly become very effective as visitors for the church, supplementing the calling done by the minister. They call in hospitals, nursing homes, and on "shut-ins" at home.

A "shut-in" needs good friends, rather than a stream of rotating strangers. The most useful calling on long-term "shut-ins" is done by those who call repeatedly on the same persons. Meaningful, supportive, and caring relationships can thus be established. The church can maximize the value of these home visitors by providing training for them.

COMMUNICATON THROUGH NURSING HOME MINISTRY

The churches have a special role in communicating with persons in nursing homes. Ministers frequently rotate to provide weekly worship services. Some ministers and representatives call regularly. Church circles, choirs, youth fellowships, Sunday school classes, and individual members have found many meaningful ways to respond to the needs of nursing home residents. Many elderly but active people serve as volunteers at nursing homes. All ages are needed in the following roles:

1. Supportive friendships: regular visits, post cards, home made treats, sharing common interests
2. Leading book discussion groups
3. Leading current events groups
4. Organizing weekly film programs
5. Game partners
6. Weekly cookie bakers
7. Helping with Bingo programs
8. Helping with craft classes
9. Putting on music programs—the "Let Me Call You Sweetheart" variety are great for everyone, including senile residents
10. Singing in the halls—every season of the year. The most effective serenading is done by choristers walking slowly through halls and responding to residents in doorways or listening from their beds. The group can stop midway in each hall, or where clusters of persons are gathered, to sing a few selections, visit, and then slowly move on again. Instrumental serenading is also very effective. This type of activity is particularly valuable because it reaches *everyone*.

Most nursing home residents will remain there or in a similar facility. It is important that the church work to keep these people included in every day life of the community to the extent possible. Residents of nursing homes tend to withdraw socially and psychologically, thus insulating themselves against disturbing events. Ministers and qualified laymen can assist the nursing home staff in reality therapy. The programs discussed help keep the residents mentally stimulated and physically active.

COMMUNICATION BEFORE AND AFTER A DEATH

The elderly expect religion to give them an adequate understanding of death. The funeral service has always attempted this. However, the present trend is to prepare those who will die, and those who will survive, for the death experience before it occurs. The churches are treating the study of death more openly than in the past. Seminars and study groups are built around "death with dignity" and "death and dying" themes. Early planning is needed regarding wills and trust arrangements, insurance matters, social security and pension information, and funeral plans. Key persons for assistance are the minister, funeral director, lawyer, banker, doctor, insurance agent, and a representative of the local social security office.

Education in how to effectively support others is needed. The church can help accumulate and communicate this knowledge. The loneliness and vacuum left by death can produce emotional cripples unless adequate communication continues following a death. Churches need to provide supportive groups as well as counseling for those in need.

Some churches have helped funeral directors find widows to provide competent follow up counseling for surviving spouses. Each minister develops his own plan of ongoing support for the survivors, which usually include the help of church members.

COMMUNICATING WITH THOSE WHO HAVE LOST A SPOUSE

The greatest single loss for most people is the loss of a married partner through death or divorce. The 6.1 million widows in the United States, and the increasing number of persons who are divorced or are going through divorce, need the support and concern of the church.

Persons newly alone need companionship, but making new friends is often difficult for grieving persons. The First Community Church of Columbus, Ohio, has organized a group of 50 widows who served as supportive friends for new widows on a one-to-one basis. In Lansing, Michigan, approximately 200 widows participate in an inter-church fellowship that rotates its monthly meetings among the Roman Catholic parishes of the area.

The Peoples Church of nearby East Lansing formed a Sunday Senior Serendipity Set for elderly widows and widowers. Approximately 20 men and women meet every other Sunday evening in the homes of members. This interdenominational church also has a weekly supper club for all single persons over 40 years of age. Paid membership numbers 150. Approximately 100 members and guests attend each Friday evening in the church social hall. This singles club was designed to meet the needs of the Peoples Church members. However, over two thirds of the present members belong to other churches or have no church affiliation. This club is led by elected officers. It is divided into five subgroups that take turns managing the dinners and programs. Weekly singles discussion groups, weekend outings, and a week at summer camp are extensions of this singles program. Subgroups based on common interests continue to develop. In 8 years, over 100 marriages have come out of the fellowship, plus many lasting friendships.

COMMUNICATION THROUGH NEIGHBORHOOD GROUPS

Supportive neighborhood groups can be set up by churches or other social agencies, as has been done in East Lansing. Fifty church and community persons keep an eye on their older neighbors, in an area defined by them. For some it is a block, for others a larger neighborhood area, and in some cases older neighbors who have moved a short distance into apartments are included. In most neighborhoods, there are key persons who know what is going on and are vitally concerned about their neighbors.

In the block where these authors live, a retired woman watches for any needs that are unmet. Transportation has been provided, groceries and prescriptions picked up, meals carried in, cleaning help secured, and arrangements made for alternative housing. A retired athletic trainer with health limitations offered his first aid skills. He bandaged sprained ankles, advised when X-rays were needed, extracted splinters, and removed foreign objects from eyes. Teenage neighbors shoveled snow from his driveway. Another retiree neighbor shoveled the trainer's sidewalk regularly and anyone else's that needed it. One young family parks a car in an older couple's driveway each winter while they are in Florida, to give the appearance of inhabitance. School children brought home because of sudden illness have been cared for by retired couples until parents arrived home. Neighborhood rummage sales and picnics are held, with a resulting feeling of friendship and goodwill. Garden surpluses of tomatoes, squash, cucumbers, and beans are shared with neighbors by retirees with large gardens.

COMMUNICATION BETWEEN CHURCHES

Churches need to communicate with each other about programs they are developing to serve the general population, and the elderly in particular. Every church does not need every kind of club or social group. However, each church needs to know where the fellowship groups are that can help its congregation.

Richard Miller, of Lansing, Michigan, publishes a monthly newsletter for Peoples Church, listing the activities and meeting places, plus general information, of about 26 clubs and organizations designed for single adults of all ages in the greater Lansing area. This is mailed to approximately 750 people, churches, and clubs.

In the three county metropolitan areas surrounding Lansing, Michigan, 26,000 formerly married persons were counted in the 1970 census in a total population of 370,000. This included 18,000 widows and divorced women, plus 8,000 widowers and divorced men. Just over 7 percent, or 1 out of 13, in this standard metropolitan area were formerly married people.

COMMUNICATION FACILITATION
THROUGH USE OF CHURCH BUILDINGS

Churches can aid communication among the elderly by offering their facilities to Senior Citizen organizations, to the heart association for Stroke Workshops, to handicapped organizations (serving all ages) for fellowship, etc. Churches render a great service by providing curb cuts, accessible entrances, and accessible bathroom facilities, thus making it possible for those with mobility limitations to participate in community functions.

COMMUNICATION FACILITATION
THROUGH TRANSPORTATION PROGRAMS

A major need of the elderly is adequate transportation to help keep them in contact with the rest of society. There comes a time for many older persons when it is no longer physically or financially feasible to drive a car.

Without transportation many are socially isolated. It is important for each community to develop transportation that allows persons the greatest degree of independence and the ability to participate in the community at the level of their ability and need.

The church has traditionally provided rides to worship and other church functions. In the past, people with buggies picked up walkers on the way to church. Now, people with cars pick up those without. But getting older people to church activities is only a part of their transportation needs.

Some churches have programs that are helping people with grocery shopping, get to medical appointments, and meet other emergency needs. National statistics indicate that older persons, regardless of income level, once they give up their cars, decrease and often cease participation in the programs and social events they have always enjoyed and that gave their life meaning. The best transportation program enables people to go wherever they want, whenever they wish.

The East Lansing Rotary Club and Peoples Church—Interdenominational, provided funds for a pilot transportation program eventually taken over by the city. This program utilized the local taxi company. Older people, 60 years and older, secure Gold Cards from the office of East Lansing Older Peoples Program (sponsored by the city and schools of East Lansing). The Gold Card entitles holders to half-price taxi fare, plus free admission to all school activities, and one dollar admission to adult education classes. The taxi service is available on demand 24 hours a day, 7 days a week. Some give up driving nights before they give up their cars. This service allows a gradual transition. Of the 2,000 persons 60 and older who are eligible, over 1,400 secured Gold Cards in the first 28 months. The taxi service has been used for doctor and dentist appointments, grocery shopping, general shopping, and visiting. Card holders have also taken trips to drug stores, hair dressers, restaurants, banks, churches, work (part time), volunteer work, hospitals, laundries, automobile service stations, bus stations, airports, libraries, adult education classes, swimming pools, weekly bridge games, theatres, entertainments, the Michigan State University football stadium, University Club, city hall, post office, schools, city parks, funeral parlors, health spas, and veterinarians. The taxis take people where they want to go at any time.

Peoples Church and the East Lansing Rotary have a second pilot program that provides half-price taxi fare service for all handicapped less than 60 years of age who are physically able to use taxis. If this program for the handicapped continues to be successful, it may also be taken over by the city of East Lansing.

Some handicapped require a lift vehicle. In the spring of 1975, the East Lansing American Legion Post 205 and Peoples Church paid the Lansing Easter Seals organization to transport adults confined to wheelchairs, using three lift vehicles when their drivers were available. This pilot program for the tri-county area around Lansing, Michigan, was partially taken over by the Capital Area Transportation Authority in the fall of 1975. This is an example of the manner in which churches, through demonstration projects, can assist the community in keeping people active and in communication with the total life of the community.

COMMUNICATION WHEN THE ELDERLY ARE ALONE

Human communication occurs within oneself. Because there need be no second or third party involved and because the elderly will spend much time alone, they need training in how to communicate and live comfortably with themselves.

The Bible and other good books will provide stimuli for thought and reflection. The accumulated wisdom of the world can be pondered and added to by the elderly. Time for reflection is one of the blessings of retirement years. Organized religion has stressed prayer, meditation, and quiet times. The self not only speaks but also listens. The importance of meditation and quietness is being rediscovered. Prayer and reflection can be of great value to the elderly; it puts them in touch with the ground of their being and builds confidence for living and dying.

RESEARCH QUESTIONS NEEDING ANSWERS

What are the most successful examples of church buildings being used as community centers for programs for the elderly? Are church buildings being made more accessible?

What types of TV and radio programs have been addressed to older people? What response have the elderly made to various types of programs? How are older persons involved in producing TV and radio programming? What programs have been innovated and produced *by* older people *for* older people?

How are churches communicating with "shut-ins"? What are churches doing to counteract the isolation that many older people feel?

What are some of the most effective ways churches are communicating with those going through the death experience?

How does the death of a spouse affect communication patterns of the survivor?

SUMMARY

Organized religion gives to all ages a sense of belonging. It helps provide the social cohesion that builds civilizations.

Honoring the elderly benefits young and old. The elderly need to be noticed. The young need to know that it is alright to grow old.

Some elderly are playing effective communication roles using skills developed over the years. More can be recruited, trained, and used. Communication by the elderly, for the elderly, and with the elderly is a goal.

Organized religion has social service stations scattered all over the world. These religious centers provide a base of operation for a world-wide war against loneliness and meaningless living. Religion has a message of hope and expectation. This message can bear good fruit in the form of happy and meaningful lives in our lifetime.

The promise of the ancient commandment holds today: "Honor thy mother and thy father that thy days may be long in the land which the Lord thy God giveth thee."

SUGGESTED READINGS

Atchley, R. C. 1972. The Social Forces in Later Life: An Introduction to Social Gerontology. Wadsworth, Belmont, Calif.

Brotman, H. B. 1968. Who Are the Aged: A Demographic View. Occasional Papers in Gerontology No. 1, Institute of Gerontology, Ann Arbor, Mich.

Butler, R. N., and M. I. Lewis. 1973. Aging and Mental Health. C. V. Mosby, St. Louis, Mo.

Cottrell, F. 1974. Aging and the Aged. Wm. C. Brown, Dubuque, Iowa.

Culver, E. T. 1961. New Church Programs with the Aging. Associated Press, New York.

Curtin, S. R. 1973. Nobody Ever Died of Old Age. Atlantic-Little, Brown, Boston, Mass.

Donahue, W. (Compiler). 1958. Free Time: Challenge to Later Maturity. University of Michigan, Ann Arbor.

Grant, F. B. 1962. Ministries of Mercy. Friendship Press, New York.

Gray, R. M., and D. O. Moberg. 1962. The Church and the Older Person. William B. Eerdmans, Grand Rapids, Mich.

Hammond, P. 1969. Aging and the ministry. In M. W. Riley, J. W. Riley, Jr., and M. E. Johnson (eds.), Aging and Society. Vol. II: Aging and the Professions, pp. 293—323. Russell Sage Foundation, New York.

Hoffman, A. M. (ed.). 1970. The Daily Needs and Interests of Older People. Charles C Thomas, Springfield, Ill.

Hunter, W. W. 1968. Preparation for Retirement. University of Michigan, Ann Arbor.

Kubler-Ross, E. 1970. On Death and Dying. MacMillan, New York.

Loether, H. J. 1975. Problems of Aging. Dickenson Publ., Belmont, Calif.

Manney, J. D., Jr. 1975. Aging in American Society. Institute of Gerontology, the University of Michigan-Wayne State University, Ann Arbor.

Maves, P. B. 1961. Aging, religion, and the church. *In* Clark Tibbitts (ed.), Handbook of Social Gerontology. University of Chicago Press, Chicago.

Rosow, I. 1967. Social Integration of the Aged. Free Press, New York.

Shanas, E., and G. F. Streib. (eds.). 1965. Social Structure and the Family: Generational Relations. Prentice-Hall, Englewood Cliffs, N.J.

Simpson, I. H., and J. C. McKinney. 1966. Social Aspects of Aging. Duke University Press, Durham, N.C.

Williams, R. 1965. Lives Through the Years: Styles of Life and Successful Aging. Aldine Publishers, Chicago, Ill.

chapter 14

The Relevance of Communication for Professionals Involved with the Elderly: Focus on Social Workers

Walter M. Beattie, Jr., M.S.

The capacity to communicate is essential for all people. An understanding by societies and their professionals of the aging processes—biological, psychological, and sociological—as they limit or change communication capacities among older persons is essential. To date, little research or documentation is available on the special knowledge and skills required by professionals in the area of communication with elderly consumers of services. Recent publications on professional responsibilities and policy formulation in regard to the aging contain little or no content on the relevance of communications for professions working with the elderly.

It is the thesis of this chapter that each of the professions must include within its knowledge and skill base an understanding of the aging processes and their special implications for communications with older persons. Only during the past several years has recognition been given to the need for the professions to address themselves to the special needs and claims of older persons. Literature on the professions and the aging is exceedingly scarce. Literature on the relevance of communication for professions working with the elderly is almost non-existent.

THE SOCIAL WORK PROFESSION

Fundamental to the work of each of the human and social professions is the capacity to communicate. Professions are characterized in part by verbal and symbolic communications that are restricted to their own members. Such forms of communication limit and restrict persons from outside a particular profession from fully identifying with and participating in the life and behavior of that profession.

Beyond special forms of communication within each profession, there is the necessity, particularly in the human and social service professions, to communicate with individuals and groups who have a wide diversity of life styles and social, economic, and ethnic backgrounds.

Probably no profession is more involved with communication skills than is social work. The profession's varied roles range from one-to-one interpersonal counseling, to work with groups in a variety of settings, to community organization, planning and advocacy on behalf of older persons with governmental and private organizations and agencies. Such a broad range of activities requires communications knowledge and skills. In working with older persons, agencies, and other professions that serve the elderly, there is required, in addition to generic social work knowledge and skills, specific knowledge and understanding of aging as a process and of the wide range of individualized needs of older persons.

Unfortunately, social work, like the other human, social, and health professions, has failed to prepare its members to work with older persons. All too often, social workers, like the majority of society, reflect negative and stereotype images and approaches to aging. Much of this is the result of a lack of a knowledge base in aging and the translation of such knowledge into appropriate concepts and goals for work with older persons. It is interesting to note in the Summary of Information on Master of Social Work Programs: 1975 (Council on Social Work Education, 1975), that of the 84 accredited schools of social work in the United States, only 26 identify concentrations or special work with the aging. Undoubtedly, more schools have some content on aging and older persons; however, it has been well documented elsewhere that, although individual social workers have pioneered in developing needed services and social policies for the elderly, social work as a profession has provided little leadership in addressing itself to the needs of our increasing aging population.

COMMUNICATING WITH CONSUMERS OF SERVICES

It has only been in recent years that the social services have given attention to the role of consumers in shaping policies concerning what services should be provided and under what circumstances. Through the inclusion of the consumer in policy and decision-making processes, attention has been focused on the fact that verbal and nonverbal communications have different meanings, as well as understandings, from the viewpoint of the provider and the consumer. There has also been increased attention given to who does and who does not utilize services and under what circumstances. It should be noted that the aging are underrepresented in most community-based services, such as individual counseling and legal services, and are overrepresented in institutional facilities. Such appraisals have given rise to the questions as to how information about the nature and availability of services is communicated to potential consumers of such services. A further question is whether information is meaningful and useful to those requiring services and can be acted on. Increasing attention also has been given to subgroupings wihin the population with the recognition that ethnicity, race, socioeconomic status, life styles, etc., represent important differences among consumers, as well as among providers.

The above considerations and questions apply to all segments of the population, including the elderly. However, among the aging population there are additional considerations. These are described below.

Generational Differences

Little attention has been paid in gerontological literature to the differences in regard to personal identities, values and attitudes, and meanings among and between the generations. While a younger person may want to be identified as "black," an older person may wish to be called "Negro." This may also be true for the older "Mexican-American" as distinct from the younger "Chicano." Each of these labels or identities carries not merely racial and ethnic identities but, equally so, attitudes, values, and meanings that relate to the person's self-conception and his "view of the world." Generational differences, as well as commonalities, are an essential framework within which the social worker must work if one of the goals of service is that of social intervention to ensure that the individualized needs of the older person are to be met.

Individual Differences

Knowledge of the aging process, its biological, psychological, and sociological factors, supports the view that aging is a continuous process of individualization. Older persons who share the same chronological age are more different than alike in regard to specific characteristics. At the same time, such persons may share common identities and events associated with the more advanced stages of life.

Age-related Changes

Important to communications is the fact that perceptual capabilities of the majority of older persons are increasingly limited and impaired with advancing age. More than 50 percent of the 65 and older population have visual impairment, with a greater proportion having auditory impairments. Those who have experienced major cardiovascular accidents may have motor impairment, as evidenced in increasing difficulty with speech and physical gesture and movement. It is also important to recognize that, in addition to perceptual and psychomotor changes within the aging individual, sociological changes occur in areas such as loss of work and family roles, as well as through bereavement resulting in loss of spouse and friends. Such changes and losses narrow the person's social world and personal identities. In addition, loss of energy forces results in a reduction in locomotion and mobility. These changes result in fewer interpersonal relationships. The life space of the aging is considerably reduced from that of younger age groups. A reduction in communications with others and the loss of significant social roles, which provide for group relatedness, mean that all too often the older person's communications are intrapersonal. They are based on past identities, memories, and situations rather than on new experiences and future orientations. What appears to the outsider, including the professional social worker, as withdrawal on the part of the older person from the social world around him is the result of sensory deprivation and societal isolation. Much like the hermit, the older person's interpersonal communication is in reality communication with self and with objects in his limited environment. One of the goals of social work practice with the aging must be that of enabling the older person to have meaningful social communications. Man is a social animal, and to be human is to participate and contribute to the social group. It must be noted that, although social isolation increases with advanced age, not all older persons are socially isolated.

Multifaceted and Interrelatedness of Problems Associated with Aging

It has been noted in gerontological literature that there is an interdependence and circular aspect of situations and disabilities identified with aging. Inadequate diet among older persons may exacerbate health problems that may, in turn, force a change from a traditional housing and living arrangement. All too often, because of a reduction in income, older persons may skimp or neglect their diets to save for an eventuality of catastrophic illness. At the same time, the elderly have been noted for their promptness in paying rents and taxes to ensure security in housing and living arrangements. Each facet of their lives is dependent upon other facets. Health status, housing and living arrangements, income, etc., are not easily separated one from the other. This interdependence of living situations and problems requires, at times, several professions to work with the individual older person and his family. For the most part, each profession deals with a separate facet of the older person's being. All too often there is a lack of communication among service providers, let alone coordination, around the individualized needs of the older consumer. For the most part, the older person must fit into the system of delivery, whether it be a health, housing, or social service delivery system.

Communications among and between the professions and with the older person and his family are essential. Most professional education neglects this most important area. This is true of social work education. Although much has been written of this interdisciplinary team, as has already been noted, each of the professions develops its own language and communications systems independent of one another. All too often, the consumer, as well as those from outside the profession, is excluded from participating in deliberations, decisions, and actions. As has been noted, the majority of professions are not prepared with a knowledge base of aging or in working with older persons.

Conceptual Frameworks and Goals of Service

Most of the professions have philosophies and goals of service that are, for the most part, irrelevant to the needs of the aging. The medical model, which is the major model in social work practice, is organized around crisis and acute, episodic forms of intervention. It is institutionally based and emphasizes cure as a predominant goal. For older persons, chronicity and long-term disability, if not illness, require assessment that is not based upon aging as a disease but rather on an assessment of capacity and function.

The ability of the professions to communicate around the needs of the aging requires new and differing approaches to professional education. Part of this education must provide for a multidisciplinary framework around commonalities in knowledge and skill about aging. It must also provide for interdisciplinary linkages to permit sharing of knowledge, skills, and values among the disciplines and professions related to the needs of older persons. Communication networks among professional schools and disciplines are essential to enable this to occur.

The issues of the professions and aging, as well as social work as one of the professions working with the aging, are issues about the organization and delivery of services. One of the major issues confronting services of older persons is the lack of communications among and between the health and social service professions. This is a critical issue not only in the United States but also in other countries.

A conceptual framework to practice with the aging must be based upon an understanding of the older person from a lifespan perspective and within an intergenerational context. The lifespan approach provides clues to an understanding of group commonalities as well as individual differences within the aging population. An intergenerational context provides a framework for understanding generational differences within the aging population, as well as between those of advanced years and those who are younger within the society. For example, in the United States an increasing number of persons more than 60 years of age may have one or more parents living. To effectively provide professional services to those in their 60s without recognizing that such persons may have another generation older than themselves within the same family context is to exacerbate the issue of separation and isolation among and between the generations. Often older people living in separate households from their children are seen as isolated from their families. Most research on the modern American family and aging indicates that, although there is a separation of households among adult generations within the same family, networks of affective support and interaction among the generations are strong (Shanas, 1968). All too often the professional in communicating with the older person fails to include other family members and from other generations.

The issues of aging often relate to intergenerational tension, conflicts, and identities, many of which are brought about by societal demands, particularly on those in their middle years. Professional communications with consumers of services must move away from the definition of the family as a household or young adults with children to a broader intergenerational and lifespan approach. Family and household are not the same, although much social science literature has confused the two.

Because many of the physiological changes associated with aging are associated with loss, as identified previously, there is an emphasis in much of professional practice, including social work, on equating loss with deficit and dysfunction in behavior, as well as in the capacities of older persons. This is, in part, based upon the medical model already discussed, with its emphasis upon disease and disability. Among persons in leadership roles in the field of aging there is an increasing awareness that professional practice with the aging must be based upon an assessment of function and capacity rather than on deficit and incapacity. The goal of practice is to enable the older person to achieve the highest function possible through the development of alternative means of meeting needs and satisfactions. This has been described by Schwartz as "compensatory intervention" (Schwartz and Mensh, 1974). The stress, in addition to that of compensation, must be on alternatives and choices if the goal of professional service is that of individualization.

To date, most services for the aging are based upon group stereotypes and mythologies about aging. The practitioner's skill, through a meaningful exchange of communications with the older person, must be that of assessment not only of the problem(s) with which the older person is confronted, but equally so in assessing his capacities, including psychosocial strengths, which will enable appropriate resolution of such problems through the use of such strengths, capacities, and abilities. Such an assessment, which must be based upon information drawn from the older person and/or his family, is also dependent upon the art of listening and the skill of hearing. All too often, practitioners, because of the lack of a knowledge base on aging and an affective understanding of the meaning of aging in our society, fail to listen to what the consumer of services is attempting to say either in verbal or nonverbal ways. Assessment also requires sensitivity to what is being communicated so that understanding may arise.

Provision of Information on Community Resources and Services

As noted previously, questions have been raised as to how information about the nature and availability of services is communicated to potential consumers of such services. While such questions apply to persons of all ages, they are particularly relevant to the elderly. Again, as already noted, one of the primary characteristics of aging in today's society is the progressive reduction in social contacts and participation. The Administration on Aging has attempted to address national policy to this concern by giving high priority to information and referral services at the local area agency on aging level over the past 3 years. It has been noted, however, that, despite the establishment of such a service, members of ethnic minorities are underrepresented among those who receive services.

Although information and referral is a traditional service established by social agencies years ago, their primary function then was to respond by telephone to requests for assistance and, in some instances, through social service exchanges, share client information among professional staffs of agencies. With older persons, however, it has become increasingly evident that the traditional approach is not effective. Therefore, outreach services that go into the home of the older person are often used. The Community Service Society of New York City, in a research demonstration program to make neighborhood and community resources more accessible to persons 60 years and older in four public housing projects, identified that the complexities of urban life for the elderly were such that it was necessary for older persons to have a trusting relationship with a significant other person in order to overcome their reluctance to seek help.

They also found that mature, in-service trained service workers, under the supervision of a professional social worker, were more effective in such outreach programs, except in the development of mutual aid programs. (Carey, 1971).

Information and referral services for the elderly involve an expanded range of communications functions. As Lester et al. (1968) has identified, these include: information, referral, counseling, consultation, coordination, planning, training, research, and interpretation. Each of these requires communications skills and also professional knowledge, including the role of research in practice. Because professional education has only given limited attention to aging and because of the special requirements of an aging population, it is essential that knowledge about the effectiveness of the emerging information and referral systems for the aging throughout the United States be developed.

Sub-populations within the Aging

The most essential characteristic of the aging is the range of age differences within the 65 and older population, that is, some 30 to 40 years. (With the Older Americans Act of 1965, there is an increasing tendency to include all persons over 60 among the older American group.) Persons in the younger age-groupings of the elderly population, those in their 60s and early 70s, are considerably different from those in their late 80s and early 90s. In addition, those included in the older age group continue to change, with about 4,000 newcomers, that is, those who celebrate their 65th birthday, being added each day (Brotman, 1974). Brotman has noted a high degree of functional illiteracy and limited formal education among today's older population; however, this is changing rapidly, and it is anticipated that within the next two decades, the older population will have a higher level of formal education. Beyond this is the ethnic and racial composition of the elderly population, which is more pluralistic than those of younger age groups who have been assimilated into the larger culture and population. Those who were foreign-born immigrants, as well as native Americans (Indians) and representatives of other racial minorities have, in addition to language barriers, cultural norms and identities that give a variety of meanings or definitions to verbal and nonverbal behavior. Carp's (1970) research on elderly Mexican-Americans identifies the fact that "age groups, ethnic groups, economic groups, and national groups 'talk past' one another." The telephone was almost never used by elderly Mexican-Americans, not because they were not available, but because their culture identified speech with facial and hand gestures from which affective meaning was associated with cognitive information. Professionals must recognize communications as a reflection of attitudes (Baldock, 1975), both on the part of the consumers as well as of the providers. Oftentimes, the consumer is hesitant about requesting assistance from professionals, and this is particularly true of the elderly whose attitudes were formulated at a time when welfare was viewed negatively and self-reliance was a primary societal value.

RESEARCH AND PRACTICE

Where literature does exist in regard to the professional and communications, it identifies the failure to relate research findings to practice. This was noted by an international committee that met following the 1971 White House Conference on Aging. This report stated that it is often a matter of years between research discovery and practice utilization. In part, responsibility, it was suggested, was that of "inadequate communication within the scientific fraternity between the researcher and the practitioner" (Kent and Fulgraff, 1972). It further suggested that there is a lack of communication among practitioners and from practitioners to researcher. It suggested that research knowledge should be made a part of the research process itself.

It should be recognized that organized research in gerontology is exceedingly recent, the majority having occurred only during the past decade. Schwartz and Mensh (1974) have further shown that we are still searching for a unifying theory of human aging or, again, as Neugarten (1968) states, "describing a meaningful context against which to view psychological change over the life cycle." As Riley and Foner (1968) state, there is, indeed, a limited knowledge base from which to communicate to professionals. Despite this, however, the issue of communications between researchers and practitioners who serve the aging is critical. Birren, Woodruff, and Bergman (1972) suggest a number of alternatives regarding the utilization of research findings to those who practice with older persons. Among these is the bringing "into play a 'translator' who understands the sophisticated language and the technical terms used by scientists and who knows about the level and the content of the practitioner's knowledge" (p. 72). Another is that, "before starting a research project, information as complete as possible must be given to the researcher about the different societal implications of the particular issue under study so that he can understand what questions his research has to answer" (p. 72).

Professional education for practice with the aging in all professions, but particularly social work, should include an understanding of research design and methodology, as well as how practice issues in working with the aging can be translated into responsible questions. The practitioner works on a day-to-day basis with the raw material of research. All too often his practice, wisdom, and knowledge fail to reach those engaged in psychological and social research. Practice, unfortunately, tends to be more intuitive. There is a need to recognize legitimate responsibility of practitioners to further the development of knowledge about older persons and the conditions under which they live. It is also important that practitioners understand experimental designs so that alternate strategies of intervention may be validated in regard to improving those unacceptable conditions found among many of today's elderly.

A related responsibility of social work practice is that of translating day-to-day practice concerns in working with the elderly into broader social policy questions that can affect institutional change. This means that paractitioners working with the aging must also, in addition to communicating with the older person, have the capacity of talking with those who formulate and administer policy. Working with legislative bodies and executive staff of governmental agencies, as well as with boards and executives of private organizations, is a critical leadership role of the profession. Institutional change, that is, societal adaptations that recognize increasing numbers and proportions of older persons rather than adjusting the older person to accept the unacceptable, must be a primary goal of practice. Theoretical and applied knowledge on aging, while essential, are not sufficient. Communications skills must also be considered as a tool of practice if such knowledge is going to affect those who make decisions about resources mobilization and allocation within the society. Manpower needs, service requirements, and facilities for the aging will continue to be of a limited, and often substandard, quality without the professional leadership required to practitioners who work with older persons.

RESEARCH QUESTIONS NEEDING ANSWERS

Communications research, particularly around professional services to the aging, is highly scattered and exceedingly limited. Much of gerontological research to date is difficult to apply to the lives of older persons. As Gans in Schwartz and Mensh (1974) states, "The high level of generality at which much of academic social science operates . . . breeds conceptual abstractedness which results in concepts that cannot be applied to the real-life situations in which the policy designer works" (p. 345).

The only identifiable discussion on research in this area is to be found in the report of an international research conference in Washington, D.C., following the 1971 White House Conference on Aging (Kent and Fulgraff,

1972). This report noted that throughout the recommendations of the White House Conference was the expressed need for effective communication and the involvement of older persons in decision making. The international group identified "the need to study the relative effectiveness of communication within varying social structures." It also raised the following questions and problems for research:

What levels of communication are optional for what persons under what circumstances?

What is the effectiveness of different media, for example, word of mouth communication versus the printed word versus television versus radio?

The problem of how to reach the so-called hard-to-reach groups: the illiterate, certain ethnic groups, and the socially isolated.

The problem of research utilization and the role of communication.

FUTURE TRENDS

As the number of older persons increases within the society, greater attention will continue to be focused on their specialized needs. As increasing numbers of people are professionally trained to work with older persons, as is the emerging trend in social work, there will be a greater understanding of the aging processes as these relate to the informational and communications needs of the elderly.

Technology is currently available to ensure a more systematized and integrated system of information about services, as well as better organizational and administrative forms for the delivery of services. However, the application of such technology will require an increasing breakdown of disciplinary and professional boundaries both in the education and training of the professions and in the delivery of services. The emergence of the translator, a person who will have the specialized skills and knowledge to identify the implications of scientific knowledge for application and service, will occur. Whether such a trained professional will belong to a particular profession, such as social work, or be viewed as a generalist in gerontology remains to be seen. Current trends in education point in opposite directions. One such trend is the emergence of schools of gerontology which place much emphasis on service provision to the elderly. The other approach is to provide for education and training within the professions but with linkages to other professions and disciplines through gerontology centers. Each of these presumes a heavy emphasis on new approaches in communications across traditional disciplines and professional lines. Within either approach, professional education will increasingly emphasize the responsibilities of the practitioner to relate practical knowledge to research and policy. Again, the capacity to communicate such knowledge must be an essential component of professional education.

Much as knowledge, education, and training are changing, so will the characteristics of the elderly. The future elderly will be better educated and more sophisticated in regard to the changing world around them. They are already emerging as advocates on their own behalf for a higher quality of life in the later years. The future will see an increasing responsiveness on the part of society and its professionals to such demands for involvement and participation on the part of the older person. The role and information and how it is communicated by the elderly themselves to those who would serve them will be an essential component of this self-advocacy approach.

SUMMARY

Aging has special implications in regard to the role of communications on the part of the helping professions. Social work, along with the other professions, has only recently begun to recognize the elderly as a legitimate area for training, as well as for the provision of service. Special issues have arisen in regard to how older persons receive information and how they act on such information about the use of community resources and services. A number of special characteristics shared by older persons require specialized approaches to the provision of service. Each of them have special implications in the area of communications.

There has, for the most part, been a failure to communicate research findings to those who work with the elderly. In addition, research is often so designed that its findings do not relate to the real life of the aging. Only limited research has been carried out in the area of how older persons receive information about services, as well as the relationship of service provision to communications skills and knowledge.

The future will see an increased emphasis on information sciences and communications skills as part of the training of professionals in working with the aging. It will also see an increased participation by the elderly in policy formulation and service delivery.

RECOMMENDATIONS

The past several decades have witnessed not only an explosion in the numbers of older persons; equally so, they have witnessed a communications technological revolution. The computer and mass media, especially television, have enabled information to be instantaneously available in a number of settings and locations. Social services have failed, to date, to adequately relate to the information and communications technologies that are available.

It is recommended that the professional education of those who work with the elderly include knowledge about the special implications of communications for the elderly. It is further recommended that professional education include training in the information sciences and communications around aging.

It is also essential that ways of adapting such capabilities to the unique needs of older persons, particularly those who are socially isolated or who cannot avail themselves of traditional means of communication, be developed. This will only take place through leadership by the human and social service professions who concern themselves with the right of older persons to continue to participate and contribute to community life and who have the right to needed services and resources.

LITERATURE CITED

Baldock, P. 1975. Geriatric Services: The Patient's Views. Gerontol. Clin. 17: 13–22.

Birren, J. E., D. S. Woodruff, and S. Bergman. 1972. Training: Issues and Methodology in Social Gerontology. The Gerontologist 12: 49–83.

Brotman, H. B. 1974. Who Are the Aged? Unpublished mimeo, 19 pp. State Association of Gerontological Educators, New York.

Carey, J. W. 1971. Senior Advisory Service for Public Housing Tenants. The Gerontologist 11: 264–267.

Carp, F. M. 1970. Communicating with Elderly Mexican-Americans. The Gerontologist 10: 126–134.

Council on Social Work Education. 1975. Summary of Information on Master of Social Work Programs: 1975. New York.

Kent, D. P., and B. Fulgraff. 1972. Planning Facilities, Programs, and Services: Government and Non-Government. The Gerontologist 12: 36–48.

Lester, E. E., P. Townsend, D. Wedderburn, H. Friis, P. Milhoj, and J. Stehouwer. 1968. Information and Referral Services for the Chronically Ill and Aged. Public Health Report 83: 295–302.

Neugarten, B. L. 1968. Adult Personality: Toward a Psychology of the Life Cycle. *In* Middle Age and Aging. The University of Chicago Press, Chicago.

Riley, M. W., and A. Foner. 1968. (eds.). Aging and Society. Vol. 1. An Inventory of Research Findings. Russell Sage Foundation, New York.

Schwartz, A. N., and I. N. Mensh. (eds.). 1974. Professional Obligations and Approaches to the Aged. Charles C Thomas, Springfield, Ill.

Shanas, E., P. Townsend, D., Wedderburn, H. Friis, P. Milhoj, and J. Stehouwer. 1968. Older People in Three Industrial Societies. Atherton Press, New York.

chapter 15

Special Living Arrangements for the Aging: The Importance of Communications

Markham T. Farrell, M.A.

The time one spends in the early years to develop a career and earn a living seems out of proportion to the efforts made in later years to reduce the pace of living, planning retirement, and anticipating old age. Passing through the various phases of life is not always tranquil. Developing from infancy to childhood, from childhood to adolescence, from adolescence to adulthood, and then on to old age can be a series of disquieting experiences that seem to intensify as the years pass. The greatest anguish, however, probably accompanies aging. That community is outgrowing all others in size and need: along with this enormous growth comes a commensurate growth in problems of special living arrangements for the aged. They oftentimes have difficulty in locating, deciding upon, adjusting to, and communicating within special living arrangements available to them.

They are, frequently, adrift on a sea of options, constantly washed farther from shore by waves of friendly advice from religious, fraternal, educational, social, and governmental organizations who are eager to help but who in their wake frequently leave confusion. The aged understandably respond with indecision, distrust, fear, and withdrawal, and even ideal living arrangements poorly communicated to the aged are unacceptable.

There is need to examine the factors involved when old people plan their living arrangements. They frequently have "special" needs that must be met in order to live their lives in relative comfort. These special needs range from a cane to complex electrical machinery that delivers oxygen from room atmosphere.

Few of the aged escape the need for some type of special assistance to living. The existence of these resources, how well their availability is communicated to the aging, and the level of motivation to use them are of major concern. This suggests that the key issues involving utilization of resources by the aging rests not only with the old and those closest to them but also with the researchers who need to know what answers are available to them.

What follows is an exploration into the six major special living arrangements for the aging. It begins with a brief description of each type and a discussion of factors that distinguish one special arrangement from the other. Focus is on communications systems involved with the varied life styles of the aged in order to identify weaknesses in these systems. Poor living arrangements for the aged are directly related to weaknesses in communications.

A discussion follows concerning the communications weaknesses, and for each special living arrangement a communications corollary is formulated. A checklist, consisting of a series of layman's questions, is the format of the corollary, and these questions are numbered consecutively.

The closing pages of this chapter offer a partial resource list keyed to the corollary questions. Also, the resource data may serve to motivate further study and to bring forth new questions that have not been presented in the corollary.

SPECIALIZED LIVING ARRANGEMENTS

There are certain constants that are inimical to living arrangements for the aged. Flights of stairs, changing temperatures, poor transportation, excessive noise, and limited communications are a few of the serious handicaps to normal living for the aging. One might conclude that they seek a warm climate and ground-level single dwellings in rural areas as near as possible to radio, television, newspapers, and people. These and other factors create the retirement centers that exist in warm climate areas.

Resistance to change, family centers, property ownership, and familiar surroundings lead many of the aged to remain in two- or more-level dwellings in urban areas across the country. These factors would appear to be detrimental to comfortable retirement living. A compromise is found by an increased number of the aged who are entering congregate living arrangements in most population centers of the nation.

This discussion examines some of the factors that determine six specialized living arrangements for the aging and relates them to communications networks that operate within those arrangements. An effort is made here to focus on the importance of communications in the decision-making process of the aged as it concerns their choice of those arrangements.

Independent Living: Husband and Wife

The most common life style of the aged in this country is husband and wife jointly occupying a private dwelling. Generally, the couple is retired, their children have left home and are living independently, and the aged couple resists relocating because of finances, resistance to change, or fear of the unknown. The specialized living arrangements to the aged in this life style usually include decreased social activity, fewer bills to pay, and accumulated assets—finanacial and material. Also, there are provisions for outside assistance in the physical maintenance of the home, reduced living expenses, and a sizable collection of personal effects related to nostalgia and personal security.

Communications input of the aged couple living alone in their household usually includes the media, neighbors, friends, religious and social organizations, the telephone, and postal service. The combination of reduced living activity, a narrowing of interests, and reduced communications input and output of the family unit results in a hesitancy to consider other options of living arrangements open to them. The communications corollary for this special living arrangement for husband and wife living independently results from lack of the intensity of communications that exists between them.

Communications Corollary

1. Have the husband and wife discussed between them the inevitable loss of the other partner?
2. Have husband and wife discussed with each other a long-range financial plan?
3. Has the decision-making partner of the marriage trained the nondecision-making partner to make decisions?
4. Have husband and wife discussed a plan to handle the confinement for long-term health care of either partner who may become ill and require long-term care?
5. Is specific information about choice of hospital, nursing home, and funeral services known by both partners?
6. Has a recent fire and safety inspection been made of the household?
7. Do both husband and wife have accurate knowledge concerning hospital, nursing home, life, and other insurances?

8. Is there some type of trust, and do other family members know about it?

Independent Living: Widow/Widower

Current statistics show that women outlive men at a ratio of about two to one, and actuarial planners predict even greater disparity in the future. A less comfortable life style than husband and wife maintaining the private household is the widow or widower occupying the private dwelling and living independently. Frequently, this life style is brought about by the sudden and unexpected death of the marital partner. The aged single person continues to live as closely as possible to the previous life style of the two partners, carrying on the family image in the community, reliving the past, living a conditioned present, and frequently failing to participate in the future.

With a loss of the marital partner, communications become further reduced as the sole occupant of the household goes about the daily chores of living, with occasional visitors and lessened communications input. Activities diminish; "cooking for one" becomes burdensome, wasteful, monotonous. Housekeeping becomes less attractive and, with reduced companionship and disrupted long-range goals, living alone becomes an endless chore. What previously was a vibrant household can become a dreary, unhealthful, meaningless cell. To a significant degree communications determine the outcome.

Comparing the living arrangements of the aged couple in the independent private home to the aged single person living in the same environment, the life styles change significantly with the loss of a partner. One must conclude that the major loss of communications within the household has a dramatic impact on the way in which the remaining partner utilizes the available special living arrangements as a sole occupant of the household. A new pattern of communications begins to emerge.

A large family living independently in a private home would tend to foster a high degree of communications quantity and quality. Similarly, a husband and wife occupying the private home without children would appear to have somewhat lessened quantity, but equal quality, of communications. A single partner living independently in a private home departs from this communications pattern by lessened quality and quantity of communications. If one were to expand this concept to a bedridden patient requiring total nursing care, a further decline in communications quantity and quality would be anticipated. The pattern that emerges, then, is one of increased communications problems (reduced communications effectiveness) in concert with increased need for special living arrangements of the aged.

The communications corollary that results from the factors surrounding the lone aged person living independently in a private home is reticence to make decisions before demand situations and failure to take actions before they become mandatory.

Communications Corollary

9. Is some type of daily communication made with the lone aged person?

10. Is the plan of handling financial, household, and health management problems communicated to next of kin or responsible parties?

11. Are plans made for home visits in the event of physical impairment?

12. Is there a communicated plan of alternatives to handle personal and financial matters in the event of mental or physical impairment of the aged?

13. Is there an agreed-upon plan between the lone aged person, next of kin, or responsible parties concerning long-term health care when needed?

14. Are specific instructions given by the lone aged person to next of kin or responsible parties concerning financial, medical, and estate management in the event of physical or mental impairment?

15. Is there some type of trust arrangement, and is it communicated to next of kin and other responsible parties?

16. Is the lone aged person disposing of excess furniture and other tangible assets so that forced or sudden disposition will not become necessary?

17. Is a power of attorney designated?

Independent Living: With Children/Next of Kin

Communications problems intensify as the special living arrangements for the aged become more complex. This is increasingly evident as the aged move in with younger members of the family. Perhaps the most serious immediate occurrence is the generation gap between first, second, and possibly third generations living in the same household simultaneously. The elderly find great difficulty in withstanding the onslaught of hard rock, and the grandchildren become equally impatient with the music of the "roaring twenties." The young adults, on the other hand, become lodged in the center of the generation gap and have some difficulty in relating to both generations. Even the precise researcher can overlook the difficulty of communications that exists within a family structure of two or possibly three generations in the same household. Because of the nature of the family structure in this type of special living arrangement, the senior male of the household tends to exert authority over other family members; hence, the grandparents find difficulty in restraining the authority they have exercised for years, and they tend to dictate policy in a home environment in which they have no real authority.

Such dominance leads to resentment in the younger generation, who find themselves host to unwanted authority and, at the same time, experience feelings of guilt over their resentment. The children and grandchildren living in this same household experience a distortion of reality when normal aged grandparents move into the home of the young family and begin to assert their authority in that household. The complexity of communications interacting among the three generations creates a serious deterrent to appropriate decision making by the aged in determining their choice of living arrangements. The existence of cultural and generation gaps added to this complexity of communications creates an interesting interruption of normal family roles and ambiguities of authority.

Special living arrangements in this type of setting include first floor occupancy for the aged, thereby limiting the necessity of climbing stairs. Often, special bathroom facilities are provided for the aged as well as additional heat, private entrances, individual communications systems (telephone, mailbox, television, radio), special lighting and temperature controls, and other conveniences.

These factors produce a communications corollary that is found in specialized living arrangements for the elderly who live within another family structure; namely, the determination of the authority role in a household where the potential exists for more than one head of that household.

Communications Corollary

18. Are the aged members of the household aware of the necessity to relinquish their authority in this specialized living arrangement?
19. Is there a trade-off of authority by the aged members for the security afforded in this specialized living arrangement?
20. Are open discussions held between members of the family to ensure the bridging of generation and cultural gaps?
21. Are financial arrangements attendant to supporting the families discussed openly and agreed upon, and are the expenses shared in a changing economic environment?
22. Are alternative living plans for the aged discussed among family

members to ensure both a feeling of security for the aged and a freedom of alternatives for the young family?

23. Are plans discussed among family members concerning possible confinement or long-term illness of an aged family member?

24. Are provisions made for emergency care of the elderly who live within this family structure?

25. Has a recent safety and fire inspection been made of the household, with emphasis on the hazards for the aged?

26. Has the family held open discussions about the possible confinement of one or both aged members of the family to a nursing home or hospital?

27. Are plans discussed openly among the family members concerning the details of the estate and burial plans in the event of death of the aged member?

28. Does some type of trust arrangement exist for both aged members of the family, and are the desires of those documents communicated to appropriate next of kin?

Independent Congregate Living

Perhaps one of the more desirable specialized living arrangements for the aging is found in apartment, condominium, town house, and retirement village types of surroundings. Several factors lead to this enviable arrangement.

At age 65 most people have reduced their pace of living. Also, because families are seldom totally intact—that is, children have usually moved from the home—there is less emphasis on home maintenance and pride. Interests turn to travel, recreation, hobbies, reduced effort, and more simplified physical surroundings. Mowing the grass, cutting the hedge, shoveling snow, raking leaves, and washing windows become less desirable in old age. And the combination of maintenance upkeep, property taxes, unneeded space, and the desire to have services performed for them leads older persons to a congregate style of living in which they can maintain independence and, at the same time, enjoy the advantages of companionship, security, and privacy. In this environment, the aged have an opportunity to enjoy life with a minimum of responsibility and physical burden.

Special arrangements in this type of living include maintenance upkeep, intercommunications with neighbors and facility management, the convenience of delivery services, group activities, fellowship with persons of similar age, planned activities and, in some instances, recreational facilities. Members of the aged community who enjoy this type of specialized living arrangement are in good health, able to move about independently, and still have the advantages of others watching over them and assisting them in their daily living.

The communications corollary produced by this specialized arrangement of condominium-apartment-retirement village living results from the unconcern of the aged about the possibility of pending confinement.

Communications Corollary

29. Has the aged individual or couple ceased to accumulate personal effects, and is there a plan toward an orderly disposal of them?

30. Has the aged individual or couple entered into a reasonable lease; in the event of death, are commitments detrimental to the survivor?

31. Are the desires and intents of a trust agreement communicated to next of kin and other responsible parties?

32. Is a power of attorney necessary and, if so, has it been assigned and communicated to family members?

33. Are financial resources, plans of management, insurance policies, beneficiaries, entitlements, and other information communicated to next of kin or other responsible parties?

34. Has the aged individual or couple indicated specific choice of a hospital, nursing home, funeral director, place of burial, executor of estate?

35. Are contingent plans made for transportation after eyesight is limited or when a driver's license is denied?

36. Is a choice evident and communicated to family and other responsible parties for living conditions under severe physical or mental impairment? Has the aged person discussed with family members the possibility of entering a long-term health care facility?

37. Have family members and other responsible parties discussed with the aged person their feelings about the necessary confinement of the aged family member?

Dependent Congregate Living

There is a paradox in this lifestyle: dependent congregate living offers the greatest hope for tomorrow's aged, but few of them are willing to accept it. It provides companionship, health care surveillance, health care services, assistance when needed with daily living tasks, and a convergence of other resources not available with independent living.

There is a great need for increased construction of congregate living facilities. Newly constructed retirement centers, homes for the aged, rest homes, church retirement homes, Christian Association homes, and the enormous growth in public housing for the elderly are examples of the attention given to a need that has outdistanced hope for immediate fulfillment.

A partial answer is the multiple dwelling, such as the high-rise, which provides the resources for the enhancement of living in an efficient manner. Another type of dependent congregate living is the retirement village.

In this type of community, as many as 50,000 aged residents, occupying independent cottages, share an affluent form of living that offers extensive services and facilities. Golf courses, boat harbors, amphitheaters, bowling alleys, tennis courts, swimming pools, campsites, restaurants, and hospitals are found among the shared public areas of these well planned, expensive operations.

The usual retirement community, however, consists of congregate living in a single facility that offers either independent or centralized food services, laundry, housekeeping, some type of nursing care, recreational facilities, and the privacy of apartment living. Physical size of these facilities is important to their efficient operation. A 100-resident facility might be considered minimum in size, one whose monthly income from residents can support needed staff and other services. On the other hand, a 200-resident facility usually operates more efficiently because of its ability to defray costs over a larger income base without having to double the staff.

The nursing services provided in the retirement facility offer security to those who consider their health an important factor in entering any type of specialized living arrangement. The decision to give up independent living, sell the homestead, dispose of furnishings, and enter a home with many other aged residents is not made easily. Often, the availability of nursing care services makes this decision more acceptable.

The dependent congregate life style of the retirement home has grown in popularity in recent years. Residents frequently purchase an apartment or have some type of lease that provides them with the privacy desired by the aged and, at the same time, affords companionship with others of similar age. The aged who enter this type of facility have usually disposed of property and furniture no longer needed. They consider this their last major move in life, and it usually is.

The transition from independent to congregate living produces the next communications corollary: the problem of adjustment that must be made as the aged move from total independence to the necessary structured, supervised life style.

Communications Corollary

38. Is the aged person prepared to accept supervision and authority?

39. Has the aged person an opportunity to live in the supervised environment on a trial basis before making final financial commitments?

40. Is the aged person living with peers with relatively similar backgrounds?

41. Is there an alternative supervised plan of living for the aged person in the event that he is unable to accept one type of supervision or dislikes the life style?

42. Can the aged person continue to have privacy in this special living arrangement?

43. Does the facility provide acceptable health care services if needed?

44. Does the facility have a close relationship with an acute care hospital?

45. Are transportation services available at reasonable rates?

46. Does the facility have established communications systems among its residents, such as a newsletter, in-house telephone system, bulletin board, disaster plan, daily attendance or condition reporting procedures, and regular resident meetings?

47. Are programs communicated that include entertainment, religious, and educational experiences, as well as interaction among residents?

48. Is there a communications liaison between the operating staff of the facility and its residents?

Dependent Health Care Living

Specialized living arrangements and communications problems intensify in the health care facility. Unlike the previous five living arrangements for the aged, this life style centers around complete confinement and includes an additional variable: physical or mental health impairment. Communications problems heighten with the convergence of professional health care staff, ancillary personnel, and specialized nursing care services in the aged person's daily living pattern.

It is not uncommon for an aged person confined to a nursing home to consider himself a prisoner, both of a disease and of a custodial staff that is assigned to care for him. In this situation, fears begin to multiply. The fear of being deserted by family members and friends, of having a terminal disease, or of death can block all other communications input. When fear is joined by anger, the patient may develop a neurotic, self-pitying attitude. This anger is often expressed toward family members to arouse sympathy, gain attention, and release emotional tension by inflicting guilt upon others.

In this frame of emotional upheaval, the aged find great difficulty in communicating within the health center. Compounding the problem, the health center has within its operations diverse and complex communications systems prescribed by law and operational at all times. These systems function to serve to safeguard against disaster; they are not, therefore, geared to the individual but to a total system of health care.

The increased involvement of government in the health care field has created some impressive new levels of expectation in patient protection systems. Life safety codes, fire protection systems, disaster plans, electronic audio-visual signaling devices are a few of the systems being advanced, and with these developments there has been a commensurate complexity of communications networks.

Communications systems in the nursing center become dehumanized. They are of the demand type, rather than informative or interpersonal systems, that report only patient condition or need. Bedside signal systems, door alarm warning gear, and fire alarm warning devices are a few examples of demand systems that add little aesthetic value to patient living.

There are more subtle communications networks in the nursing home. Patient condition measuring devices used in determining blood pressure, heart beat rate, pulmonary, and other functions are individual communications systems, and this input is further transmitted through patient progress reports, doctors' orders, charts, graphs, and other materials that comprise the patient chart of progress or decline. Perhaps it is accurate to say that the aged persons living in the dependent health care environment are as much an assignment as they are a resident, and communications become distorted.

In this life style, the aged are usually confined either to bed, wheelchair, or the building. And confinement distorts communications. In fact, in a dependent health care living environment, there is a displacement at the very basis of communications. The excitement of a world series win, for example, succumbs to the triumph of bodily functions.

Many of the aged are further confined by diet. They must have their daily intake weighed and measured and their output accounted for. Often medicine is a confining factor: patients must have medicine administered by a professional nurse at a given time and in measured quantity. And appliances become limiting factors. High volume oxygen administration units are not portable, and because oxygen is essential to survival of some patients, their ability to communicate is limited by their disease-related immobility. These and other factors require the aged to be confined to a given area at a specified time, and at best their communications input systems include television, radio, newspapers, staff conversations, letters, and visitors from outside the facility. Communications output systems are similarly limited to staff, family, visitors, and letter writing.

Because the aged person occupying a bed in a health-related living arrangement becomes part of a total health care community, his communications become less direct and are substantially slowed down. For example, if three people have a specific need and signal simultaneously for the assistance of a staff member, the aide must determine priority and answer the calls in order of importance. Communications slowdown also occurs because information takes time to filter upward from patient through staff personnel and downward through health-oriented channels. And information that passes from one person to another loses accuracy and detail. This is especially evident among the aged who tend to be impatient with detail. Thus, one may expect communications output to lack both accuracy and timeliness.

Staff members and physicians do not contribute to the improvement of communications. Historically, physicians do not spend a great amount of time discussing patient-condition subjects with the patient or his family. This is brought about by two factors: first, the physician's time is usually limited, because he must treat many patients in a busy schedule; and second, physicians have learned that discussion with family and patient frequently arouses needless apprehension because the patient or family fail to perceive accurately what the doctor has told them. Staff members also are discouraged by their supervisors from discussing a patient's condition with him because they lack professional diagnostic training.

It is interesting to note that communications considered desirable in previously discussed specialized living arrangements for the aged are often harmful in the health care life style.

A family member may carelessly report to the patient the death of a neighbor. This news may create serious anxiety in the patient, resulting in the patient identifying the neighbor's death with his own condition. In health care living environments negatives appear to attract negatives, and communications of adversity to patients often lead to depression and increased anxiety. The neighbor's death, however, remains an important communications fact to the aged resident. But the communicator must be concerned with the quality of this type of communication as well as with the importance of his visit to the confined aged person. A decline in visits results in further diminished communications input. Dependent health care living requires the resident to function within the structure of the organization. This distorts interpersonal communications and, therefore, creates the corollary that, in dependent health care living, the resident loses a degree of individuality and becomes a part of the total inpatient body.

Communications Corollary

49. Does the resident aged person have some familiar personal effects close to him, such as a radio, pictures, furniture, and knicknacks?

50. Are personal interrelationships with friends and next of kin communicated as much as permitted by visits, written greetings, gifts, and other remembrances?

51. Are the resident's likes, dislikes, interests, fears, and other individual characteristics communicated to staff and other residents?

52. Are there frequent communications with the aged person about his needs—physical and emotional?

53. Have family members and other responsible persons discussed openly with staff and administration any guilt feelings that may exist among family members as a result of the aged person's confinement?

54. Are trust arrangements communicated to family and other responsible persons?

55. Are alternate plans for entering the aged person into a less confined living arrangement communicated to others in the event that physical improvement permits transfer?

56. Are plans communicated to staff for choice of funeral director, burial, hospital, and disposal of on-premises personal effects should this information be needed?

57. Are the amount and location of all assets of the confined aged person communicated to next of kin or other responsible persons?

58. Is there only one family member or other responsible party responsible for decision making concerning the confined aged person, and has that authority been communicated to other interested persons?

59. Are all insurance entitlements known and communicated to the decision-making authority in charge of the aged person's care?

60. Are communications with the confined aged person positive, rehabilitative, and encouraging in intensity?

SUMMARY

This chapter has set forth six types of specialized living arrangements for the aging. Each arrangement has produced a communications corollary.

The married couple living independently in a private dwelling lacks intensity of communications between the two people. Decisions are delayed.

A lone surviving spouse occupying a single dwelling, but having limited communications, often delays decisions too long, and this forms the corollary for independent, lone-aged, living arrangements.

Two and three family generations occupying the same dwelling present increased communications problems. Generation and culture gaps between them create the corollary of obscured authority within the household.

Independent congregate living in apartments, town houses, and mobil homes produces a more subtle communications corollary: the complacency of the aged in failing to plan for pending confinement.

Dependent congregate living in retirement centers, homes for the aged, and rest homes introduces the corollary that security is required at the cost of independence.

Finally, dependent health care provides the most complex form of specialized living arrangement. Communications problems multiply; the corollary becomes a trade-off of individuality for health care.

If this chapter has been successful, it has developed interest and concern for the relationships that exist between the six specialized living arrangements for the aging, the communications systems that are operational within them, and the great potential that exists for the enhancement of the aged through knowledge of these relationships.

The greatest test for this potential lies in the talents of students in the field of communications whose search for knowledge will lead them, as well as the aged, to a more enriched life.

ADDITIONAL RESOURCES

The following suggested readings and additional resources are keyed to the corollary question of the chapter. Corollary question numbers are indicated parenthetically following the relevant reading, and resources are listed alphabetically.

American Red Cross

Blood
Disaster aid
Transportation (to doctor, clinic, hospital)
Household items available
Appliances available

American Cancer Society

Cancer treatment supplies
Counseling

Transporation to treatments (clinic, hospital, radiologist)
Sickroom supplies

Accountants—CPAs

Assistance with financial management
Aid in tax management and reports
Advisory services in financial matters
Help with reconciling bank accounts, reviewing invoices

Accounting Schools

Junior accountants help with minor financial matters

Antique Dealers

Help in disposal of personal effects—often on consignment

Apartment directories

Available in most cities—help in locating housing

Appraisers

Serve in process of real estate disposal
Assist in disposal of personal effects

Art Galleries

Help in disposal of personal effects

Attorneys

Assist in preparing trust agreements
Assist in disposal of real property
Assist in disposal of personal effects
Defend aged persons in consumer protection matters
Advise on purchases, insurance, rentals, leases, life leases
Prepare power of attorney documents
Notarize transfers of property—assist in transfers

Auctioneers

Help in disposal of personal effects; sometimes complete household

Bankers

Administer trust agreements
Serve as trust officers
Counsel on investments

Assist in handling bank accounts
Assist in general financial management
Serve as guardian of valuables—safe deposit box, etc.

Barber Schools

Provide economical grooming services to aged men

Beauty Schools

Provide economical grooming services to aged women

Book Dealers

Aid in disposal of personal effects (books, papers, stamps, etc.)

Bookkeeping Services

Aid in financial management
Aid in tax preparation
Counsel on tax and related financial matters

Bus Lines

Offer special transportation services and rates to aged
Greyhound Bus Line "Ameripass" for senior citizens

Catholic Social Services—local county agencies

Counseling
Transportation
Home help
Meals
Sick room supplies

Churches and Religious Organizations

Religious services
Transportation to and from church—other transportation
Senior citizens programs
Meals
Home help
Helping hand in funeral arrangements
Assist with personal needs
Counseling services

Clergymen

Counseling services
Assistance with funeral arrangements

Visitations to the infirm
Help with most personal problems in the community

Colleges and Universities

Classes available for the aged—extension services
Resource (students) for home maintenance help
High school completion courses offered
Visitations by students with aged as part of learning programs
On-campus events: concerts, sports, theater—with reduced senior rates

Civic Players Groups

Entertainment at reduced cost—dinner theaters
Enrichment of leisure time
Opportunity for acting in senior parts

Commission on Aging—state agencies

Varied services ranging from transportation, meals, health services, counseling, and many others for the aged

Consumers Council—state agency

Provide information on consumer-related subjects
Counseling services available on consumer matters

Consumers Protection Agency—state agency

Negotiate consumer problems between aged and merchant
Mediate complaints regarding landlord, grocery store, utilities, etc.
Defend aged in consumer fraud matters

Credit Counseling Services—independent

Debt counseling
Money management
Establish budgets

Dental Assistant Schools

Provide economical minor dental services: adjustment, cleaning, etc.
Diagnostics for the aged

Dental Schools

Provide economical evaluations
Provide literature and resources for dental hygiene

Economic Opportunity Program—local agency

Provides nutrition program
Makes emergency clothing available to aged in need
Provides transportation
Provides meals
Provides medical services

Employment Agencies

Provide domestic help
Provide professional home care help
Assist in screening help
Assist in recruiting help
Provide job placement services for the aged

Equipment Rental Agencies

Provide temporary health care equipment: beds, appliances, supplies
Provide oxygen rental on temporary basis

Family and Child Services Centers

Provide counseling services
Provide foster care
Assist with money management
Provide social and job adjustment counseling
Provide travelers aid information

Funeral Directors

Assist with funeral arrangements
Assist with burial arrangements
Assist in donation process of human organisms to research
Loan chairs to elderly programs
Donate flowers for floral arrangement classes and activities of the aged

Furniture Dealers—used

Help in disposing of personal effects
Help in acquiring needed items at low cost
Assist in temporary storage

Health, Education, and Welfare Department, Washington, D.C.

Provides compendium of data on Medicare and Medicaid
Publishes voluminous data on the aged
Determines criteria for local, state, and federal health programs

Health Department—state

Provides directory of nursing homes, homes for the aged, and hospitals
Investigates complaints regarding health care, sanitation, abuse
Provides local health center for public health services: culture tests, immunizations, health care information, and infection control

Home inspection services

Provide inspection information concerning health, safety, and insurance

Hospitals

Provide emergency care on premises
Provide emergency vehicles for transfer
Social Services personnel provide counseling, admission, transfer, location of nursing home, homes for the aged, family guidance, and other patient-related services
Provide out-patient clinic services

Insurance Companies

Provide home safety inspection services
Assist in preparing annuity and trust programs

Labor Organizations

Most organizations have senior citizens' programs throughout the country, and participants must not necessarily be members
Activities at local union halls—speakers, meals, and entertainment

Libraries

Provide substantial information services on diverse topics
Record rentals—book loan
Library programs—usually inexpensive to the aged
Provide assistance in locating people, places, and things
Provide mobil book service

Real Estate Companies

Provide assistance on disposal of real property
Assist in rental properties
Provide part-time employment to the aged by assignment to showings

Social Services—state

Provide specific information on Medicare and Medicaid insurance
Assist in locating health care

Assist in financial matters
Serve as liaison between the aged and the nursing home
Investigate complaints on health care
Process Social Security matters
Provide counseling services

Taxi Companies

Provide emergency deliveries: medications, oxygen, sick room items, etc.
Offer reduced rates to the aged
Helpful in location of streets in unknown areas

SUGGESTED READINGS

Commerce Clearing House, Inc. 1974. Social Security and Medicare Explained, Including Medicaid. Commerce Clearing House, Inc., Chicago.
Donahue, W. (ed.). 1954. Housing the Aged. University of Michigan Press, Ann Arbor.
Facing Retirement: A Guide to the Middle Aged and Elderly by a Country Doctor. 1960. Allen and Unwin, London.
Frush, J. Jr., and B. Eschenbach. 1968. The Retirement Residence. Charles C Thomas, Springfield, Ill.
Giles, R. 1949. How to Retire and Enjoy it. Whittlesey House, New York.
Gross, F. 1972. Your Retirement Housing Guide. Modern Maturity Journal, Long Beach.
Jacobs, H., and W. Morris. (eds.). 1966. Nursing and Retirement Home Administration. The Iowa State University Press, Ames.
Miller, D. 1969. The Extended Care Facility: A Guide to Organization and Operation. McGraw-Hill, New York.
Nulsen, R. 1972. The Mobile Home Manual, Vols. I and II. Trail-R-Club of America, Beverly Hills.
Nutrition Service of the Iowa State Department of Health and Iowa Dietetic Association. 1961. Simplified Diet Manual—With Meal Patterns, 2nd Ed. Iowa State University Press, Ames.
Pollock, S. 1975. Give Now, Pay Yesterday. In Senior Advocate. July/Aug. Senior Advocates International, Inc., St. Petersburg, Fla.
Roy, W. 1972. The Proposed Health Maintenance Organization Act of 1972. Science and Health Communications Group, Washington, D.C.
Stern, E. 1952. You and Your Aging Parents. A. A. Wyn, New York.
Stoler, P. 1975. New Outlook for the Aged. In Time. Vol. 105, No. 23. June 2. Time, Inc., Chicago.
Streib, G., and C. Schneider. 1971. Retirement in American Society. Cornell University Press, Ithaca.
Sunshine, J. 1973. How to Enjoy Retirement. 2nd printing. Library of Congress, New York.
Tica, P., and J. Shaw. 1974. Barrier-Free Design Accessibility for the Handicapped. Institute for Research and Development in Occupational Education, New York.

U.S. Department of Health, Education, and Welfare Public Health Service, Office of Nursing Home Affairs. 1975. Long-term Care Facility Survey, Interim Report. U.S. Department of Health, Education, and Welfare, Rockville, Md.

U.S. Department of Health, Education, and Welfare. 1974. Social Security Handbook. U.S. Government Printing Office, Washington, D.C.

U.S. Senate Special Committee on Aging. 1974. Adequacy of Federal Response to Housing Needs of Older American. *In* Hearings Before the Subcommittee on Housing for the Elderly. January 17–19. U.S. Government Printing Office, Washington, D.C.

chapter 16
Communication Specialists in Aging-related Organizations

James Danowski, Ph.D.

Today, it is uncertain whether gerontology, most typically conceived as the study of old people, will continue to flourish or will soon transform so radically that it will no longer be known as it is now. In support of continued growth, social gerontologists often raise the standard of the changing age structure of the population, predicting a nation of old people dependent on the dwindling young for survival within the "foreseeable" future.

However, an important counter trend presses against this perspective. Functional theories of aging abandon chronological age as the important variable and look to indexing how people operate within the micro-environment as the criterion for grouping people into sets. Thus, simple demography loses importance, and perhaps psychographies, sociographies, or even infographies become critical. One way to view functional age is from an information processing perspective (Danowski, 1975a). Informational aging increases as the complexity of information seeking and processing decreases. In short, variance makes a person functionally young. Variance, or entropy, can be measured in the use of channels and the processing of content, as well as form in messages. The key predictor of this entropy is a person's perceived control over environment.

Note that the social policy implications of such a perspective are far reaching, calling for a rethinking of the social order and how it relates to social service delivery. The theoretic implications of this perspective call out clearly for a developmental approach to human behavior, turning the social science of aging back in upon itself, resulting in the study of all human behavior over the lifespan. Thus, the study of old people as an isolated group becomes scientifically irrational. In short, this theoretic trend raises many questions about the future organization of scientific activity in aging, and thus the role of communications specialists in gerontology. This uncertainty about the future of the science of aging underscores the tentativeness of that which follows.

It must also be noted at the outset that, given the variety of kinds of organizational structures forming the basis for aging-related organizations, it is unreasonable to think that all of this variety could be accounted for in a single chapter of this size. As Ashby (1968) suggests with his "law of requisite variety," in order for the uncertainty in one system to be reduced by another system, the reducing system must have a corresponding level of uncertainty within it. Therefore, this author is able to outline here only the basic structure of the role of the communications specialist from a personal perspective. Specific applications must be left to the readers. In this perspective, of course, the author makes specific assumptions about the nature of the organization providing the context for this explication. First, are particular assumptions about an organization structured around aging, and second, theoretic assumptions about organizational characteristics and processes.

The particular assumptions about aging-related organizations are that they:

1. Are interdisciplinary, ranging from the physical and biological sciences to the social sciences and the social services and humanities
2. Are engaged in research, service, and instruction
3. Have disciplinary as well as interdisciplinary subunit specialization
4. Are affiliated with an institution of higher learning

INFORMATION PROCESSING THEORY OF ORGANIZATIONS

Any organization focused around research, service, or instruction regarding aging may be viewed from an information processing perspective as an uncertainty expansion and reduction system. From this view derives a useful framework for examining the communications specialist.[1] From a macro perspective, the organization may be considered to be oriented primarily to reducing uncertainty about the processes of aging. This is basically the knowledge generation function of scientific and other evidential systems. However, the organization may also engage in expanding other organizations' awareness of their uncertainty about aging, if those organizations are not currently aware of their uncertainty. In exchange for reducing the uncertainty of others about aging, resources may be obtained.

---

[1] For a discussion of how elderly advocate groups may view news organizations as uncertainty reducers, see Danowski, 1975b.

Given this information processing view of organizations, the aging related organization, as well as other organizations, may be considered to have three primary types of uncertainty: 1) uncertainty about the input process, 2) uncertainty about the transduction process, and 3) uncertainty about the output process. Essentially, viewing the organization systemically, it takes inputs from the environment, operates upon them, and then eventually outputs information into the environment. Within each of these three groups of functions of input, transduction, and output are three sublevels: 1) channel uncertainty, 2) content uncertainty, and 3) form uncertainty (Danowski, 1975c). Each of the three primary functions of input, transduction, and output requires the exchange of information among either elements of the environment and elements internal to the system, or only internal system elements.

Furthermore, the aging organization may be viewed as both constituted by and embedded within communication networks. As an element of a larger social system, the organization is linked with other organizations in its environment, such as funding agencies, educational institutions, elderly advocate groups, social service agencies, and so on.

The testing of information processing theories of organizations shows (Danowski, 1974, 1975d) that the more complex the information processed from the environment the more complex the internal communication of the organization. A more complex communication network within the organization has greater numbers of communication subgroups within it, more integrated inter-group linkage patterns, and less connectedness within groups. This research shows that key components of environment related to communication network complexity are: openness, i.e., the amount of information exchanged with the environment, information content diversity, and system size.

Currently, it appears that a number of aging-related organizations are growing in size, are exchanging more information with their environments, and have greater diversity in the content of information they process. All of these processes seem to be spurred by the increased funding to aging-related problems and the movement upward of aging on the agenda of national problems. Simply by themselves, these are interesting phenomena. Moreover, they have direct implications for the role of the communications specialist in the aging-related organization. With the increase in the internal complexity of communication networks in the organization, there is increased need to manage information processing effectively.

Given these assumptions, the important question that must be addressed is: How can the communications specialist aid the organization in expanding and reducing its uncertainty? The answer to this question

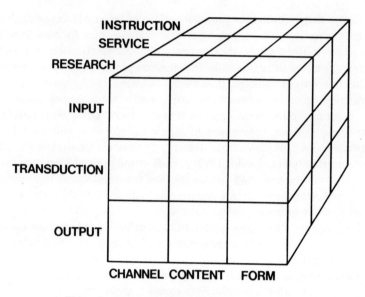

Figure 1. Communication functions and structure.

cannot be derived simply, because in light of the three-dimensional model (Figure 1) there are at least 27 specific communications subfunctions. Clearly, it is not reasonable that a single individual could effectively cope with 27 major responsibility areas in a large organization. Thus, a multiplicity of communications specialists must be considered in the organization. The discussion of these various communication activities is organized below into three major groups, defined by the input, transduction, and output processes.

Input

First to be considered are the input processes of the aging-related organization. Within input are three levels of communication structure: channel, content, and form. Also assumed for the organization are three major groups of activities, labeled: research, service, and instruction. The cells dealing with form uncertainty can be effectively set aside here, because the organization has no real control over input form, once a particular channel and content is selected. Basically, however, although the organization might use form criteria as a message selection rule, it would probably not be cost effective to do so, because adapting to changing input form requires little effort. That leaves input channel and content decisions to some unit of the organization. Functionally, this unit of the system might be called the environmental scanner and selector (ESS). Typically, this requires the input of printed information from sources such as bibliographies, publisher brochures, government document directories, specialists in a particular area of research, and so on. This type of communications role might best be filled by a person with qualification and experience in the area of library and information sciences.

The information needs of persons primarily performing research tasks will be somewhat unique to the people filling these roles, as is the case for those filling service and instruction roles. Thus, the ESS must be skilled at seeking information through interpersonal channels, whether this is mediated through memos or telephones, or occurs through face-to-face interaction. Also, the person(s) must be skilled at filtering information from these sources to create an efficient decision-making structure, yet meet the needs of the respective constituencies. Organizational personnel in all areas will, of course, be continually gathering their own environmental information as well as having unmet information needs. One difficult skill for the ESS is to effectively gather and process this environmental information from members of the respective groups. This requires training in basic research methods for gathering quantitative and qualitative information, suggesting a very active communication role for the person(s) most typically labeled "librarians" in such organizations.

Perhaps the organization could hire a liaison person skilled at organizational change and development and personnel research to serve as a link between an existing librarian staff and its three groups of constituencies. In short, the ESS has a two-part role—one is gathering information from the organization's external environment, while the other is gathering information from the internal environment—concerning both information gathered directly by other personnel, as well as data on their unmet information needs. It is this latter role for which librarians are typically least prepared. Thus, the organization might want to recruit a person trained in library work as well as familiar with basic social science and communications research methods.

Transduction

The organization has a great deal of control over the transducation processes, for this is the core of its operations and involves the basic "production" processes within research, service, and instruction. This raises the question of what role the communications specialist can play in aiding the organization to reduce its transduction uncertainty. In all three transduction subfunctions, there are two levels of communications functions to be performed. At the intrasystem level, there is a need to integrate the three subfunctions within as well as among one another. This unit, the transduction communication specialists (TCS), might coordinate meetings among the three groups, coordinate colloquia, and develop in-house exhibits and multi-media displays focusing on the work taking place within each of the subfunctions. This unit would also create an internal newsletter and information system, provided the organization does not have a computer system and operator to manage a teleconferencing system. If there *is* an in-house computer system, then these activities ought probably to come under this functional unit, because it deals primarily with transduction. An advanced computer system would also be used for ESS activities, as well as the output activities to be discussed shortly. Probably of great importance to the organization would be a teleconferencing system linking persons within and across research, service, and instruction. Thus, some of the responsibility for interlinking these elements of the system can be programmed into the computer software and managed by the TCS.

The second level of communications transduction specialization is the link between environment and organization, within research, service, and instruction. For example, the researcher must interact with the larger environment in order to gather and analyze data, particularly social data. There are roles here for researchers in communication theory itself specializing in areas such as:

1. Intrapersonal communication, in areas such as verbal and nonverbal communication, speech, and hearing
2. Interpersonal communication, primarily the study of dyadic relationships and attitude change
3. Small group communication
4. Organizational communication, including both formal organizations and informal voluntary associations and community organizations
5. Mass communications
6. Communications technology

An additional area of communication specialization is probably of great importance in the study of aging although, currently, there is little systematic training of students to perform such a role. This is the social policy of communications. Some schools of communication are beginning to evolve programs that develop skills in the policy processes. This particular specialization is somewhat of a hybrid between the basic theoretician and the service specialist, and it may require a separate organization unit to ensure effective management.

In the service areas there is a need for functions such as information and referral, community communication, and communication training workshops. Essentially, the person filling such a role should have training in communication and social change, diffusion of innovations, and group communication management. Typically, persons in areas such as social work have had somewhat similar training. However, the organization is likely to have a more effective service function if they employ a person with communications training in a professional masters program, or it might consider sending persons already working in the area for advanced communications training.

In the instruction area, there is a need for information about curriculum, communication education in aging, and instructional media production. The first requires skills in gathering information about student information needs, and perceptions and opinions of faculty and staff. The second requires an instructor trained in communication education to teach courses and seminars and to run workshops. Also, researchers would be available to teach theory and research courses, as well as topical seminars for advanced undergraduate and graduate students. The third requires the skills of a media production and technology use staff for developing and producing instructional media materials.

Output

Often academic research organizations leave the output of information back to the environment solely to the transducers. Typically, however, these people are untrained, and often unmotivated, to develop and implement information dissemination strategies skillfully. Thus, more effective organizations establish a unit whose responsibility is largely the output of organizationally generated information back into the environment.

In this mode of information processing, the organization has a great deal of control over all three levels of communication structure: channel, content, and form. It may decide whether to use channels such as publications, mailing lists, mass media dissemination, interpersonal dissemination, conferences, and so on. In essence, this organizational unit conducts information campaigns for the system. In this process, the unit can select from the pool of content developed through the transduction processes in research, service, and instruction, deciding what content to disseminate to particular audiences. Likewise, it decides how to organize messages within the particular channels and content used. In effect, this is composing the encoding of information into a selected form or structure. The functional specifications for these output function communications specialists are: 1) skilled in developing strategies for selecting audiences, and the channel, content, and form of messages to be used; 2) skilled in actively seeking information from transducers, who typically do not initiate dissemination; and 3) competent with advanced communications technologies.

Typically, a unit performing some of these functions in the organization is called the "publications" office, or the "public affairs" office, or the "community relations" office. Frequently, however, persons filling these communications roles are often not well trained in the theory and methodologies of information dissemination, particularly with research methods akin to marketing. They often have no theoretical basis for making decisions about communications.

Because it has already been assumed that there is a communications production facility located in the organization used by instructional personnel, the information disseminator must also be conversant with the language of the production personnel in order to effectively use their services for constructing messages and using communications technologies in information dissemination and diffusion.

RESEARCH QUESTIONS NEEDING ANSWERS

The task of considering research questions regarding the roles of communications specialists in aging organizations at the outset seems rather fruitless. As much as social scientists research other phenomena, they are highly reluctant to research themselves. Beyond explanations symbolized by folk stories of the poorly heeled feet of the shoemaker, or the leaky pipes of the plumber, are explanations perhaps more cognitive than motivational. Given that the key tenet of the scientific world view is one of control over variables, perhaps social scientists are reluctant to give a group of their peers greater information, and most likely control, over portions of their environments. If nothing else, social research is often intrusion into the consciousness of others, and the social research community is not likely to subject itself to this frequently. Nevertheless, this chapter does not seem quite complete without a treatment of research priorities in the sociology or, as it were, communicology, of knowledge related to aging.

Probably the most essential research question is: Does communications management work, i.e., does an organization focused on aging benefit from perceiving and administering itself as an information processing network with the attendent concepts and principles being deriving from communication theory? Logic suggests an affirmative answer to this question, although some will require systematic empirical evidence.

If communications management does, in fact, contribute to organizational well-being, as we suspect it might, then a tier of questions may be addressed regarding the relationship between variations in communications management systems and different components of organizational well-being. Because the concept "well-being" is highly dependent for meaning on the world view in which it is embedded, and communications management systems inseparable from ideology, a clear-cut research answer will be relative to the dominant ideology of the times. Currently, organizational well-being is defined by a range of variables, exemplified by: morale, economic efficiency, client perceptions, and so on.

The next level of research questions deals more with the problem-solving aspects of organizational communication research and, thus, the questions are as varied and diffuse as the daily, or perhaps quarterly, or even 5-year problems of aging-related organizations. In a sense, this policy research is aid and counsel in the maturation of the aging-related organization itself. If social gerontology is to succeed, it must develop and grow beyond the questions and problems of aging to which it is addressed. The study of the maturation of organizations themselves is now beginning to be identifiable (Johnson, 1975).

Research can answer questions about the very specific adaptive utility for the aging-relating organization of problem solving organizational communication research, and particularly network analysis theories and research techniques. Given the wide range of possible communications management problems that aging-related organizations might face, it is not feasible to delineate all of them here. However, some general groups of research questions are:

1. What environmental factors lead to the effectiveness of alternative locations in the organizational structure for the various communications specialists? For example, under what conditions ought a communications theory and research specialist be placed in a multi-disciplinary unit or a disciplinary unit closest to the researcher's interest?

2. Under what circumstances are various techniques for gathering data on internal information needs of the aging-related organization most valid and reliable? For example, when are personal interviewing, group meetings, self-administered questionnaires, a "suggestion box," a computerized tele-conferencing system, etc., most appropriate for information needs assessment?

3. How frequently and through what modes should instruction, research, and service people communicate with one another? For example, how often, if at all, should communication take place through group meetings, routing of print material, in-house exhibits, and so on?

4. What dissemination strategies for information on aging are useful with different target audiences? For example, in diffusing information to older people, what are the relative cost/benefits of mass mailing, use of standard mass media, conferences, "outreach," and so on?

Meaningful answers to these types of questions require the cooperation of many aging-related organizations, so that cross-system comparisons can be made that may be generalized. Otherwise, all that can be done is to conduct isolated case studies, which typically do not yield general principles applicable to other cases. A necessary condition for reliably obtaining research answers is communication among aging-related organizations. However, while necessary, this inter-organizational communication is not sufficient to deal with these problems. There must be coordination as well.

FUTURE TRENDS

This chapter began by raising critical questions about the future of the study of aging, pointing to the uncertainty created by the movement toward functional theories of aging and current national policy considerations and experiments in using functional criteria as a basis for deciding the elegibility for social service provision. These trends, if they continue upward, will lead to the death of gerontology as it is known, and thus the roles of communications specialists in the aging-related organizations will be rather precarious.

Assume for the moment that gerontology leads a full life. Then, a very important structuring agent of the future will be communications and information technologies. Already advanced communications technologies, such as computer managed data gathering, analysis, and display; tele-conferencing systems; and video applications, are being used in aging-related organizations, as in other research, service, and instruction organizations.

What does this imply for the future role of communications specialists in aging-related organizations? Clearly suggested is a vital and integrated role in managmeent of the organization and its subsystems. We are learning that communications technologies cannot be designed only under the neon of the laboratory. Communications systems designers must move out into "natural light" and consider the characteristics, needs, and preferences of the human user if the technologies are to be used without coercive sanctions. In addition to the functional roles and skills discussed earlier in this chapter, this new hybrid group of communications specialists must be skilled in communications needs and functions analysis, cost/benefit analysis, communications hardware and software systems design, user training, and evaluation. Unfortunately, currently few of these "new renaissance" communications persons are being trained, although the seeds of a techno-scientific humanism have already been sprouting in the field of communications. Innovative aging-related organizations will recognize these trends, recruit these future specialists, and advance both the study of aging and communications.

SUMMARY

In conclusion, the basic purpose of this chapter has been to examine the organization focused on aging from an information processing perspective. This theoretic viewpoint has suggested a way to organize functionally the internal components of the organization in light of environmental characteristics. The reason for this framework is that it is increasingly recognized that communications and information processes are, as it were, the "nervous system" of the organization—the basic life supporting network. If this is indeed a useful perspective, then the effective management of organizations should be enhanced by the grouping of units based on shared communications activities and providing adequate linkages among these functional units to foster system-wide coordination and integration. Thus, a well managed communication system in aging-related organizations ought to foster accelerated progress. The challenge for the aging-related organization is to manage its own informational aging processes as a system. The goal is to become in functional terms, "informationally younger."

DEFINITION OF TERMS

PSYCHOGRAPHICS is the measurement and mapping or representation of individuals' psychological orientations, attitudes, values, and life style, etc. In recent years psychographics has gained increasing use in marketing, which previously almost exclusively used demographics.

SOCIOGRAPHICS is analagous to psychographics except that rather than focusing on psychological characteristics of people, it focuses on social characteristics. Examples of sociographics are the measurement and mapping of friendship and opinion leadership patterns of individuals, the social roles a person performs, organizational relationships, etc.

INFOGRAPHICS is a term coined by the author to refer to the measurement and mapping of patterns in the communications behavior of persons or other systems. Examples of infographics are the individual's interpersonal communications network patterns, profiles of media use, profiles of functions and gratifications of mediated and interpersonal communication over various phases of the life span, etc.

CHANNELS are "carriers" of information which link a source of information with a receiver of it. Channels are relatively independent of the kinds of information flowing through them. Examples of channels in mediated communication are television, newspapers or journals, newsletters, convention papers, etc. In interpersonal communication, channels are typically represented by the relationship or link between specific pairs of individuals. Thus, if two persons talk with one another, a channel exists connecting them by an information flow. This interpersonal channel may occur informally, or be more formalized where one or both of the participants represent some larger social system such as a group or organization.

CONTENT is the messages flowing through communication channels. It is what is being communicated about, and typically this information has symbolic meaning. In short, it is largely the semantics of communication. Examples of content in mediated communication are the types of information in aging publications such as life satisfaction, social activities, psychological orientations, health, etc. In interpersonal communication, examples are messages about the self, about work, about friends, about events in the news, or about aging, etc.

FORM is the organization of messages or content within a communication channel. In other words, it is the structural characteristics of messages— patterns which are not specific to content. It is analagous to syntax or grammar in language. For example, in mediated communication, in a newsletter, form is its lay out—the use of space, positioning, size, paragraphing, etc. Examples of form in interpersonal communication are the "stimulus" and "response" patterns constituted by the sending and receiving of messages by participants in the communication activity. The structure of these message exchanges can shed light on control and dominance in the relationship. In short, here form is the "style" of interpersonal communication, aside from its content.

ENTROPY is a term originally developed in the physical sciences to conceptualize heat processes or thermodynamics. In the social sciences, entropy is typically defined as the lack of predictability in a specified set of alternatives. A maximally entropic situation occurs when it is equiprobable or equally likely that any one of a given set of possible alternatives actually occurs over time. Uncertainty is closely linked with entropy. Uncertainty is the perception of entropy by an individual. The more entropic a set of alternatives the greater uncertainty a person has in predicting the patterns of those alternatives. In short, entropy or uncertainty is a positive function of: a) the number of alternatives in a given set, and b) the relative probability of the occurrence of those alternatives.

TRANSDUCTION is the operations that are performed on information as it is processed by a system after input and before output—what happens to information while it is "inside" a system. In being transduced, information may be compared to other information, may be stored, may be recoded, may be filtered, etc. Thus transduction is the processing of information within the boundaries of a system, distinct from the gathering or input of information, and the dissemination or output of information.

REFERENCES

Ashby, W. R. 1968. Principles of the self-organizing system. *In* W. Buckley (ed.), Modern Systems Research for the Behavioral Scientist, pp. 108–122. Aldine, Chicago.

Danowski, J. 1974. An Information Processing Model of Organizations: A Focus on Environmental Uncertainty and Communication Network Structuration. Presented at the International Communication Association Meetings, New Orleans.

Danowski, J. 1975a. Informational Aging: Implications for Alternative Futures of Societal Information Systems. Presented at the International Communication Association Meetings, Chicago.

Danowski, J. 1975b. An Uncertainty Model of Media Access by Elderly Advocate Organizations. Presented at the Gerontological Society Meetings, Louisville.

Danowski, J. 1975c. Informational Aging: Interpersonal and Mass Communication Patterns in a Retirement Community. Presented at the Gerontological Society Meetings, Louisville.

Danowski, J. 1975d. Communication Network Analysis and Social

Change: Group Structure and Family Planning in Two Korean Villages. Presented to the East-West Communication Institute, June 28–July 12, Honolulu.

Johnson, K. R. 1975. Comparative Analysis of the Age Structure of Organizations. Presented at the American Sociological Association Meetings, San Francisco.

chapter 17
Summary

E. Jane Oyer, Ph.D.

Multidisciplinary dimensions characterize the study of both communication and aging—two concepts that are very important in human existence. Although each has been studied singly, only recently have the two begun to be studied at their interface.

The importance of communication to older persons is noted by writers of the various chapters. Communication is central to successful transactions throughout the span of life, and it may assume an even greater place in the lives of older people who have retired from the work force. As life space decreases, satisfaction must be gained from a shrinking number of communication alternatives.

For purposes here, communication has been defined operationally to include the sending and receiving of messages, both verbal and nonverbal, within, between, and/or among people. Persons communicating within themselves or with another person, with small or large groups or people, or through one of the mediums of mass communication such as radio, television, cablevision, newspapers, magazines, or books are included. A general model of communication embraces a (1) source, (2) code, (3) transmission medium, and (4) receiver. There is no age-specific model for communication as it occurs within any sector of the population.

Gerontology, a word that literally means the logic of aging, is a social scientific area of study that focuses on the science of aging in our society. Gerontologists are generalists with an interest in the ways that the various components of older peoples' lives intersect. Aging has been considered to be a process of slow but continuous change that is manifested throughout life. This book, however, has concentrated on the population that is 65 years of age or older.

The United States at the present time is an aging society in that the segment of older people is increasing at a greater rate than that of younger people. Perhaps this multiplication in numbers will give what, heretofore, has been a rather powerless group an increasing influence in societal affairs. Beginnings of a trend in this direction appear to be the formation of and coalition between organized groups of older persons. Examples are the American Association of Retired Persons and the Grey Panthers.

Presently, almost 11 percent of the United States population is 65 years of age or older, that is, approximately 21 million people. The proportion has almost tripled since 1900, and some demographers predict that by the turn of the next century the proportion may rise to 20 percent.

The social-psychological study of aging has been approached from several vantage points. One theoretical position has been called disengagement theory, and its development has been purported to explain the social withdrawal of many older people. However, many older people who do not disengage have been found to adjust well (perhaps at a higher level) to the aging process and have not been accounted for by this approach. Activity theory grew from studies that revealed that a large number of older people maintained fairly constant amounts of activity or social participation in keeping with their past life styles and socioeconomic status. But activity theory is not comprehensive enough to account for the multiple social-psychological variables involved. Another developing framework for the study of aging has been called the ecological systems approach. Here, focus is placed upon the interfaces of man's environmental support systems as they affect his life.

Because communication among older persons is such an important and under-researched area of study, a conference was called at Michigan State University to bring together professionals from a number of disciplines for the purpose of identifying researchable questions concerning communication and aging. Hopefully, some of the questions identified here will be answered in the near future.

When communication was considered from the standpoint of a retiree-author, eight important areas were noted. A need was seen to make vocabulary more accurate and complete, thereby reducing or hopefully eliminating, ageism from language. The heterogeneity that exists within the group of people 65 and older was recognized as an important facet. People age very differentially, and their preferences are manifested through a variety of life styles. Ethics (or truth in communication) is an exceptionally important aspect of communication and is especially so for older people who must depend upon others for vital services. A related aspect of this is the completeness of the information presented. Wise decision-making requires knowledge of each alternative. Some of the recent self-disclosure regulations appear to hold promise that that type of information will be forthcoming more as a matter of course. Extension of communication networks was proposed through such innovative means as information banks housed, perhaps, in a university and staffed by older volunteers. Equality in communication can be better maintained if senders and receivers share information as if each were a resource for the other. Creative ways to keep older persons continuously involved in society need to be implemented. Suggestions include an annual re-involvement day at which recognition is given for the social contributions of older people in the community. Such a program could stimulate others to follow suit insofar as community contributions are concerned and holds considerable promise for enriching the quality of the lives of people of all age groups.

Certain factors related to the lives of older people serve to facilitate or to deter their communication within the family. Included are variables such as the generation gap, changes of residence, types of housing, attitudes, schedule conflicts, health, values conflicts, social mobility, and the division of labor within the family. The kin-family network, which is essentially a series of communication links between members, functions as a medium for the exchange of material goods, services, and social-psychological satisfactions. Older people can be very effective senders and receivers when this family communication system is maintained.

Changes in the structure of society have modified formerly established communication patterns. One of the most pronounced effects or changes has been the reduction in the extent to which people of various age groups communicate with each other. Perhaps the older segment of the population has been most dramatically affected by this exclusionary trend which deprives society of one of its greatest human resources. Quantitative, basic knowledge about social communication processes is a necessary first step toward the reversal of this trend.

Communities house a number of formal and informal organizations that are vital parts of a communications network available to older people. Economic organizations, such as large corporations and chambers of commerce, are examples of formal organizations that very often make special provisions for older people. Vocational groups such as nurses' associations, labor unions, farmers' cooperatives, banks and professional organizations such as the American Medical Association are others. Government sponsored organizations are led by the office of the Administration on Aging and the Social Security Administration with their various regional and area branches.

Educational organizations are finally recognizing their responsibilities to older citizens and are making strides toward providing for them. Religious, cultural, fraternal, recreational, civic, health and welfare community service and planning, as well as advocacy, lobbying, and research organizations all provide special services and opportunities to communicate. Informal organizations are typified by the neighborhood group, the concerned block police officer, the landlord, or the telephone reassurance caller, all of whom share a degree of old fashioned neighborliness. Their human touch may be more effective at the grass roots level than the most sophisticated of mechanized communication systems. Even though a number of formal and informal organizations that can be utilized by older people exist in every community, there remains a great need to communicate their availability and specialized services to those older people who are their potential audiences.

Studies reveal that older people spend more time watching television each day than they devote to any other activity other than sleep. The 3 to 6 hours each day spent watching television serves in one of several ways to meet their needs. Television provides a link to the outside world and sometimes substitutes for direct experiences and social interactions. Knowledge is needed about ways that mass media, including television, affect older people. The media's effect upon attitudes of younger persons toward their elders is another facet awaiting further investigation. Some aspects of cablevision, such as its interactive potential, have just begun to be tapped. The next decade should provide dramatic improvements in the ways that the mass media serve older people.

Consumption needs and resources are influenced by aging, and their impact on consuming processes is vital to the development of public and business systems planned to meet their needs. Constraints upon consuming processes that are related to aging include income, immobility, diminished physical capacity, and changes in living environments.

As life space constricts over time, consumption tends to become more specialized and more dependent upon past experience. Generally, less confidence is placed in unfamiliar sources of information about goods and services. Loss of or changes in consuming roles such as might be experienced when moving into a nursing home probably contribute to social disengagement. Being a consumer helps to keep one integrated into the on-going life of a community.

A number of research questions regarding the interface between communication and the aging consumer are unanswered. For example, do changes in various sensory processes, such as sight, hearing, or touch, influence need recognition? How does financial stress influence decisions as to which needs to satisfy first? The importance of being a wise consumer is highlighted for older people, and more knowledge is needed at this juncture.

Communication related to the health care or older people is influenced by such age-associated physiological phenomena as hearing and vision changes and impediments in physical mobility. Interpersonal environmental changes also influence communication about health needs. Changes in the neighborhood, for example, may mean a loss of concerned, longtime friends who would notice if one were not up and about. Moves to a retirement home, loss of a spouse, forced relocation to a family member's home or institutionalization all change established communications with health-related personnel. Knowledge obtained through research studies can be directly applied to aid older persons who must make dramatic adjustments in their advanced years. For example, what patterns of communication would minimize the stress felt by many older people who are forced to undergo major environmental changes?

Speech and language functioning among older people is affected to a great extent by physical health, which may vary considerably. Age-related alterations in speech include a slightly higher intensity for older persons with normal hearing and a reduction in the speed of utterances. Researchers have found that most people are able to estimate the approximate ages of talkers by listening to recordings of their speech. This finding tends to confirm the notion that people also *sound* their ages.

Neurological diseases affect speech production, and perhaps the most familiar problem here is a condition called aphasia that often follows a stroke or cerebral vascular accident. Persons sustaining this condition may have difficulty sending and/or receiving speech. Post-stroke victims and their caregivers require specialized instruction. Knowledge regarding language behavior in the older-aged population is limited, and further research is required.

Hearing impairment can be the most devastating sensory problem to afflict older people because it interferes so directly with social communication. This quite common problem varies in degree from mild to moderate, to severe and to deaf.

Hearing losses are classified according to the site of the lesion as conductive, sensorineural, central, and mixed. Rehabilitative procedures, therefore, vary somewhat and, contrary to common opinion, a hearing aid is not the solution for all. Hearing aids make sounds louder, but do not necessarily assist wearers in distinguishing or discriminating among speech elements. Other rehabilitative procedures include special instruction in lipreading, auditory training, and counseling and may include a combination of these approaches. For those hearing-impaired older people who want to remain "tuned-in" to the daily round, auditory rehabilitation is extremely important.

Data support the fact that age in and of itself is not a barrier to learning, and a new day seems to be dawning for educational opportunities for older persons. Lifelong education is an idea whose time has come, and a number of educational institutions are making special provision for older learners and teachers. In fact, innovative and experimental approaches are surfacing that promise to attract older people with a greater range of interests and with more varied backgrounds. For example, some older people appear more responsive to educational opportunities when they are presented in the facilities of community, religious, and business organizations rather than in the more traditional school settings. The increased leisure time that retirement affords and changing societal attitudes toward leisure (no longer considered sinful) permit older audiences to avail themselves of increased educational opportunities. However, the information that educational opportunities exist must be communicated to more older adults. Mass media's potential has yet to be realized in this important area.

A number of legal and public policy problems in communication concern the aging sector. In fact, the current thrust toward lifelong learning may be viewed as a societal effort to ensure that all age groups are informed about the social structure and share in its maintainance—in effect, an implementation of public policy. Law and public policy can provide for communication among older people to support their individual and collective needs. For example, improvement of the general exclusionary attitudes toward aging can be made through the law and policy implementation. Age-discrimination laws are finally being written and enforced.

Older people have a responsibility to communicate to the larger society as well and to share in the formation of law and public policy. If ways that communication might be used to assist them in formulating policy are learned, older people can contribute their wisdom and experience and thereby maintain meaningful participation in social (legal) affairs.

Organized religion assists older people in meeting communication needs through various activities, programs, and approaches. Some that have been discussed are formal worship services, radio and television programs, distribution of printed materials, telephone calls, ministerial visits, counseling sessions, nursing home services, and small-group meetings. Recognition of older members and expressions of appreciation for their long years of service may encourage communication between members of differing age groups. Older, experienced people may provide a great service by participating in visiting programs designed to reach secluded or home-bound persons. Retired ministers often continue to serve communities by utilizing their particular communication skills.

At times of great personal crisis, such as the loss of a spouse through death or divorce, many older people depend upon religious beliefs and church-related persons to sustain them. Funerals, special meetings of bereaved persons, and study sessions that explore ways of coping provide means for communicative expression.

Religious groups often foster communication within a community by permitting and even encouraging organizations to share their facilities. Generally, provision is made for easy access for persons with mobility problems. Organized religion has long been concerned about members' communication needs. Perhaps future research will reveal ways to improve and extend these efforts.

Examples of the relevance of communication for professionals involved with the elderly were discussed with the focus upon key professionals: social workers. Perhaps no profession is more involved with communication skills, because social workers' roles range from interpersonal counseling and group work in various settings to community organization, planning, and advocacy.

The importance of listening to consumers of services and establishing ways for them to participate in policy formation dealing with older people was noted. Only within recent years have the social service professions given attention to the direct inclusion of consumers in this kind of decision-making. Other aspects of communicating with consumers of services that merit special attention include generational differences that may mean, for example, that an older "Chicano" would prefer to be thought of as an older "Mexican-American." Views of the world may also vary by generation, and individual differences related to the biological, psychological, and sociological aspects of aging also merit special thought. Age-related changes include sensory decrements in a large proportion of the older population and may result in visual and/or hearing problems that interfere with communication.

The multifaceted or interrelated nature of problems that beset the elderly provoke providers to use a systems mode of thinking. One cannot, for example, suggest changes in housing without considering income, health, and social-psychological factors as well. Leaders in professional practice now more frequently base programs for the elderly upon assessment of function and capacity, rather than upon the former model of deficit and incapacity.

Providing information to older people relative to the availability of community services is a key communications problem for social workers. Another communications problem involves the researcher and the practitioner. Where research evidence does exist concerning the professional and aging, there is a common failure to relate it to practice. Creating the role of "translator," a person who can speak the language of both the researcher and practitioner on their own terms was suggested as one strategy for overcoming this communications gap. The future portends an increased emphasis on the communication scientist's role in the education of professionals.

Communication is influenced to a considerable degree by the type of living arrangement selected by or for older people. Six types of specialized living arrangements have been discussed followed by communications corollaries. Independent living, typified by a husband and wife occupying a private dwelling, is the life style of the greatest number of older people. Loss of a spouse may prompt a widow or widower to continue independent living or to seek the companionship of others. Independent living may then mean sharing a home with children or other relatives. Congregate living is found in apartment, condominium, town house, and retirement village types of surroundings, and meets the needs of a rather large number of older persons. Another type of congregate living, dependent congregate living, also has many advantages, and a great need exists for the construction of more facilities of this type. Of particularly great importance to the adjustment of residents is an established communication system, which usually involves resident meetings, daily attendance reporting, disaster plans, bulletin boards, in-house telephones, and news bulletins. Dependent health care living provides the most complex form of specialized living arrangement and individuality may become a trade-off for health care. Special attention to residents' communication needs is essential for successful adjustment. More information is needed about the ways in which communication is influenced by the social structures that evolve from these types of living arrangements so that the lives of older persons living in them may be enhanced.

Institutes and centers designed for gerontological study are placing communications specialists on their faculties. This may be viewed as a recognition of the importance of communication to older people. The discussion concerning a communications specialist's role in an aging-related organization employed a framework that viewed the organization as an uncertainty expansion and reduction system. Organizations planned by or for older people are primarily oriented toward the reduction of uncertainties about aging processes through their teaching, research, and service programs.

Complex information processed from the environment requires a complex internal communication system within an organization. The expertise of communication specialists is needed to manage information processing effectively in the more complex organizations. Presently, computer-managed data gathering, analysis, and display, teleconferencing systems, and video applications are being used in various organizations for the aging. The communications network of an organization has been likened to a basic life support or nervous system. On a micro-scale, the same principles might apply to individual people—and to older people in particular.

With the foregoing summary in mind, the importance of communication as related to aging can be seen. Much thought has been given by a wide range of specialists to the problem as they see it from their perspectives. However, many questions yet remain to be answered if the full implications of communication as related to older people are to be understood. A more complete understanding cannot help but contribute to the quality of the lives of older people.

SUGGESTED READINGS

Bagdikian, B. H. 1971. The Information Machines, Their Impact on Men and the Media. Harper and Row, New York.

Boyd, R. A., and C. G. Oakes (eds.). 1973. Foundations of Practical Gerontology. University of South Carolina Press, Columbia.

Cottrell, R. 1974. Aging and the Aged. W. C. Brown, Dubuque.

Curtin, S. R. 1972. Nobody Ever Died of Old Age. Little Brown, Boston.

Howells, J. G. (ed.). 1975. Modern Perspectives in the Psychiatry of Old Age. Brunner/Mazel, New York.

Huyck, M. H. 1974. Growing Older. Prentice-Hall, Englewood Cliffs, N.J.

Kimmel, D. C. 1974. Adulthood and Aging. Wiley, New York.

Mortenson, C. D. 1972. Communication: The Study of Human Interaction. McGraw-Hill, New York.

Neugarten, B. L. (ed.). 1968. Middle Age and Aging. University of Chicago Press, Chicago.

Palmore, E. (ed.). 1970. Normal Aging. Duke University Press, Durham.

Rose, A. M., and W. A. Peterson. (eds.). 1965 Older People and their Social World. F. A. Davis, Philadelphia.

Smith, A. G. (ed.). 1966. Communication and Culture: Readings on the Codes of Human Interaction. Holt, Rinehart, and Winston, New York.

Smith, A. G. 1973. The Shadow in the Cave: The Broadcaster, His Audience, and the State. University of Illinois Press, Urbana.

Smith, B. K. 1973. Aging in America. Beacon Press, Boston.

Index